# THE GOSPEL ACCORDING TO JESUS

Book Design: Paul Ferrini and Lisa Carta

Library of Congress Number: 2010901555

ISBN # 978-1-879159-82-2

Heartways Press
9 Phillips Street Greenfield, MA 01301
413-774-9474

info@heartwayspress.com
www.paulferrini.com

Manufactured in the United States of America

# THE
# GOSPEL
# ACCORDING TO
# JESUS

*A New Testament for Our Time*

BY PAUL FERRINI

*For My Children:*
*Arianna, Misha & Shanti*

# TABLE OF CONTENTS

## BOOK THREE: MIRACLE OF LOVE

## BOOK FOUR: RETURN TO THE GARDEN

# Preface

The words in this book were written down during a five year period from 1993–1998. These messages are the fruit of my personal relationship with Jesus which developed in the 1980s and intensified thereafter. Opening my heart and mind to my teacher and writing down his words was an experience of profound communion. It was essentially ecstatic in nature.

During the last 15 years, these messages have been shared with men and women around the world. They have been translated into numerous languages and have been published in many countries. Readers have told me how touched they have been reading these words. They have told me that they feel that Jesus is speaking directly into their hearts. Through their experience of communion with him, their faith has grown and their willingness to trust has deepened. This is perhaps the greatest blessing this work brings to its readers.

This work also brings clarification and correction to the body of teachings that have been attributed to Jesus. That body of teaching includes not only what we read in the Gospels, but the concepts and positions adopted by the church hierarchy at the Council of Nicaea —when Christianity became the official state religion of the Roman Empire—and thereafter. Many of these later add-ons are challenged by Jesus in the messages you will read in this book.

Those of you who are interested in the differences between the teachings that appear in this book and those of traditional Christianity are referred to my book *Love is My Gospel: The Radical Teachings of Jesus* (2006), which further elucidates these differences.

The material in this book comes from the following previously published books: *Love Without Conditions, The Silence of the Heart, Miracle of Love,* and *Return to the Garden.* Assembling these writings together in a single volume has been a challenging but exciting task.

Having all of these teachings together in one place reinforces their power, congruence, and integrity.

Even if you have read the individual books in this series you will be surprised by the power and authority of these teachings when collected together in one place. You may find that they have a new and more profound impact on you now than they did when you read them for the first time.

If you are encountering these teachings for the first time, please take your time. There is a lot here to understand and integrate. As you read these words, take them into the silence of your heart and let them abide there. Cultivate your own personal connection with Jesus and allow Him to guide you into a deeper relationship with yourself, with Him, and with God.

For me, truth is revealed when it resonates in my heart and mind and, sometimes indeed, in every cell of my body. I invite you to put these teachings to the same test.

While there is a universal Truth that threads its way though all scripture and sacred writings, each of us must decide what speaks to us and what we will use as a compass to guide our journey through life. It is therefore with trust and humility that I share these messages with you.

Some time ago, my teacher told me, "You are responsible for any teaching you accept as truth. No one else has that responsibility." In the end, experience is the best teacher. Experience shows us what works and what does not, what helps and what hurts.

Words can inform and uplift us. At times they even reverberate in the silence of our hearts. But in the end we have to join the dance of life to understand its mysteries.

May the seeds of this teaching be planted in your heart and blossom in your life. May you drink deeply from the well and quench your thirst for love and truth. May you heal, forgive and come into the fullness of your power and purpose.

*Namaste,*
Paul Ferrini, December, 2009

# Introduction

*Mine is a teaching of love, not of fear. Jesus*

The great majority of my teachings have come down to you intact. However, there are some errors and distortions that need to be corrected. Mine is a teaching of love, not of fear. The language of fear cannot be used in any testament that comes from me.

Do not be surprised that some—even those as wise as my apostles—would have you believe in a vindictive God who punishes you for your sins. I assure you that they are mistaken. Our God is not an angry God, but a compassionate One who helps you to find forgiveness for your errors and those of others. By learning compassion and practicing forgiveness, you move through your fear, correct your errors and relinquish your judgments. Gradually, your shame is washed away in a baptism of acceptance and love.

Please just do your part. Ask forgiveness from all whom you have harmed in thought, word or deed, extend forgiveness to others who ask it from you, and be willing also to forgive yourself. God will do the rest.

There is nothing that you have done or that has been done to you that I have not done or suffered to be done to me. Moreover, I tell you that I am not only the one impaled on the cross of the world. You too are crucified for your mistakes. And you are also the one who wields the executioner's hammer.

All of you have come here to learn to love without conditions. When you can love yourself unconditionally, it is not difficult to love others. When you can accept others with all of their faults, it is not difficult to accept your own.

Those who misunderstand and misinterpret my words would have you place me above you. Please do not do this. Whoever places me on a pedestal also places me on the cross, for you cannot have one without the other. Therefore, do not address me or anyone else as less than or greater than you, for to do so is to create the one and only sin against the son of Man.

I teach and have always taught the Spiritual Law of Equality. Adhere to this teaching and all that separates you from one another will fall away and you will rest in the Heart of God where all beings are equally loved and blessed.

I do not teach one thing to one person and something else to another. My teaching is the same for all of you. Think well, therefore when anyone asks you to judge, blame, libel, cheat, harm, or reject any of your brothers and sisters in my name. I tell you this is a blasphemy and an inversion of truth. It can lead only to suffering.

I have told you once and I will tell you again, all are welcome in my house: rich and poor, black and white, straight and gay, women and men, children and old people, tall and short, skinny and fat, healthy and sick, the able-bodied and the handicapped.

I do not have one church for those who live in their minds and another for those who live in their hearts. I have one church for all and the door to that church is always open to anyone who wants to enter. Whoever closes the door or blocks the way to any brother or sister takes my name in vain and distorts my teaching.

Do not heed the words of such a person but observe his actions to see if they are consistent with what he says. As I have told you before, you would be wise to examine the tree before you eat the fruit dangling from its branches.

The door to my church and the door to my heart is always open to you, dear brother and sister. Indeed, I welcome you even as I hear your footsteps approaching. If I so honor and care for you, how could our God, who is far greater than I, do otherwise? No, my friends, God's love for you is more profound than any love you will ever know. Even my love for you pales by comparison.

We are both children of a loving God. Of that you may be certain. All that God has given to me will be given to you when you are ready to receive it. By then it will not matter from whose hands you receive the Gift, for all who serve Him share His love for you and extend His blessing to you now and for all time.

Do not despair, dear ones. Open your hearts and feel my Love for you. Take my hand whenever you need it. Although at times it seems that you walk this path alone, know that I am at your side whenever you call to me.

Godspeed on your journey. Soon you will be home. Until then, know I am holding this place for you.

# BOOK 1

# Love Without Conditions

*I am the door to love*
*without conditions.*
*When you walk through,*
*you too will be the door.*

# Author's Preface

*The light of Christ is within us all.*

To think of Jesus as being outside of and independent of your mind is to miss the point. For it is in your mind that Jesus addresses you. He is your most intimate friend speaking to you, sometimes in words, often beyond words. Your communication and communion with him is essential to your practice of his teaching.

Each of us has a tiny spark of light that illuminates the darkness of our unconscious. This is the divine spark of awareness which keeps our connection with God alive. This spark also connects us to the divine teacher in our tradition and to the divinity within our brothers and sisters.

As Jesus points out in this book, were we to see only that spark of light within each one of us, all darkness in our perception and experience would dissolve, and the world as we know it would disappear. This is how love is established in our own heart and in the hearts of our brothers and sisters.

Do not make the mistake of thinking that any reflection of the Christ Mind seeks anything other than the establishment of the kingdom of love in our minds and hearts. That is its single goal. St. Francis works for this. The Baal Shem Tov works for this. Rumi works for this.

Divisions into religions are relics of this world. Such boundaries do not exist in the Christ Mind, where all beings join in a single goal. It is hard for us to imagine this, but it is so.

There is no one brought up in the Judeo-Christian tradition who does not have to come to terms with the life and teachings of Jesus. This is true for Christians and Jews alike. It is also true for atheists or agnostics.

All who have rejected Jesus or placed him on a pedestal have misunderstood his teaching. That is why correction must take place for all of us. To each one of us, Jesus has a specific message that will help us dissolve our guilt and walk through our fear.

A follower of Jesus does not advocate any kind of separation. He practices love and forgiveness for all beings, including himself. He embraces the Jew, the Muslim and the Hindu as his brother. He does not seek to convert others, but rests secure in his own faith. Nor does he believe that those who choose a different path will be denied salvation. A true follower of Jesus knows that God has many ways of bringing us home and never doubts the outcome.

Each of us has available to us a personal relationship with Jesus. That relationship comes into being simply as we begin to want it and trust it. There is no technology, no invocation, no esoteric spiritual practice involved in it. The simple but authentic need for his friendship and his guidance is all that is required.

Let's be clear that Jesus does not wish to become an authority figure for us. Indeed, he stands against all authority save God's. He asks merely that we take his hand as an equal, and that we reach out to each one of our neighbors with the same mutual respect and intention of equality. His teaching may be simple, but it requires all of our attention, all of our energy, all of our commitment to put it into practice.

Ultimately, the end of human suffering comes when we decide together that we have suffered enough. Each of us, in our own way, is beginning to ask for a better way. Do you think that Jesus will abandon us now? Do you think the little spark in your heart and mind will shrink and grow dim, a casualty of our fear, our guilt, and our pain? It cannot be so.

Because the light is within us, it cannot refuse to shine when we call upon it. The light of Christ is within us all. Let us invoke it together, in the name of love.

Paul Ferrini
Santa Fe, New Mexico
December, 1993

## CHAPTER ONE

# Mastery of your Thoughts

*A single true thought restores the kingdom.*

My teaching has been and will continue to be distorted because it threatens every thought which is false. And so threatened, false thoughts take hold of the teaching and seek to mold it to fit their ends. It does not take long before the words attributed to me are the opposite of the ones that I have said.

This is why I ask you to be vigilant. Do not resist this distortion, attack it or seek to discredit it, for that will just make it stronger. But be clear in your own mind and reject the false for the sake of truth.

A single false idea can bring the mind that thinks it to despair. But a single true thought restores the kingdom. Therefore, choose your thoughts wisely. And if you are uncertain what to think, bring your dilemma to me.

Mastery of your thoughts is essential for your enlightenment. For it is in your thoughts that you choose to walk with me or to walk away from me.

If you would be like me you must learn to think like me. And if you would learn to think like me you must place every thought you think in my hands. I will tell you if it is helpful or not. Unhelpful thoughts must be eliminated. That is the essence of mind training. Only thoughts that bless and recall us to truth shall be retained.

## THE CORE ISSUE

*You are using everyone in your experience as a mirror
to show you what you believe about yourself.*

Like all your brothers and sisters, you suffer from a basic sense of inadequacy and unworthiness. You feel that you have made terrible mistakes which will sooner or later catch up with you. You expect to be punished for your sins and are waiting for the shoe to drop.

These unresolved issues of self-worth are the conditions of your embodiment. In other words, you are here to work them out. You selected your parents to exacerbate your shame so that you could become conscious of it. Thus, blaming them for your problems will not help you remove the conditions you have placed on love.

Seeking someone special to provide the love your parents weren't able to provide will not help either. It just raises the temperature in the pressure cooker. Don't be surprised if the mate you choose is the perfect embodiment of the parent with whom you most need to heal. Your life is set up so that you will come face to face with your wounds. Parents, spouses and children are here to help you see your need for healing, and you are performing the same function in their lives.

Looking for unconditional love in a world of conditions must inevitably fail. Since all your brothers and sisters are acting out of shame-based patterns, they cannot offer you the love you know that you deserve, nor can you offer it to them. The best that you can do is raise each other's awareness of the love that is necessary and begin taking responsibility for giving it to yourself.

If you do not take responsibility for bringing love to your own wounds, you will not move out of the vicious cycle of blame and shame. Your feelings of rage, hurt and betrayal, all of which seem justified, just fuel the fire of interpersonal conflict and continue to reinforce your unconscious belief that you are unlovable.

You must learn to see the extent of your own self-hatred. Until you look in the mirror and see your own beliefs reflected there, you will be using every brother or sister in your experience as a mirror to show you what you believe about yourself. While this practice may eventually produce awareness of the pattern, it is not the shortest or the easiest way home, since there is always the tendency to think that what you see is somebody else's lesson.

If you want to step outside the vicious psychology of the world, you must stop the game of projection. It is ironic, indeed, but at the very instant at which you are proclaiming your innocence at your brother's expense, you are also reinforcing your unconscious shame and inferiority.

There is no way out of the circle of blame but to stop blaming. Yet, be prepared. If you would step off the wheel of suffering, you may find that you aren't very popular. Those who don't join in the world's game of projection are the very first to be attacked. If you learned anything from my life, you must have learned this!

## THE FUTILITY OF PUNISHMENT

*You cannot love in an unloving way.*
*You can't be right and attack what's wrong.*

In human society there is a right and a wrong. Those who do right are rewarded and those who do wrong are punished. This is how it has always been.

My teaching threatens this basic assumption. At the most superficial level it challenges the idea that wrongs should be punished. In the face of the call for retribution, I have stood and will continue to stand for forgiveness.

At a deeper level my teaching challenges the very idea that someone should be condemned by his behavior. If someone acts wrongly, it is because he thinks thoughts that are false. If he can realize the untruth of his thinking, he can change his behavior. And it is in the interest of society to help him do this. But if punishment is brought, his false ideas will be reinforced, and guilt will be added to them.

You have heard the expression "two wrongs do not make a right." That is the essence of my teaching. All wrongs must be corrected in the right manner. Otherwise correction is attack.

To seek to overpower or to argue with a false idea is to strengthen it. That is the way of violence. My way, on the other hand, is nonviolent. It demonstrates the answer in its approach to the problem. It brings love, not attack, to the ones in pain. Its means are consistent with its ends.

To make wrong is to teach guilt and perpetuate the belief that pain and suffering are necessary. To make right is to teach love and demonstrate its power to overcome all suffering. To put it simply, you are never right to make wrong, or wrong to make right. To be right, make right.

You cannot love in an unloving way. You can't be right and attack what's wrong. Error must be undone. And since the root of all error is fear, only the undoing of fear will bring correction.

Love is the only response that undoes fear. If you don't believe this, try it. Love any person or situation that evokes fear in you and the fear will disappear. This is true, not so much because love is an antidote to fear, but because fear is "the absence of love." It therefore cannot exist whenever love is present.

## SELF-FORGIVENESS

*Without self-forgiveness, there is no release from guilt.*

Your feelings of inadequacy and unworthiness create your fear of retribution. If you believe that there is something wrong with you or that you have done something wrong, you will be afraid of being punished. And if you are afraid of being punished, you will defend yourself against all imagined attack. Whenever you feel that someone is questioning your self worth, you will be ready to pull the trigger.

This whole drama of guilt and retribution is happening only in your mind. If you project it, you will bring others into it and you will need to work it out together. This just ups the ante. Working something out with another when you are not aware of your own complicity in the event is unlikely.

Better to begin by bringing awareness to your own thoughts. For not only will you find that guilt is the root of all suffering, you will also find that self-forgiveness is necessary. Without self-forgiveness, there is no release from guilt.

The drama of redemption is also happening in your mind. Judge and jury live within your own thoughts. You established your guilt and now you must dissolve it. Until you undo your guilt, you cannot find your innocence. That is what the forgiveness process is all about. It has nothing to do with forgiving others. It has everything to do with forgiving yourself for establishing your guilt.

## YOUR BROTHER

*Those who withhold forgiveness from others*
*only withhold it from themselves.*

Forgiving your brother for his trespass on you only helps him if it enables him to forgive himself. Likewise, receiving your brother's forgiveness for your trespass on him only helps you if it enables you to forgive yourself.

The forgiveness of others is necessary only if you believe that it is. If you do, as most people do, making amends is important. Asking others for forgiveness demonstrates that you are ready to change your own mind about what happened

However, do not make the mistake of giving your brother the "power" to forgive you. This places power outside of yourself, where it can never be. Ask for his forgiveness but, if he withholds it, do not assume that forgiveness will never be yours. Indeed, it is always yours. Those who withhold forgiveness only withhold it from themselves.

You have a simple choice: to find your brother innocent or to find him guilty. This choice occurs over and over again, every day, every hour, every moment. Thought by thought, you imprison your brother or release him. And as you choose to treat him, so do you deliver the same judgment upon yourself.

You cannot get to heaven by holding your brother down, nor will you get there if you try to carry him. Each of you has been given the means to discover your own innocence. Simply acknowledge your brother and bless him upon his journey. If he asks for your help, give it gladly. But do not try to do for your brother what he must do for himself.

Proper boundaries are necessary if you are to move beyond them.

Don't make your peace and happiness your brother's responsibility, or make his peace and happiness yours. He is not here to save you, nor you to save him.

On the other hand, release your brother from every grievance you have of him. Do not withhold love from him in any way. For to try to hold him back from his happiness is but to attack him and imprison yourself in the grip of fear and guilt.

Do not avoid your brother's call for help. Let him work by your side as long as he will. And when he is ready to leave, wish him well. Give him food and water for the journey. Don't make him beholden to you or force him to stay against his will.

Your brother's freedom is but a symbol for your own. Therefore, let him come and go gracefully. Welcome him when he comes and bid him farewell when he goes. More than that you cannot do. Yet this much is enough. Care for each stranger in this way, and I will show you a world where trust has returned and charity rules.

Love your neighbor as you would love yourself. Make him equally important. Do not sacrifice for him or ask him to sacrifice for you, but help him when you can and receive his help gratefully when you need it. This simple dignified exchange is a gesture of love and acceptance. It demonstrates mutual confidence and mutual regard.

More than this is too much. Less than this is too little.


# INTERPRETATION

*Just because you have inverted truth*
*does not mean the truth ceases to be true.*

You interpret what happens in your life according to your core beliefs and the emotional states that arise from them.

When your expectations are not met, you are merely receiving a correction. You are being told that you do not see the whole truth of a situation. You are being asked to expand your perceptions. Correction is not attack. It is not punishment.

The perception that you are being attacked or punished when things do not go your way is entirely guilt-driven. Without that guilt, the correction would be received with gratitude, and perception would be expanded to include the new information.

All experience happens for one purpose only: to expand your awareness. Any other meaning you see in your life experience is a meaning that you made up. You may not decide at a conscious level what will happen to you, but you most definitely interpret what happens according to your beliefs.

Your primary freedom lies in learning from the experiences that come your way. Of course, you can refuse to learn from your experiences. But this choice leads to suffering. If you don't know this yet, it won't be long before you do.

On the other hand, you can end suffering by accepting your experience and learning from it. When you embrace your life as it is, correction is received and your thoughts are brought into alignment with the Divine Mind.

Life is either resistance or surrender. These are the only choices. Resistance leads to suffering. Surrender leads to bliss. Resistance is the decision to act alone. Surrender is the decision to act with God.

You cannot experience joy in life by opposing the ideas or actions of other people. You can experience joy only by remaining faithful to the truth within your own heart. And this truth never rejects others, but invites them in.

Truth is a door that remains open. You cannot close this door. You can choose not to enter. You can walk in the opposite direction. But you can never say: "I tried to enter, but the door was closed." The door is never closed to you or anyone else.

If you feel that the door has been shut in your face, you have interpreted your experience in a fearful way. And your belief may become a self-fulfilling prophecy.

You are all masters at taking truth and inverting it. You have the creative ability to make anything mean what you want it to mean. You can take yes and make it no, wrong and make it right. That is how strong your beliefs are.

But just because you have inverted truth does not mean the truth ceases to be true. It means only that you have succeeded in hiding the truth from yourself.

So how you interpret your experience is rather important. When your expectations are frustrated, will you accept the correction or will you insist that you are being unfairly treated? Are you the victim of what happens or the one who learns from it? Do you experience what happens as a blessing or as a punishment? These are the questions you must ask.

Every experience is an opportunity to embrace truth and reject illusion. One experience is not better or worse than another in this respect. All experiences are equally potent. They exist only as a birthing ground for your divinity.

## THE NEED FOR MIRACLES

*Every miracle demonstrates that love is stronger than fear.*

Miracles are demonstrations of the Divine Mind in action within your mind and experience. To experience a miracle, you must know that you need it, ask for it sincerely and be willing to receive it. Then it is possible for it to manifest in your consciousness and your experience.

Unfortunately, even if the miracle has manifested in your life, you may not know it because you have a preconception of what it is supposed to look like. So even though it is sitting right next to you, you may not recognize it.

What good is a miracle if you can't find it? To bring God's solution into your heart and mind, let go of your pictures and expectations. Be open to change and allow it to reveal itself to you.

Some of you may ask: "Why doesn't God give me the miracle I ask for?" That is because the miracle you ask for may not free you from your fear. Therefore, it is not miraculous, and your fear will just recreate the conditions you were hoping to change.

Without a shift within consciousness, there cannot be a shift in your outer circumstances. So be humble and receptive. Do not try to tell God how to meet your needs. Let go of your solution and open to His.

## FORM AND CONTENT

*Each moment is new and each situation
asks something different from you.*

If you are trying to find the perfect form—the perfect job, the perfect relationship—you will be continually frustrated. The world does not offer perfection in this respect. It simply offers you an opportunity to grow and to change, which is not hard if you are not attached to the form of your expression.

If you are not attached to form, your focus remains in the present, where each moment is new and each situation asks something different from you. Your attention stays with what is happening. You are able to accept and respond to what is.

If you are looking for perfection or predictability you must realize that the world cannot offer you this. Everything in the world is in the process of change. Nothing is steady or predictable. Nothing can give you anything other than temporary security. Thoughts come and go. Relationships begin and end. Bodies are born and pass away. This is all the world can offer you: impermanence, growth, change. Permanence cannot be found at the level of form.

## LOVE IS WITHOUT CONDITIONS

*When you establish conditions on love,
you experience the conditions, not the love.*

What is all-inclusive, all-accepting, all-loving cannot be limited to form. Love does not choose its beloved or the moment of its expression. Love extends to all at all times. Love is without conditions; that is to say it is "without form."

Does this mean that you cannot experience love in the world? Of course not! However, your experience of love will be diminished in direct proportion to your need to interpret or control it. Interpretation places conditions upon that which must be without conditions. When you establish conditions on love, you experience the conditions, not the love. You encounter the form, not the content.

To understand anything in the world, you must learn to look beyond the form to the creative intention behind it. When the intentions change, the form that carries those intentions changes too.

Every situation in your life provides you with an opportunity to experience greater intimacy and freedom. As you love more people more deeply, you become less attached to them individually. You begin to align with the energy of Divine Love which is beyond the body, indeed beyond form of any kind.

In each moment you are challenged to use the form that is available to you. To do so, you need to be flexible and receptive, yet in alignment with your intention. Move into intimacy without trying to define it or control it, and you will not be limited by form or obsessed by it. You will be free to create spontaneously.

## OPENING TO THE DIVINE

*There is no human being who does not deserve*
*your forgiveness and your love.*

In a world where there are only "good" thoughts, comparison is impossible. Without comparison there is no interpretation, so there can be no failure, punishment, sacrifice or suffering. Can you imagine such a shining, guiltless world? It may seem strange to you that such a world can exist, yet it is no harder to create than the world you inhabit!

You can begin to create this new world by understanding that there is no bad, but only good in you and in your brother. Not one of God's children can be bad. At worst he is hurt. At worst he attacks others and blames them for his pain, but he is not bad.

Yes, your compassion must go this deep. There is no human being who does not deserve your forgiveness. There is no human being who does not deserve your love.

Only one who is in fear judges another. Are you beyond the grip of fear? If not, then recognize your fear. If you recognize your fear, you will not judge others, for you will come to see that fear always distorts your perception.

Recognize your fear and be truthful with yourself and with others. Confess: "I am in fear now, so I cannot see rightly."

Give up the judgments you would make, for they are but a meaningless attack against one whose goodness you cannot see. Surrender those judgments to me. Tell the truth: "Jesus, I cannot see this brother rightly, for I judge him. Help me to drop my judgments and understand what fears his behavior brings up for me."

Every judgment you make on your brother states very specifically what you hate or cannot accept about yourself. You never hate another unless he reminds you of yourself.

That is why every attempt to justify anger, fear and judgment fails miserably. It is merely an attempt to indict another for your own mistake. It lacks honesty. It lacks responsibility.

You have the means to end fear and judgment totally, yet you would still justify them. Why? Because you cannot admit your mistake.

You would prefer to suffer rather than to admit that you had made a mistake. You would rather pretend to be perfect than recognize that you are a learner here. What incomprehensible pride! How can I take the hand of one who, in spite of his pain, insists that he is perfect? I cannot help you if you do not let me.

To be mistaken is not so terrible a thing. It will not deprive you of love and acceptance. You think that it will, but that is a fiction. What deprives you of love is your insistence on being right when you are not. That prevents correction from being made.

Please try to understand this. Being wrong does not mean being "bad" and being right does not mean being "good." Every one of you will be both right and wrong hundreds of times in a single day. I tell you that you cannot count the number of times you are right or wrong in the course of your journey here.

This world is a school and you have come here to learn. Learning means making mistakes and correcting them. Learning does not mean being right all the time. If you were right all the time, why would you need to come to school?

Be humble, my friend. You are here as a learner and must accept that this is so if you are to master your lessons. Lest you recognize that you have made a mistake, I cannot help you correct it.

But admit your mistake and correction will be there, along with forgiveness. That is the path I have set out for you.

Do not try to be perfect, my friend. That is an inappropriate goal. Only those who choose to suffer long and hard desire to be perfect. Desire instead to recognize every mistake you make that you might learn from it.

Perfection comes spontaneously and without effort only when you tell the truth, when you let go of your desire to impress others, when you surrender your false pride.

Those who ask for correction will receive it. This is not because they are better than others, but merely because they ask.

Do not judge those who are not ready to admit their mistakes. Simply admit your own and give the rest to God.

Share what your experience has been, but do not seek to thrust it upon others. For you do not know what others need and it is not up to you to know.

Remember the good in your brother. Remember the good in yourself. Let all fears and judgments dissolve where they arise. Admit your mistakes and be tolerant of the mistakes others make. That is what I ask of you.

It is simple, is it not? It is so simple you will keep forgetting it. But do not be discouraged. Once you have decided that this is what you want, you cannot fail to come home.

CHAPTER TWO

# Learning to Listen

*There are times in your life when you need to be quiet and listen.*

You are wasting so much time looking for answers to your problems outside of yourself. If you just took the time to be with yourself, the answers would arise spontaneously.

Learn to be present with your experience. "Being with" is not an analytical activity. Indeed, recognize that you cannot figure your experience out. You can either be with it, or you can intellectualize it, which of course is an escape.

Every moment you are receiving helpful suggestions which can aid you in steering the ship of your life back on course. But you cannot hear these suggestions if you don't take the time to listen. Ironically, it is precisely at those times when you are most frantic trying to figure out and "fix" your problems that you most need to be quiet and listen. You may not realize that at first. But you can't help but notice that the more you try to figure things out the more confused they get.

When you give up trying "to make your life work" the way you think it should, you can be open to receive spiritual guidance from within. Usually, when you are on a collision course, the answer that you receive is something like: "slow down, look around." That might not seem like such profound guidance, but it is the beginning of correction.

As long as things are flowing smoothly in your life, you need not seek correction. But when the waters get turbulent, you would do well to pause and consider your course.

Timely introspection can make a profound difference in your life. There are times when external reality simply closes down around you and the only appropriate place to go is within.

I am not asking you to meditate for two hours every day. Nor am I saying that regular meditation isn't helpful. I'm just saying that there are times in your life when you need to be quiet and listen. If you learn to honor those times, you will save yourself a lot of grief.

The more you learn to listen within, the more you will begin to "be with" your experience as it happens. You will develop a partnership with your life, a willingness to participate, to feel and experience what comes along.

The truth is that life is neither blessing you nor punishing you. It is working with you to help you awaken to the truth. Life is your teacher. It is giving you constant feedback and correction.

## LOVE WITHOUT CONDITIONS

*One who loves without conditions*
*places no limits on his freedom or on anyone else's.*

You have learned conditional love from people whose love for you was compromised by their own guilt and fear. These have been your role models. You need not be ashamed of this. You need only be aware of it as a fact.

From the time you were an infant, you were conditioned to value yourself only when people responded positively to you. You learned that your self-worth was established externally. That fundamental error has perpetuated itself throughout your life.

Your parents' experience was no different from yours. Your children's experience may be similar. All of you need to heal from the same wounds. All trespasses/violations must be made conscious and the emotions attached to them must be released. This is the way that all wounded beings move from the experience of conditional love to the experience of love without conditions.

In the process of healing, you learn to give yourself the unconditional love you never received from your biological parents. In this process you are re-parented, not by other authority figures, but by the Source of Love inside yourself.

Learning to give love to the wounded person within begins to reverse your belief that your self-worth must be based on how others respond to you. Slowly you retrain yourself to value yourself as you are, here and now, without conditions. No one else can do this for you. People can assist and encourage, but no one can teach you how to love yourself. That is the work of each individual soul.

Each soul comes into physical experience intent to grapple with these issues of self-worth. However, very early on in the soul's sojourn here conditions are placed on its natural ability to love and include others in its experience.

Reversing these conditions is essential. If the soul leaves the physical world believing that it is the victim of its experience here, it will be drawn back again to unlearn that belief. However, if the soul awakens to the truth that its worth is not dependent on anything or anyone outside its mind or experience, it will establish itself in the Source of Love and awaken from the dream of abuse.

Awakening from abuse means rejecting the illusion that you are not lovable as you are. You demonstrate love by giving it to yourself unconditionally. As you do, you attract others into your life who are able to love you without conditions.

Your attempt to find love outside yourself always fails, because you cannot receive from another something you haven't given to yourself. When you withhold love from yourself, you attract others into your life who are doing the same thing.

The experience of unconditional love begins in your heart, not in someone else's. Don't make your ability to love yourself conditional on someone else's ability to love you. Don't place your faith in the conditions that surround love or in the form in which it presents itself. For these are impermanent and subject to the vicissitudes of everyday life.

Real love does not change. It exists independently of the form through which it expresses. The Source of this eternal, omnipresent, formless Love is within you. This is where your faith must be placed, for this Love is as certain as anything you will ever know. Once it is firmly established in your heart, you will never need to look for happiness outside of yourself.

People will come and go in your life. Some people will treat you well. Others will treat you unkindly. You will accept the love that its there and see lack of love for what it is, a cry for help from one who is hurting. You will encourage others to find the Source of love within as you did, knowing fully that you cannot fix their little problems. The tragedy of their lives can only be addressed by their willingness to look within their own hearts and minds.

One who loves without conditions places no limits on his freedom nor on anyone else's. He does not try to keep love, for to try to keep it is to lose it. Love is a gift that must constantly be given as it is asked for in each situation. And the giver always knows when and to whom the gift is to be given.

There is nothing complicated about the act of love. It becomes complicated only when one starts to withhold love, and then it ceases to be love that one offers.

One who loves unconditionally does not love in degrees or with strings attached. He does not search for someone special to love. He loves everyone who stands before him. One person is no more worthy or unworthy of his love than another. This is the kind of love that I offer you and that I ask you to extend to others.

Love takes no hostages. It makes no bargains. It is not compromised by fear. Indeed, where love is present, fear with all its myriad conditions cannot be.

## DEATH AND REBIRTH

*What dies is everything that you thought you were.*

The experience of Real Love ends your experience of the conditional world. When you experience it, you no longer feel separate from others. You open to a larger reality that includes the well being of others. Judgment falls away and acceptance rules.

When I told you "Lest you die and be born again you shall not enter the kingdom of heaven," I wasn't talking about reincarnation.

I was talking about the death of the ego, the dissolution of all beliefs that separate you from others.

What dies is not you. What dies is every judgment you ever made about yourself or anyone else. And what is born again is the Christ that has eternal life, in you and in me.

You are afraid of the death-rebirth process. Yet what dies on the cross is not you. You are not the body. You are not your ego.

You cannot avoid the death of the body or the death of the ego. But these are not necessarily the same. Do not make the mistake of believing that your ego dies when your body does, or that your body dies when your ego does.

Your ego dies when you no longer have use for it. Until then, it will not be taken from you. You can hold onto your ego almost forever, but you will not do this. For this is hell, and you will not want to live in hell forever. There will come a time when the pain will be overwhelming. There will come a time when you will call out to me "Please help me. I am ready to let go." That time comes for every being, I assure you.

Until then, all you can do is walk though your fears. Acknowledge every fear you have and turn each one over to me. That will quicken your awakening. That will take you directly to your core issues, to the fear beyond all your fears. Be assured, when you come to that place, I will stand beside you.

Gentle brother and sister, I ask only for your trust. Give it to me and we shall walk together out of this place of shadows. I cannot save you from your fear, but I can take your hand as you learn to face your fear and move through it.

Rest easy. The outcome of your journey is guaranteed. Where I am now, you shall also be. And then you will know with absolute certainty that Love is who you are. It is inseparable from you. It is your only true Identity.

## OPENING THE DOOR

*I am the door to love without conditions.*
*When you walk through, you too will be the door.*

To bring attention to any person or situation, you cannot have an agenda of your own. If you have expectations of yourself, of another, or of the situation in general, you cannot be fully attentive in that moment. Your ability to be attentive depends on having an open mind, a mind that is free of judgment and free of expectation, and an open heart, a heart filled with compassion for yourself and others. It means that you see and treat others as equals and understand that your well-being and theirs are one and the same.

Having an open mind and an open heart opens the door to love. But this is a door that opens and closes. When it closes, one needs to be patient and forgiving, or the door will not open again.

One needs to feel not only the presence of love, but its absence as well. Feeling its absence, one learns to listen, and to soften in the heart. Feeling separate from others, one learns to look for the subtle judgments that are being made. The shift from judgment to acceptance, from separation to empathy is the essence of healing.

Being a healer or miracle worker means accepting your inherent capacity to be free of conflict, free of guilt, free of judgment or blame. If you accept this capacity in yourself, you will demonstrate miracles in your life just as I did.

Healing is not only possible, it is necessary. Every one of you is a healer of your own perceived injuries and injustices, and a witness to the power of the miracle. Healing is your only purpose here. The sooner you realize it the better.

Please remember that all authentic spiritual practice begins with the cultivation of love for and acceptance of yourself. Don't try to love other people before you learn to love yourself. You won't be able to do it.

When someone comes into your life who pushes all your buttons, don't try to love that person. Just refuse to blame him or make him your enemy. Simply acknowledge that he pushes your buttons and ask for time to be with your feelings.

When you are alone, remind yourself that what you are feeling belongs to you only. The other person has nothing to do with what you are feeling. Disengage from all thoughts that would make the other person responsible for what you are feeling.

Now be with your feeling and say to yourself: "What I am feeling shows me some aspect of myself which I am judging. I want to learn to accept all aspects of myself. I want to learn to bring love to all the wounded parts of me."

Practice this again and again and be patient and compassionate with yourself. Take small steps. Begin healing your own thoughts and feelings. Every time you heal a judgmental thought or feeling of separation, it is felt by every mind and heart in the universe. Your healing belongs not just to you, but to all beings.

When you come to peace, world peace becomes immanent. If you have a responsibility to others it is only this one: that you come to peace in your own heart and mind.

An open heart and an open mind are the door that opens to love's presence. Even when the door is closed, it bids you open it. Even when you are judging and feeling separate from another, love calls to you from within.

I have told you that, no matter how many times you have refused to enter the sanctuary, you have only to knock and the door will be opened to you. I have said to you "Ask, and it shall be given you," but you refuse to believe me. You think that someone is counting your sins, your moments of indecision or recalcitrance, but it is not true. You are the only one counting.

I say to you, brother, "Stop counting, stop making excuses, stop pretending that the door is locked. I am here at the threshold. Reach out and take my hand and we will open the door and walk through together."

I am the door to love without conditions. When you walk through, you too will be the door.

## RELINQUISHING EFFORT

*I tell you that you cannot fix yourself.*
*Awareness is the only effective tool for transformation.*

What happens in your life is neutral, neither positive nor negative. You decide whether it is positive or negative, spiritual or mundane.

Everything in your experience can be endowed with spiritual qualities by bringing your love, acceptance or forgiveness to it. Even a terminal illness or a murder can be transformed by the power of your love.

When you give the situation your own meaning, you will always view it as a punishment of you or someone else. That is what your fear does to any event that happens in your life. Don't be surprised when this happens. Indeed, expect it.

Don't try to live without fear. To try to live without fear is the most fearful proposition you can imagine. Just acknowledge the fear and move through to the other end of it.

There is nothing you can do that will procure your salvation. In fact, everything that you do will simply keep you from finding what is already there. Salvation is already there. You are already saved. You do not have to buy your salvation from me, from your brother, or from some church or synagogue.

You practice forgiveness not to buy your salvation, but because the practice of forgiveness allows you to experience salvation right here, right now. You learn to accept what comes as a gift, not because it brings you brownie points with God, but because acceptance reminds you that there is nothing wrong now, nor was there ever anything wrong.

Your entire spirituality is lived in this moment only. It has nothing to do with anything you have ever thought or felt in the past. It is happening right now, with the circumstance that lies before you.

You experience darkness and scarcity only when you find fault with the situation you are presented with in the moment. When you see the situation and feel gratitude for it, you experience only bliss.

Do not try to move out of darkness. Do not try to move into bliss. The movement takes place of itself. Just be willing to move and let that willingness move you.

Most of what you try to do for yourself will not succeed because you do not know who you really are. Your self-image is limited. You do not know or feel the extent of God's love for you. You think that somewhere along the line something in you got broken, or perhaps you are just missing some parts. But that isn't true. You have no missing or broken parts. All of your wholeness is fully present right now.

Many of you study prosperity consciousness, yet what you do does not seem to prosper. Why is this? Because you do not know your true worth. If you knew your true worth, you would not feel that something was missing from your life. You would feel grateful for everything you have.

The truth is that every thought prospers. Each thought that you think adds its energy, positive or negative, to the situation at hand. Because you have a mixture of positive and negative thoughts, your external situation reflects both.

However, you won't be able to make negative thoughts go away by focusing on positive ones. In fact, the more you focus on positive thoughts, the more power you give to your negative thoughts. You cannot escape this paradox.

That's why saying affirmations doesn't work. Stop trying to change your negative thoughts and just be aware of them. Awareness is the only effective tool for transformation.

How will you learn to be supported by Divine law if you are always interfering in its workings? I tell you that you cannot fix yourself. Your attempt to fix yourself just fractures your consciousness into smaller pieces.

## MOVING OUT OF CONFLICT

*Love accepts the validity of both sides.*

When you watch your thoughts you become aware that part of you wants one result and another part of you wants another. You feel that you have to choose between these two parts and that brings pressure and conflict.

When your mind is in conflict, you do not move out of conflict by choosing between two opposing positions. That just sets up a more intense conflict.

You move out of conflict by accepting both positions. This is a loving act. Love always transcends any kind of dualism. Love never chooses sides. It always accepts the validity of both sides.

You believe that you must choose between right and wrong. But are you or anyone capable of determining what is right and what is wrong? As soon as you think you know, you have lost the thread of truth. So don't try to choose. Don't embrace one side and reject the other. Embrace both, or embrace neither. Be neutral and you will meet life on its own terms.

Lest you find this place of neutrality, you will continue to impose your own meaning on what happens in your life, and there will always be some aspect of scarcity or punishment in it, because you do not know your own worth.

Even if there were something about you that needed fixing—and I am not suggesting that this is the case—you would not know how to do the fixing. If you are broken, how can you fix yourself? If you are divided or in conflict, how can you create wholeness? Only that which is not broken can experience its wholeness.

Understand that here, in this moment, there is nothing wrong with you or with your life. Everything is as it should be. Right now, in this moment, you are completely loved.

Are you in pain or conflict? Okay. But that does not mean that you are not completely loved. The idea that being in pain cuts you off from love is an idea you have imposed on the situation. In truth, nothing cuts you off from love, save your own beliefs.

You invert the truth of the situation. You make cause an effect and effect a cause. Your fear inverts the truth and makes you a victim of the world. But you are not a victim.

However, do not beat yourself because you do this. Simply see and accept what you do and let it shift of itself. Simply bring your awareness to it. When you see the world in its utter neutrality, you will understand that it exists only as a tool for your own learning.

Pray for those who trespass against you. Do not hold them to you with thoughts of retribution, but gently release them in forgiveness.

And know that as you release them, you release yourself.

I can preach to you about the power of forgiveness, but you will never know how great that power is until you experience it. The willingness to forgive yourself and release others from your judgment is the greatest power you can know while you live in this embodiment. The only power that is greater is the power of love itself. And without the gesture of forgiveness, which removes the veil of fear, the power of love remains unharnessed.

Yet take heart, my friend. Every time you forgive, you dissolve a condition you have placed on your capacity to love. Every time you forgive, love is awakened in you more deeply and your capacity to extend that love is increased. That is the nature of the journey. Be at peace with it and it cannot fail to bring you home.

CHAPTER THREE

# Transparency

*You are one facet in the many-faceted jewel
of God's love and grace.*

When you have nothing to hide, shame can dissolve. Lies no longer need to be upheld. Simplicity and clarity rule in your life, for there is no deception or hidden agendas.

This clarity is available to you right now if you have the courage to communicate honestly. If you have a fear and share it, that fear and the guilt beneath it no longer remain hidden. If you have a judgment, you can see it and examine it. You can hide your attack thoughts or you can confess them.

The ritual of confession, like most rituals, has ceased to embody the purpose behind it. It has nothing to do with receiving absolution from another. It has everything to do with rejecting the density of deceit and bringing fear and guilt into conscious awareness. The one who hears the confession is not a judge, but a witness. He or she does not have to wear robes or be in a position of authority. Any witness will do, so long as the witness understands that her role is not to judge or condemn, but merely to listen with compassion.

There is no one who does not make mistakes. Trespass one against another, with or without intention, is commonplace.   Mistakes will be made and each error is a gift because it brings you to correction. Celebrate the opportunity to bring all manipulation and deceit to the surface. Be thankful for the invitation to reach into the dark places of your mind and bring the contents to the light of conscious inspection.

When you justify your mistakes, you hang onto them, forcing yourself to defend them over and over again. This takes a great deal of time and energy. Indeed, if you are not careful, it can become the dominant theme of your life.

Why not confess your errors so that you don't have to spend all your time defending them. Own your deceit so that it doesn't chain you to the limitations of the past. Let each trespass be openly acknowledged. If you think poorly of your brother, tell him so and ask him to forgive you. Do this not to raise him on a pedestal, but to keep yourself from falling into the bottomless pit of self-hatred and despair.

The density of this world is a result of your lack of courage to admit your mistakes. Do you really think it possible that you could be more moral or more correct than anyone else? The best that you can do is to be more skillful at hiding your mistakes. This is a sad and self-defeating game. I ask you to stop playing it.

Trust your brother and sister and know that they do not stand above you in judgment, but side by side, as your equals. They cannot condemn you without condemning themselves.

Confess to yourself. Confess to your mate, your boss, even to the stranger on the street. Do not be concerned about what people think. This is a revolutionary teaching. Your confession gives others permission to look at their own mistakes with compassion.

One who admits her mistakes is a beacon of light to others. She has shed her cloak of darkness. Light shines through her, for her mind is transparent, a clear channel through which truth flows without effort.

Others immediately know that she can be trusted and they reach out to take her hand. Having forgiven her own sins, she can extend that forgiveness to others. Her authority does not come from outside, but from within. She has been ordained by no authority of the world. Yet each person who comes to her recognizes her, trusts her, and confides in her.

This is the truth about confession. And any man or woman can be a minister or a priest. Do not believe in the lies that are offered up to you in my name. Use your common sense.

You are right to reject false teachings. I too would have turned away from a church that offers nothing but deception, exclusivity, and guilt. But do not allow your anger at the hypocrisy to take you away from your direct relationship with me. Forget everything you have been taught by others and consider the truth now in your own heart. That is where we must meet, not in some pretentious building that mocks my teaching and my life.

Now consider the truth, my friend. You cannot have secrets from me or from your brother and leave your suffering behind. To end suffering, you must end all forms of deceit in your life. And that can only be done by telling the truth, to yourself, to me, and to your brother and sister.

What do you have to lose, except the density and confusion of the world? Would you keep your secrets and remain in the labyrinth or would you confess them and be free of the dark, twisting streets? The choice is yours.

But do not fool yourself. There is no salvation in secrecy or darkness. Salvation is offered openly to everyone in the light of truth. And in that light no shadows of shame or sin can remain.

Have the courage to admit your mistakes so that you can learn from your errors and release yourself from pain, struggle, and deceit. Do not deny the truth or pretend that you have not heard it. For I have told it to you here in simple words that you can understand.

The rest is up to you. For Truth is not embraced until it is put into practice in your life.

Each of you is one facet in the many-faceted jewel of God's love and grace. Each one of you has in your own way a simple dignity of expression. The beauty of one facet does not interfere with the splendor of another, but adds to it in both breadth and intensity.

What makes one facet shine is available to all. The light that is in me is also in you. I am no more beloved by God than you are. You must come to know this in your own heart. No amount of teaching or preaching will cause you to believe it.

That is why I ask you to practice. Remove the impurities of judgment that block the clarity of your perception. Remove the obstacles of competition, envy, and greed which block the flow of love through your heart. Confess your fears, your feelings of inadequacy, your trespasses and your grievances. Bring the darkness of your secret thoughts and feelings into the light of conscious attention.

There is no mistake that cannot be corrected. There is no trespass that cannot be forgiven. That is my teaching. It is not just through my words that you can understand it. Everything I taught I also demonstrated in my life. How then can I ask less of you, my friend?

## THE AWAKENING HEART

*You are the dreamer of the darkness
and the one who brings the light.*

Unconditional love comes naturally to you. It is your nature to feel compassion for yourself and others. It is natural for you to want to reach out and comfort a friend. It is natural for you to receive the love of those who care about you. None of this takes any effort or learning.

Why then is your experience of unconditional love so rare? The answer may surprise you.

In the beginning you were one with God and shared in the omnipotent power of His love. Nothing was impossible for you. But then you began to wonder what would happen if you created apart from God.

Since you had never done this before, you weren't too sure of yourself. Doubt came in and you wondered "What if something goes wrong?" This doubt was just separation anxiety, but it gave rise to many other fearful thoughts. Among these thoughts was the thought "If I make a mess of things, God might be mad at me and withdraw His love from me." And that thought was the clincher.

It didn't take long to go from that thought to the experience of feeling guilty and cut off from God's loving presence. Now this separation was artificial and self-imposed, but it felt real to you and you believed it.

And so all that you created after that was the result of the belief: "I am not worthy of God's love." So in your own mind you "fell from grace." You went from sharing in the omnipotent power of God's love to being afraid of that love. Another way of saying that is that you became afraid of your own creative power. So you hid it away where you couldn't see it. You stopped being a creator and became a victim. You stopped being a cause and became an effect. In other words, you turned reality inside out. You made love fearful.

When you are feeling separate, it's hard to remember what it was like before separation occurred. Yet that seems to be your peculiar dilemma.

And to find your way back to God, you must retrace your steps and realize that the "separation" was your choice, not His. You asked "What if I abused this power?" Then you proceeded to make a world in which your power was fearful. You did not stop and wait for God's answer to your doubt and fear. Had you listened to His answer, you would have heard something like this: "You are loved without conditions. I will never withdraw My love from you. Remembering that you are loved, you can only act in a loving way."

Had you listened to God's answer, your dream of separation would have come to an end. For God's answer immediately challenges your assumption that you are not loved. This assumption is the original neurotic idea. All victimhood begins with this idea. You cannot think "bad" things or perform "bad" acts unless you believe that you are "unworthy of love." All attack proceeds from this one assumption.

Adam and Eve asked the same "What if?" question: "What if I ate of the apple and became as powerful as God?" They too gave their own fearful answer, felt shame and hid themselves from God. You are asking the same question right now. You are chewing the same apple. You too are playing hide and seek with God.

Indeed, it is the continual asking and answering of this question which keeps your experience of victimhood in place. In your self-created world, you are either a victim or a victimizer. As you explore these roles, you see that there is little difference between them. The victim needs the victimizer and vice versa.

The question of evil does not arise until one doubts one's own worthiness to give and receive love. That is your existential state. You doubt that you are lovable . . . you and everyone else in your world.

Now comes the choice, the only choice that you need to make: are you going to answer the question "am I lovable" or are you going to wait to hear God's answer? Are you going to let God correct your original faulty assumption, or are you going to accept this assumption as truth and build your life on its foundation?

It's never too late to stop chewing on the apple. It's never too late to realize that your answer to your own fearful inquiry is unsatisfactory. It's never too late to turn to God and say: "God, my answer has filled my mind with fear. My answer has brought only pain and struggle into my life. It must be the wrong answer. Will you please help me find another one?"

You see, your spiritual life on Earth does not begin until you ask that question. It does not matter what religion you are. It does not matter what your social or economic standing is. Each one of you will come to a point in your life when you are ready to challenge your false beliefs and assumptions. And that is the beginning of your healing, and the restoration of your power and purpose.

The doubting of your own doubt, the negating of your own negativity is the turning point, the end of the descent into matter and the beginning of the ascent into heaven. It is the renewal of your partnership with God, the New Covenant.

You can't be a partner with God so long as you see yourself or anyone else as a hapless victim. The New Covenant asks you to recognize the Kingdom of God in your own heart. That is another way of saying that you reject the idea that God is separate from you. You reject the idea that you are unlovable or that your brother is unlovable. You reject the idea of evil as an idea created in fear. You reject the idea that God's power can be abused.

The New Covenant is the acceptance of God's answer to the question "What if?" It is the beginning of your own personal salvation and the beginning of human reception of the Kingdom of God on Earth.

Once upon a time, you rejected your creative partnership with God. Now you are ready to reclaim it. Once upon a time you entertained the idea that you could be unlovable in God's eyes. Now you reclaim your eternal love communion with Him.

When you accept God back into your life, your whole experience of the world and all the people in it changes. You are a father and a mother to every child who approaches you, a son or daughter to every elderly person. You are a friend to friend and friendless alike. You are a lover to the one who remembers he is loved and to the one who has forgotten.

There is no place where your loving presence and testimony to God's love is not needed. All are crying out for your gentle words. All would drink from the cup that quenched your thirst.

The dream of unhappiness comes to an end when it is questioned and rejected. If you are questioning your unhappiness, you are awakening to the unconditional love that lies in your heart. If you are not questioning your unhappiness, you are deepening your experience of it so that you can hit bottom. For, until you hit bottom, you are content with your own answers.

No one can force another to awaken. Each person experiences the futility of giving and receiving conditional love when he or she is ready. Each person clings to separation and control until the pain of it is unbearable. The pain threshold is different for each individual, but everyone crosses it in the end.

That is why I ask you not to preach to others, but merely to extend love to them. Those who are ready to receive it will ask your help. Those who are not ready will continue on their journey without interfering with yours.

A minister of love extends love to those who ask for it, silently or in words. He does not browbeat unbelievers with words or concepts promising some future salvation.

Salvation is available now for those who would be saved. Do not judge the others for it is not for you to judge. Those who come later into the lap of God's love are not less worthy than those who come sooner.

In truth, it is not God who lifts you up. Nor is it me. You lift yourself up as you remember how lovable you are and accept your role in God's plan.

Accepting your omnipotence is impossible without your reconciliation with God. For all power comes from Him. You share in that as an equal partner, but you can never exercise that power apart from Him. Even in the "What if" dream, you could never separate yourself totally from His love. In that dream, you crossed the threshold of pain and chose to return. So it is with everyone.

The power of God's love cannot be abused. It can be rejected, denied, hidden. But all rejection, denial, and secret guilt have limits. Truth can be distorted but it can never be completely eradicated or denied. A tiny light always remains in the deepest darkness, and that light will always be found when the desire to find it arises.

You, my friend, are the hero of your own dream. You are the dreamer of the darkness and the one who brings the light. You are tempter and savior rolled in one. This you will come to know if you do not know it already.

In this self-created drama, your only argument is with God. It seems to be with your brother, but it is not. The tree of good and evil grows in your own mind, and it is in your own mind that you explore the questions of inequality and abuse.

There will come a time when your answer and God's answer will be one and the same. And then the tree of good and evil will transform into the tree of life, indivisible and whole. Love will no longer have an opposite, but will extend freely in all directions.

When someone approaches you who would place a condition on your love or his, you will say to him: "Brother, I have dreamed that dream and I know its outcome. It leads only to suffering and death. It does not do justice to either of us. Let us question the assumptions that give birth to it. I am confident that together we can find a better way."

If you ever wonder what your purpose is here on Earth, please remember that your purpose is merely to answer the call for love wherever you hear it. This is not difficult to do if you are willing. It requires no special abilities or talents. The hows and whys of love take care of themselves, as you walk through the door that opens before you.

I never said that you should walk through brick walls or even that you should walk on water. I merely pointed to the open door and asked you if you were ready to enter. And that is all that you need to ask your brother.

One who loves without conditions is never attached to the outcome. People come and go and you will never know the whys and wherefores. Some you think will easily pass through the gate, yet they will turn suddenly away. Others you are convinced will never come within sight of the gate, yet they will cross the threshold with unexpected grace.

Do not be concerned. It is none of your business who comes and who goes. The covenant is made in every heart and only God knows who is ready and who is not. Leave the knowing to Him and merely place yourself in His service. Life goes more smoothly when you do His will. And in your trust of Him your heart is filled to the brim and overflows with love and acceptance.

Thus do you come to know that the supply of love is limitless. It has no beginning or end. All the limits of Earth are absorbed in the boundless love of Heaven as the Kingdom of God is established in your heart.

## ELIMINATING SCARCITY THINKING

*If you do not understand the meaning of the gift,*
*be still and wait. God does not give questionable gifts.*

Scarcity thinking results from your perception that you are not worthy of love. If you do not feel worthy of love, you will project lack outside you. You will see the glass as half empty, rather than half full.

If you see the glass as half empty, do not be surprised if before too long there is nothing left in the glass. Lack is the result of negative perception. Of course, the same principle works in reverse. See the glass as half full and it won't be long before it is filled to the brim.

When you know that you are worthy of love, you tend to interpret the words and actions of others in a loving way. You do not easily take offense. If someone is rude to you, you consider the possibility that he or she may be having a bad day. You don't feel victimized or abused.

How you view life depends on whether you feel lovable or unlovable, worthy or unworthy. Either way, you will create an external situation which reinforces your opinion of yourself.

All preoccupation with supply comes from living in the past. Lack is simply the remembrance of old wounds. These are too easily projected into the future.

To end scarcity thinking you must forgive the past. Whatever it has been no longer matters. It no longer has effect, because you have released it.

Do you feel unfairly treated? If so, you will project lack into your life. Only one who feels unfairly treated will be unfairly treated.

To end scarcity thinking, start with the awareness that you feel unfairly treated. Realize that this comes from your deep sense of unworthiness. Understand that you do not feel lovable right now.

Don't try to change your thought. Don't repeat the affirmation "I am lovable right now," hoping that it will reverse your conditioning. Simply be aware: "I'm not feeling lovable right now. I feel unworthy. I feel mistreated. I feel scared that the bad things that happened in the past are going to happen again."

Just be aware of how your heart has tensed and tightened. Be aware how you have emotionally shut down. Information came to you and you had a choice as to whether to see it as negative or positive. You chose to see the glass as half empty. You chose to be a victim.

That's okay. Don't be ashamed. There is no need to tense up any further. There is no need to beat yourself up. Just be aware of what you chose to see and how it made you feel. See that it made you unhappy and realize that you must make a different choice if you want to be happy.

You have practiced hard being a victim and have learned that role well. Don't think invincibility comes without practice. Just see your choice to be a victim and be willing to make a different choice. That will be enough.

Abundance thinking means you feel loved and worthy right now. Now you can say that you feel this way, but if the phone rings and you find out that you just lost a lot of money or that your partner is leaving you, how worthy do you feel? Is the glass half empty or half

50

full? Do you know that right now, in the moment that you heard this apparently bad news, you are completely worthy and lovable?

If the answer is yes, then you have learned abundance thinking. If the answer is no, then you are wrestling with scarcity thinking. Just acknowledging your own fear-based thinking goes a long way toward transforming it.

That is why emotional honesty is important. You can't force yourself to think positively, but you can acknowledge your negativity. Acknowledging your negativity is a loving act. It is a gesture of hope. It says: "I see what is happening and I know there is a better way. I know that I can make another choice."

Giving yourself another choice is the work of individual redemption. Forgiving the past and letting it go sets the stage for choosing differently. No matter how many times you have made the same mistake, you have a fresh opportunity to forgive yourself.

Without forgiveness, it is impossible to move out of scarcity thinking. And to forgive, you must become aware of all the ways in which you are hurting. You must acknowledge the wound. Then you can forgive it.

Hidden wounds have hidden agendas that hold us hostage to the past. Deep wounds may require bandaging at first, but to complete the healing process they must be exposed to air and sunlight. Conscious awareness must be brought to all unconscious beliefs and assumptions.

Scarcity is an important teacher. Every perception of lack in your surroundings mirrors an inner feeling of unworthiness that must be brought into conscious awareness.

The experience of scarcity is not God punishing you. It is you showing yourself a belief that needs to be corrected.

You have the capacity to love yourself. And that capacity must be awakened in you for authentic spiritual growth to take place.

You learn to love yourself by seeing how you withhold love from yourself. And you often see how you withhold love from yourself by seeing how you withhold it from others.

Abundance comes into your life, not because you have learned to memorize some mumbo jumbo incantation, but because you have learned to bring love to the wounded aspects of your psyche. Love heals all perception of division and conflict and restores the original perception of wholeness, free of sin or guilt.

When you have seen yourself as you really are, you know that love cannot be taken away from you. Love belongs to you eternally, formless yet ever-present, unconditional yet responding easily to the conditions at hand.

Whenever news comes that seems bad, consider this. Would God give you a questionable gift? Do not be misled by the wrapping on the box, but open it with an open heart. And if you still do not understand the meaning of the gift, be still and wait. God does not give questionable gifts.

Often you will not know the meaning of the gift until the gift is put to work in your life. That can be frustrating, but it is inevitable.

The gifts of God do not feed your ego expectations. Their value is of a higher order. They help you open to your true nature and purpose here. Sometimes they seem to close a door and you don't understand why. Only when the right door opens do you understand why the wrong door was closed.

Yours is a partnership with the Divine Mind. Please do not try to make abundance your responsibility or God's alone. If you are willing to love yourself, you will open the channel through which God's love can reach you.

Open the door to abundance within your own mind and see the gifts of love reflected all around you. And please, do not judge the value of these gifts or the form that they take in your life. For the value is beyond question, and the form is too easily misunderstood.

## GRATITUDE

*Gratitude is the choice to see the love of God in all things.*

You cannot mention abundance without also mentioning gratitude. Gratitude stems from worthiness and supports the experience of abundance. On the other hand, ungratefulness stems from unworthiness and reinforces the perception of scarcity. Each is a closed circle.

To enter the circle of grace, you need to bring love to yourself or another. To enter the circle of fear, you need to withhold love from yourself or another.

When you stand inside of one circle, the reality of the other circle comes into question. This is why you often have the sense that there are two mutually exclusive worlds in your experience.

The grateful cannot imagine being unjustly treated. The resentful cannot imagine being loved by God. Which world would you inhabit? It is your choice.

In every moment you must decide to play the victim or remember that you cannot be unfairly treated. In the former case, you will resent the gift and see it as a punishment; in the latter, you will accept what comes your way knowing that it brings a blessing you cannot yet see.

Gratitude is the choice to see the love of God in all things. No being can be miserable who chooses thus. For the choice to appreciate leads to happiness as surely as the choice to depreciate leads to unhappiness and despair.

One gesture supports and uplifts. The other devalues and tears down. How you choose to respond to life shapes your own continued perception. If you are living in despair, it is because you are choosing to depreciate the gifts that have been given you.

Each person who walks the earth reaps the results of the thoughts he has sown. And if he would change the nature of next year's harvest, he must change the thoughts he is thinking now.

Think a single grateful thought and you will see how true this simple statement is. The next time you are about to depreciate a gift that is given you, pause a moment and open your heart to receive that gift with gratitude. Then notice how your experience of the gift and relationship with the giver is transformed.

The next time you are poised to judge or condemn another, pause a moment and let that person into your heart. Bless where you would condemn. Judge not and be glad that you have not judged. Feel the release that comes to you when you let another be free of your narrow perceptions.

When I said to turn the other cheek, I instructed you to demonstrate to your brother that he could not hurt you. If he cannot hurt you, he cannot be guilty for his attack on you. And if he is not guilty, then he does not have to punish himself.

When you turn your cheek, you are not inviting your brother to hit you again. You are reminding him that there is no injury. You are telling him that you know that you cannot be unfairly treated. You are demonstrating to him your refusal to accept attack, for you know you are worthy and lovable in that moment. And knowing your worthiness, you cannot fail to see his.

The violations and trespasses of this world will end when you refuse to be a victim or a victimizer. Then you will step out of the circle of fear and all that you do and say will be filled with grace. This you will each experience.

Christ will be born in you as It was in me. But first you must set aside all unworthiness, all scarcity thinking, all resentment, all need to attack or defend. First, you must learn to turn the other cheek.

It seems that there are two worlds, but truly there is only one. Fear is but the lack of love. Scarcity is but the lack of abundance. Resentment is but the lack of gratitude.

Something cannot be lacking unless it was first present in abundance. Without presence, absence has no meaning.

This is like a game of hide and seek. Someone has to hide first. Who will it be? Will it be you or me? Perhaps it will be the Creator Himself.

In truth, it matters not. When it is your turn, you will hide, and your brother will find you, as I found him. Everyone gets a turn to hide and everyone eventually is found.

The world of duality emanates from wholeness and to wholeness returns. What is joined separates and comes together again. This is a simple dance. It need not be fearful.

I invite you to enter the dance without taking yourself too seriously. None of you are professional dancers. But every one of you is capable of learning the steps. When you step on someone else's toe, a simple "sorry" will do fine. You're all learning at the same time and mistakes are to be expected.

CHAPTER FOUR

# Freedom from Attachment

*Where there is no resistance, there is no unhappiness.*

Supreme Reality cannot be apprehended from a dualistic frame of reference. It is the creation of total acceptance, surrender, all-inclusive love. In contrast to the flow of Supreme Reality, there is Resistance, which gives birth to various conditions. Distinctions, comparisons and judgments arise and the natural flow is interrupted.

The nature of Supreme Reality is to say "Yes." It has a natural exuberance and enthusiasm. It is happiness personified, for it takes everyone and everything as itself. Resistance, on the other hand, tends to say "No." By nature it brings conflict and struggle. It opposes life and so it is unhappiness personified.

Where there is no resistance, there is no unhappiness. Unhappiness always resists some condition. It establishes itself in some interpretation for or against. The root of unhappiness is attachment.

Now I am not asking you to give up all your attachments. That is not a realistic goal. I simply ask you to become aware of your attachments, your perceptions, your interpretations for or against.

If you want to understand the unconditional, look at the tree moving in the wind. That is the best metaphor you will find. The tree has deep roots and wide branches. It is fixed below, flexible above. It is a symbol of strength and surrender.

You can develop the same strength of character by moving flexibly with all the situations in your life. Stand tall and be rooted in the moment. Know your needs, but allow them to be met as life knows how. Do not insist that your needs be met in a certain way. If you do, you will offer unnecessary resistance. The trunk of the tree snaps when it tries to stand against the wind.

Move in the wind. Your life is a dance. It is neither good nor bad. It is a movement, a continuum.

Your choice is a simple one. You can dance or not. Deciding not to dance will not remove you from the dance floor. The dance will continue on around you.

There is a simple dignity in this. I encourage you to enjoy the simple grace of being alive. If you are seeking a greater meaning in life, you will be disappointed. Beyond the dance, there is no meaning.

All conditions open of themselves to the unconditional. Simply be open and present, and you will fall into the arms of God. But resist even for a moment and you will get caught in a needless tangle of your own making.

Human beings cannot be free of conditional reality, because conditional reality is a creation of human consciousness. Stop trying to escape your own creations. Simply accept them, as the tree accepts the wind. Your dignity lies in becoming fully human, fully receptive to your own needs and those of others. Compassion comes not by cutting yourself off from the range of emotional experience, but by participating fully in it.

Some have said that this world is a painful place. That is not true. This world is neither joyful nor painful, or you may say it is both at once. This world is a birthing place for the emotional and mental body. Physical birth and death simply facilitate the development of a thinking/feeling consciousness which is responsible for its own creations.

It is absurd to deny the importance of this birthing work and it is equally absurd to glorify it. There is no human being who participates in the journey of birth who does not experience both joy and pain.

Are both necessary? Absolutely. Without pain, the mother would not expel the baby from the birth canal. Without the joy of the newborn life, the pain would have no meaning.

But do not say "this is a place of pain, or this is a place of joy." Do not seek to make of your experience what it is not. Stay away from interpretations which would have you embrace only one end of the spectrum of life.

My experience here was no different than yours. I did not conquer pain. I surrendered to it. I did not overcome death, I went willingly through it. I did not glorify the body, nor did I condemn it. I did not call this world heaven or hell, but taught that both are of your own making.

I entered the dance of life as you have entered it, to grow in understanding and acceptance, to move from conditional love to the experience of love without conditions. There is nothing that you have felt or experienced, dear brother and sister, that I have not tasted. I know every desire and every fear, for I have lived through them all. And my release from them came through no special dispensation.

You see, I am no better dancer than you are. I simply offered my willingness to participate and to learn, and that is all that I ask of you. Be willing. Participate. Touch and be touched. Feel everything. Open your arms to life and let your heart be touched. That is why you are here.

When the heart opens, it is filled with love and its ability to give and receive is no longer based on anything external. It gives without thought of return, because giving is the greatest gift. And it receives, not for itself alone, but that others may experience the gift too.

The laws of this world no longer limit the man or woman whose heart is open. And so miracles happen, not through any special activity, but merely as an extension of love itself.

Miracles do not come from linear, sequential thinking. They cannot be planned. One cannot learn to perform them or to receive them. Miracles come spontaneously to the heart that has opened and the mind that has surrendered its need to control or to know.

For the Mind of God is innocent and all-giving. It cannot withhold its supply from you, for you are part of it. "Reach out and receive these gifts," it calls to you. But you do not heed its call. In your frustration, you do not hear the Divine voice calling to you.

Yet, no matter how far you may feel from God, you are but one thought away. And right now is the moment of your salvation.

Remember this, dear friend. Right now, in this moment, you are either listening to the voice of God or you are needlessly enmeshed in your own psychodrama. You are either happy or you are finding fault with the circumstances of your life.

As you learn to be open to the present moment, you will become increasingly aware of the Divine Presence in your mind and experience. Your personal goals will open up in this expanded consciousness, helping you to understand how you can best be of service to yourself and others.

Circumstances will unfold before your eyes. The appearance will often seem perplexing, but you will not judge. You will not find fault with yourself or with others. You will learn to surrender to the situation at hand, doing the best that you can and trusting the outcome to God. You will increasingly understand that your gift is acceptable as it is. It is always enough.

Thus, the time of self-crucifixion will come to an end, and peace will return to your mind. Then you will see me as I really am, for then you will have given birth to the Christ within. I await that moment with great joy and certainty. For that is the moment of truth. That is the end of separation. That is the end of suffering.


## THE GLORY OF GOD

*God is without form. He abides in all things.*
*There is no place where His presence cannot be found.*

God is not some abstraction. God is a living presence, all-good, all-giving, happy, whole, and without fear. Can you imagine such a Being?

Let go of the limits you place on what is possible. God is beyond these limits, for He is without form. Being formless, He abides in all things. There is no place where His presence cannot be found.

God is neither male nor female, for He has no body and therefore no gender. God is often referred to as "he" because He is masculine in relationship to us. We are the womb in which his Spirit is carried, nurtured and brought forth.

Although we stand in relation to Him as the bride to the bridegroom, God does not conform to some masculine image. He is neither warrior, nor shaman, nor savior. He is not the wise man with white hair, nor is He the wise woman either. All such images are anthropomorphic.

God is a loving presence that combines all of the positive masculine and feminine qualities. He is nurturing and also protective, gentle and kind as well as strong and assertive. He has the wisdom of the sage and the innocence of the child, the strength of the warrior, as well as the sensitivity of the young mother.

God is all this and more. He is beyond definition. He cannot be limited to the concepts we have about him.

As a non-limited presence, Spirit of God moves through our minds and our experience. The Spirit is not born and does not die. It exists before physical birth and after physical death. It is not subject to the highs and lows of mental-emotional experience. It is a steady, loving presence, to which you return when you have stopped crucifying yourself or attacking others.

The Spirit within you is not different from the Spirit within your brother or sister. It is a single essence. Bodies seem to make you separate from each another, but Spirit unites you. Minds may disagree, judge and attack each other, but Spirit holds all minds in simple harmony.

When you identify with the body or with thoughts of separation, you forget your essence. You think you are separate from your brother. You think you are separate from God. You could not judge or attack each other otherwise.

When you remember your essence, you also remember your spiritual connection to all Beings. Attack is impossible when you remember who you are.

When you are in touch with your essence, you know that you are acceptable exactly as you are. You know that there is nothing about you or anyone else that needs to be improved or fixed. To know your essence requires that you discard your self-judgments and criticisms of your brother or sister.

## KEEPING THE SABBATH

*From that place of peace within, you will arise
and be a peacemaker among women and men.*

The more you learn to rest in this state, the easier your life will be. God-communion is good for the nerves. It is essential for your overall well-being physically, emotionally and mentally.

I do not ask you to meditate or pray for an hour a day. I simply ask you to remember your essence for five minutes out of each hour, or for one thought out of every ten. Let your remembrance of God be continual, so that you do not get absorbed in the drama of your life. Nine thoughts may be about needing to fix yourself or someone else, but let the tenth thought be about that which does not need fixing.

This was the rhythm the Sabbath was to establish. For six days you could be absorbed in the drama of work and struggle, but on the seventh day you were to remember God. The seventh day was to be a day of rest, of turning inward.

Let the wisdom of the Sabbath be brought into your daily life. That way you will not forget for very long who you are or who your brother is. Enter into the ritual of remembering and your days and hours and minutes will be transformed.

When you eat, God will sit at your table. When you speak with your brother, God will remind you to say something encouraging to him.

Be easy with the choice your brother makes, even if it differs substantially from your own. Know that what helps him remember God cannot hurt you or hold you back. Put aside any words or beliefs that separate you from others. Overlook the differences you see, find what you can share with others and focus on that.

Truth comes in all shapes and sizes, but it remains one simple truth. You must learn to see the truth in every form and in each situation. That is what a man or woman of peace must do.

You are entering a time when the barriers of culture and religion will be transcended. With tolerance for diversity will come the perception of universal values which can be embraced by all. This is a time of great importance. Each one of you has a significant role to play in the dismantling of the barriers to peace.

I encourage you to find the place within where you are whole and complete. From that place, you will celebrate and accept all people who come into your life. From that place of peace within, you will arise and be a peacemaker among women and men. This is my teaching.

## THE LESSONS OF EARTH

*The seeds of transformation have already been sowed.*
*Your job is to water and nurture them.*

You are here to learn that all beings are equal regardless of their apparent circumstances. Men and women, black and white, Hindu or Catholic are all equal in their existential worth. All inequalities are of your own making and must be abolished.

Many of you have been working on this curriculum for some time. Some of you live in poverty conditions, while others have riches. Some have too much food to eat, while others go hungry. If you had already mastered the curriculum here, these conditions of inequality would not exist.

You are here to overcome your shame-based belief that you are superior or inferior to any other human being. You are here to learn to meet your needs in a way that is not unfair or hurtful to others. You are here to learn to make your own choices and to respect the choices that other people make.

The practice of equality is a profound one. It can transform your consciousness and your world. Then, when you have mastered these lessons, you will be ready to move on to greater challenges.

When you leave your body, you will move into a non-physical classroom, where learning will be accelerated and you will experience a creative freedom unknown on Earth, except perhaps in the dream state. In your dreams, you create your reality quite recklessly. You kill and are killed, make love to all kinds of people, move through incredible danger and have miraculous escapes. Few of you would ever attempt in your waking state what you attempt in the dream state. Non-physical experience is even more dramatic than the dream state. The creative possibilities are endless.

Earth school then becomes an environment for testing the skills you develop in the non-physical classrooms attached to Earth. You can't graduate from Earth school until you have demonstrated your mastery of the curriculum. All beings know this, and so all are anxious to incarnate in physical bodies to demonstrate the fact that they have learned their lessons.

Why do they have so much trouble? The dense conditions of physical experience are difficult to master. It takes time to develop physically. You start in your mother's womb totally dependent on her. When you are born, you are physically helpless. You have to learn to feed yourself, to walk, talk, and manipulate your environment. For someone who has recently experienced a non-physical environment where the effects of thought are instantaneous, this is pure torture. In time, consciousness contracts and moves to more fully inhabit the physical body, thus shutting off awareness of other dimensions with their creative possibilities.

Put simply, consciousness gets absorbed into the density of the physical environment. There it feels trapped and victimized. It does not remember its less limited state. It does not remember that it is not a body.

In a few rare cases, consciousness does not fully contract when it enters the physical classroom. These people inhabit bodies, yet still retain the memory of the non-physical dimension. They know that they are not limited to the body. They know that they are not the victim of other people's thoughts and actions. They know that they can create reality through the power of their thought.

These people are master spiritual teachers. Without the presence of these teachers, the density of the earth plane environment would overshadow the collective consciousness and block out most of the connection to spiritual knowledge. There have been times in human history when the Earth experience has been dark indeed.

The time that you now inhabit the physical classroom is a time of transition. Technologically, you have the ability to destroy the physical environment many times over. Yet there is more light available on the planet now than there has been in any other time in history.

Your lessons on planet Earth now are clear. You are here to overcome your victim consciousness and step into the fullness of your power and purpose. You are here to create and to learn to be responsible for your creations. You are here to learn to treat your neighbor as you want to be treated, to create equality and justice on the planet.

As you learn to establish equality with your brothers and sisters, you will also establish equality with me, for there is no brother or sister who is not dear to me. I see into the soul of both the criminal and his victim and I will not withhold love from either of them. Do not be shocked that I ask the same of you.

Be patient and steadfast, my friend. Our work will not be done until there are no more victimizers or victims. Everyone is to be embraced, as she is, so that she may let go of her fear and her need to retaliate against others. Everyone is to be loved without conditions so that she may open her heart to love.

To walk with me is to serve all of your brothers and sisters.

When the lessons of equality are learned, Earth will give birth to a more glorious curriculum. The seeds of this transformation have already been sowed. Your job is to water and nurture them.

CHAPTER FIVE

# The Tyranny of Agreement

*Your enemy is a mirror into which you look*
*until the angry face that you see smiles back at you.*

The ego's notion of love is based on agreement. It cannot conceive of love being present when two people disagree.

Yet unless you are free to disagree with your brother in any given situation, you cannot love him. If your brother insists to you that he is a victim of someone else's actions, will you agree with him? Of course, you won't. You will say "Sorry, brother. I do not see it that way."

Many of you cannot imagine that saying "no" can be a loving act. Yet it is very easy to say "no" in a loving way. If your child is putting his hand on a hot stove, you say "no" quickly and firmly. You do not want him to hurt himself. And then you put your arm around him and reassure him that you love him.

How many times does your brother come to you with his hand on the stove? You cannot support behavior that you know will be hurtful to another person and you don't want your friends to support that kind of behavior in you.

A friend is one who is free to agree or disagree. A friend will speak to you truthfully. She may or may not perceive the situation accurately, but she is not afraid to tell you what she thinks. A friend tells the truth and then reminds you that you are free to make your own choice.

This is love in action. A friend loves you equally when he is saying "yes" or "no." He does not withhold his advice, nor does he try to impose his opinion on you. A friend wishes to be helpful. He treats you with respect and dignity, and he tells you the truth.

You can't be a friend if you are not willing to be honest. But this doesn't mean that you are right.

Being right and being honest are not necessarily the same thing. When you are honest, you are giving the best that you can give with the awareness that you have. But honesty alone is not enough. Honesty and humility must go hand in hand. Your humility says to your brother "This is the way that I see it. I may be right or I may be wrong. How do you see it? After all, you are the one who must make the choice."

A humble person understands appropriate boundaries. He never seeks to usurp another's right and responsibility to make his own choices.

Because you constantly seek agreement, you rarely experience love without conditions. Agreement is the ultimate condition and therefore the ultimate codependency or collusion. It says "If your ego and my ego agree, I'll support you."

When two egos agree, you should be wary. That is because it is the nature of the ego to separate, to divide, to conflict with other egos. So when two egos agree, you can be sure that they are joining together to oppose another ego. This is not genuine agreement, but a temporary alliance. As soon as the common enemy is conquered, the alliance ceases to serve a purpose, and each ego returns to its own agenda.

Looking for love in agreement is not a very wise move. It is bound to bring you disappointment. You would do much better to look for love through disagreement.

You will remember that I told you "love your enemy." I did not say this to be perverse or difficult. I said this for several important reasons. First, it is easy for you to love your friend. Most of the time your friend agrees with you and supports you. So it is not hard to love him.

But your enemy disagrees with you. He believes that you are wrong. He sees your weaknesses and would do his best to exploit them. If you have a blind spot, you can be sure he sees it. To put it simply, your enemy is not willing to give you the benefit of the doubt. He is therefore your very best teacher.

Your enemy reflects back to you everything that you do not like about yourself. He shows you exactly where your fears and insecurities lie. If you listen to what your enemy is saying to you, you will know exactly where you must make corrections in yourself. Only one who opposes you thus can be such an effective teacher.

Why do I say "love" your enemy? I say love your enemy because if you do not love him you won't value the gift he brings to you.

No one can go through life without both allies and opponents. A good ally is willing to oppose you. And a good opponent is the best ally.

When you learn to love your enemy, you demonstrate your willingness to look at all of the dark places within your mind. Your enemy is simply a mirror into which you look until gradually the angry face that you see smiles back at you.

To make peace with your enemies, you must learn to see through their eyes, as well as through your own. Then you will develop compassion and move beyond conflict.

Remember, you do not have to agree with your enemies to make peace with them. But you must learn to love them.

Peace does not come through the agreement of egos, for it is impossible for egos to agree. Peace comes when love and mutual respect are present. When love is present, your enemy becomes like a friend who is not afraid to disagree with you. You do not cast him out of your heart just because he sees things differently from you. You listen carefully to what he has to say.

When you listen to your enemy the same way that you would listen to your friend, it is not your ego doing the listening. The Spirit inside of you is listening to the Spirit inside of him.

The cause of all human conflict is a simple one: each side dehumanizes the other. Each side sees the other as less worthy. As long as each side perceives the other this way, even the simplest details cannot be negotiated. But let each side bring to the other the attitude of respect and acceptance, and even difficult details will be resolved.

Miracles come from love. The solutions that come from loving minds are without limit. The willingness to love—to regard each other as equals—is the essence behind all miracle making.

Out of a diversity of perspectives comes the one perspective that honors everyone. Yet this perspective will not be available until everyone has been heard. Your job, my friends, is to give every person a fair hearing. This is the essence of democracy, which is not only a spiritual ideal, but a living process. When the process breaks down, the ideal is corrupted. But when the process remains strong—as awkward and ungainly as it seems—the ideal cannot fail to manifest.

A society that tolerates differences of perspective is a society that is based on the practical demonstration of love and equality. Those who seek agreement build totalitarian systems where individual freedoms are sacrificed and the whole never benefits from the wisdom of the parts. Such systems are doomed to failure.

It takes courage to disagree. It takes wisdom and foresight to maintain an environment of equality in which all perspectives can be considered. The path to truth has never been an easy one. It certainly has never been one based on expediency.

The expedient solution to conflict is to exterminate all those with whom you disagree. The goal here is not to love, or even to understand, but to destroy your enemies. That has been the prevailing value system on your planet throughout its history.

The democratic approach is a brave new experiment. It says, "Let all voices be heard." It welcomes diversity and has faith in the essential worth of individual human beings. It asks you to love, respect, and learn from your opponents. It assumes that the human heart and mind is deep and wide enough to contain all these perspectives. It trusts in your open-mindedness. Indeed, it entrusts its entire success on your ability to consider different points of view and, when appropriate, change your mind.

Totalitarian and fundamentalist ideas play to your fears. They are always creating enemies and seeking to overcome them. They believe that there is one side that is good and another side that is evil. They are oversimplified and dualistic in their perceptions of the world.

On the other hand, the path of compassion challenges you to love and accept all beings as equals. It makes no exceptions, for it knows that to condemn one person is to condemn all. It is not an easy path, for it recognizes that there will be continual challenges to your commitment to equality. And each challenge must be met with the full depth of your commitment if you are to demonstrate the truth.

Many people use my name in vain. They attribute abusive, judgmental ideas to me and use them to justify all manner of vile acts. That is why I must tell you clearly: do not use my name in vain. Do not use my name to judge any man or woman. I have never taken one brother's side against another's. Nor would I ever ask that of you.

I have asked you to come to peace within your own mind. And I have asked you to come to peace with all of your brothers and sisters. How can anyone distort this simple teaching?

If you have heard me in your heart, you know that you cannot use these ideas to justify any judgment or attack on another human being. When you would judge another, look within and ask "Would I judge myself in this way?" For any judgment against your sister is also a judgment against yourself and a judgment against me.

Understand, my friend, that you will not find love if you seek agreement. Love runs deeper than that. As you learn to love the one who opposes you, you will find the Source that goes beyond judgment or fear. In that Source we are all joined as equals, free to think and act in accordance with our guidance.

I support you in your freedom to choose, even when you make a different choice than I would make. For I trust you; I trust God's plan for your awakening. And I know that you can never make a mistake that will cut you off from God's love or from mine.

## CRIME AND PUNISHMENT

*Those who hurt others feel that they have no choice.*
*Those who know they have a choice do not hurt others.*

The seeds of all actions are to be found in your thoughts. What begins as thought quickly becomes speech and what becomes speech eventually becomes action.

Society says, "Only the physical action is reprehensible. Verbal attacks are unfortunate, but inevitable. No one would be foolish enough to try to hold another accountable for his thoughts."

You are outraged by the act of murder, but the thought of murder is acceptable. You have all had it. You are outraged by the act of rape or sexual abuse, yet you are not greatly disturbed by the thought of it.

Yet the difference between you and the one who rapes and murders is not as big as you think. I do not say this to make you feel bad. I say this to help you wake up to your responsibility to your brother.

If you can forgive yourself for having thoughts of revenge, why can't you forgive the man or woman who acts with vengeance? This person merely acts out what you have thought about.

I am not justifying the act of vengeance. I cannot justify any attack, and I am not suggesting that you do. I am simply asking you why do you cast this brother out of your heart? He is perhaps even more desperate for love and forgiveness than you are. Would you withhold it from him?

Your brother has been wounded deeply. He has grown up without a father. He has been addicted to drugs since he was nine years old. He has lived in a project where he has never felt safe. Do you not feel some compassion for the wounded boy in the man who commits the crime?

If you were to step into his shoes, would you do that much better? Be honest, my friend, and in that honesty, you will find compassion, if not for the man, for the boy who became the man.

I will tell you right now it is not the man who pulls the trigger, but the boy. It is the one who is overwhelmed and sacred. It is the little one who does not feel loved and accepted. It is the wounded boy who strikes out, not the man.

Do not let your sight be distorted by the angry, disdainful face of the man. Beneath that hard exterior is overwhelming pain and self judgment. Beneath the mask of mismanaged manhood and vicious anger is the boy who does not believe he is lovable.

If you cannot embrace the boy in him, how can you embrace the boy or the girl in yourself? For his fear and yours are not so different.

Let us first take away your mask of moral superiority and then let the boy or girl in you look out at the boy in him. That is where love and acceptance begin. That is where forgiveness has its roots.

Criminals are just one group of untouchables in your society. You do not want to look at their lives. You do not want to hear about their pain. You want to put them away where you do not have to deal with them. You do the same with the elderly, the mentally ill, the homeless, and so forth.

You see, my friend, you do not want the responsibility to love your brother. Yet without loving him, you cannot learn to love and accept yourself. Your brother is the key to your salvation. He always was and always will be.

Just as the individual denies and represses the negative tendencies he does not want to accept in himself, society denies and institutionalizes the problems it does not want to face. Individual and collective unconscious are filled with unspeakable wounds. The behavior that results is driven by the unacknowledged pain, guilt and fear embedded in these wounds.

Forgiveness brings a searchlight into these dark, secret places in self and society. It says to your own guilt and fear, "Come out and be seen. I need to understand you." And it says to the criminal, "Come out, meet the victims of your crime, express your regret, ask for forgiveness, make amends, begin the process of healing."

Acknowledging the wound is always the first step in the healing process. If you are not willing to face the fear behind the wound, individually and collectively, the healing process cannot begin.

It is hard for you to look at your own repressed pain. It is hard for society to look at the pain of its outcasts, but this must be done.

Everybody lives in a prison of reactivity until the wound is made conscious. It is not just the criminal who is behind bars. The men and women who put him there live behind different bars. If you don't bring your unconscious material into conscious awareness it will express on its own distorted terms. If you don't work intentionally with the criminal to help him come to love and accept himself, he will re-enter society with the same anger and vindictiveness.

Building more prisons or putting more police on the streets will not make your neighborhoods safer. These actions just exacerbate the situation by raising the level of fear.

If you want to improve these situations, bring the work of forgiveness into the prisons and the neighborhoods. Hire more teachers and counselors and social workers. Feed people, challenge them emotionally and mentally. Offer them experiences of safe emotional bonding. Provide them with opportunities for education and training. Give them hope. Give them acceptance. Give them love.

This is the work of a peacemaker. This is service. This is embracing your brother as yourself.

Please remember, in giving to others, you will be giving to yourself. Nobody gives love without receiving it. Nobody gives a gift he does not simultaneously receive.

It is time that you stopped trying to punish the sinner in yourself and the criminal in your society. Punishment simply reinforces rejection. That is the opposite of what is needed. Feelings of rejection must be mitigated and alleviated. Judgment and attack must be brought into the light of conscious awareness. Guilt and fear must be seen for what they are.

The work of rehabilitation is a work of integration. The darkness must be brought to light. All that is unacceptable must be made acceptable so that we can look at it without fear. The seeds of action must be found in thought, and addressed there. You cannot change actions without changing thoughts.

If you make certain thoughts taboo, you will be afraid to look at them. This is not constructive. Be willing to look at the murderous thoughts in the psyche so that you don't have to bury them in the unconscious.

Help people take responsibility for the thoughts that they think and the effects of those thoughts. Personal power and authentic self-esteem begin with the realization that you have a choice about what to think, what to say, and how to act.

Those who strike out at others feel that they have no choice. Those who know they have a choice do not strike out at others.

This is the key. Show a man the choices he has and he will not commit a crime. Crime is another form of self-punishment, unconsciously chosen to address unconscious guilt. The criminal commits a crime because he is still trying to punish himself. Society obliges him, by punishing him and reinforcing his guilt.

The only way out of this vicious cycle is for society to drop the agenda of ostracism and punishment and commit to healing. Every person in pain must be offered a path out of pain. Each must be helped to consciously identify his shame and unworthiness, as well as the patterns of abuse and betrayal that run through his life.

The lepers of your society are no different than the lepers of my time. They bear everyone's wounds on their skin. They are bold witnesses to the pain we do not want to deal with. Society should be grateful to them, for they are way-showers. They point to the path of healing all human beings must take.

## THE SEARCH FOR HAPPINESS

*The world cannot make you happy.*
*The sooner you learn this, the easier your struggle will be.*

This is the world of "conditions." It cannot give you what you want. It can only reflect back to you what you don't want.

The search for happiness in the world is a grim one. The world cannot make you happy. The sooner you learn this, the easier your struggle will be.

Please spend some time looking at your goals. How many of these goals have to do with accomplishing something in the world? You will see that many of them do. Don't be ashamed. Just realize that your attention is directed outward.

Once you accomplish one goal, you have to set another goal. You can't be happy with what you have done. You keep looking for happiness in the future.

Yet real happiness happens only in the present moment. If you are happy now, there is nothing else to accomplish. Indeed, if you become concerned about whether you will be happy tomorrow or even five minutes from now, you will forget to be happy now. All your scheming and dreaming takes you away from your present happiness.

Many of you have very important jobs serving others. Yet you are not happy right now in this moment. I must ask you: at what price would you serve others?

Do you really believe that you can bring happiness to another when you yourself are worried and stressed? Surely, you know that this is not possible.

There is nothing glamorous about the process of awakening. People who awaken do not become wealthy or famous. They do not sell salvation. They simply look into your eyes and ask "Are you happy right now?" If you answer "yes," then they smile back at you, because they know you are already in heaven. If you answer "no," then they simply ask "Why not?" Because they know that you have a choice to be happy right now, and there is nothing except your own stubborn need to wallow in the past that prevents you from making that choice.

All the master can do is ask "Why not?" He cannot tell you what to do or what not to do, for the responsibility for both doing and undoing belongs to you.

## NOT WITHHOLDING LOVE

*All anyone wants is to be loved and accepted as s/he is.*

Your brother only wants your love, but he does not know how to ask for it. Indeed, he is confused about what love is. So he asks for money, or sex, or something else. He tries to manipulate you to get what he wants.

Of course, you don't want to be manipulated. You don't want to reinforce his inappropriate behavior by giving into his demands. But you don't want to reject him either. So what do you do?

You give him the love that he really wants. You give to him what you can give freely and you don't worry that you aren't meeting his demands.

You say "yes" to loving him and "no" to being manipulated. You say "no," but you do not cast him out of your heart. You do not judge him, or separate from him. You refuse to be a victim or a victimizer.

You say: "No, friend, I cannot give you what you ask, but I will find a way to support you that affirms both of us. I will not reject you. I will not pretend that you are less worthy than me. Your need for love is as important as mine and I honor it."

This is how the lover talks to the beloved. He does not say "I will do anything you want." He says "I will find a way to honor us both." The lover is equal to the beloved. They are the mutual expression of love.

It is important that you understand this. Many of you believe that if you do not say "yes" to another's demands you are not acting in a loving way. That is not true. Saying say yes to another's demands is not loving yourself. Do not place another's needs before your own. Love has nothing to do with sacrifice.

On the other hand, some of you believe that you must say "no" to everyone to protect yourself from trespass and manipulation. That is the other extreme. If you have to say "no" to everyone you just reinforce your fear of intimacy. You build a wall around your heart to keep other people out.

It is important to see your pattern of codependence or isolation. Do you abandon yourself to try to keep others? Or do you reject others to try to hold onto yourself? Both gestures are a denial of authenticity and intimacy.

Only the authentic person—one who honors his own truth—is capable of intimacy with another. Only the respectful person—one who honors the other person's truth—is capable of being himself fully.

Do not capitulate to each other's demands or allow yourself to be manipulated. Set healthy boundaries with others. On the other hand, don't push people away when they approach you with respect. Keep your heart open.

Let your "no" to manipulation become a "yes" to love and support. Let your "yes" to love and support become a "no" to manipulation. Honor yourself and others equally.

Let love replace your grievances. If you feel attacked, say "no" to the attack, but do not attack back. If you attack others, realize it and make amends. Correct the problem in the moment.

The more you give love, the more love you will attract. That is because you stay in the vibration of love by loving. As you learn to say "yes" to people's need for love and support, their behavior toward you will no longer be motivated by fear.

Do not speak or act in a way that makes the fearful more afraid. Instead, speak and act in a loving way, for love alone redeems. Fear and condemnation have no place in a ministry of love.

All anyone wants is to be loved and accepted as she is. Give her that and she will not be afraid. Give her that, and she will have no need to attack you.

CHAPTER SIX

# Relinquishing Judgment

*Be patient with yourself and the barriers to truth will come down.*

All "objective" reality is based on subjective agreement. Yet, explore this area of agreement rigorously, you will see that it is paper thin, like a flimsy membrane draped over the world that you perceive. Behind that membrane, nobody agrees on anything.

Events occur with a certain rhythm and grace. But then you step in and try to give them meaning, and the rhythm and grace are lost. As soon as you think you know what something means, you cease to be able to understand it.

If you would know "reality," you must remove your judgments from it. This can and must be done with every situation in your life. Do not decide what something means. Just let it be and dwell with it, move with it, breathe with it. In time, insight will come.

When people come to you saying "I have the answer," send them politely away. Their answer is just as toxic for you as your own judgment of the situation.

Let others know that there is nothing in you or in your life that needs to be fixed. Remind yourself of this too. You don't need to change what it is. You need to learn to accept it and learn what it has to teach you.

The purpose of each situation will be revealed to you when you are ready to accept it. Until then, be patient and gentle with yourself, and the barriers to truth will come down.

## AUTHENTIC SPIRITUALITY

*Each path has its own simple beauty and mystery.*

The nature of mind is unlimited. It does not conform to time or space. It goes beyond all boundaries. Yet you experience only that portion of the mind that fits into your experience. Other aspects of mind operate beyond your understanding or awareness.

Those who have come close to death know that there is a reality which is beyond the limits of perception in this world. In that reality, communication is spontaneous and all-inclusive.

The interesting thing is that right now, without struggle or effort, you are in communion with unlimited being. Your body is bathed in light. Your heart is capable of receiving unconditional love and your mind is capable of apprehending truth directly.

This is the ultimate destination in the journey of consciousness. All forms of spiritual practice invite you to the experience of unconditional love and grace here and now. When you throw out the dogma and ritual you come to the essential invitation to connection and oneness. It is there in every tradition.

All beings are called to peace, joy, and happiness. To answer this call is to enter the path. It does not matter what form it takes or how you express it. Each path has its own simple beauty and mystery.

Authentic spirituality is not linear. It is not prescriptive. It cannot tell you "Do this and do that, and such and such will happen." Whatever is done must come from deep inside. It must be fresh, clear and centered in the heart. It must be done spontaneously.

The path home is never what you think it is. Yet it is never beyond your own ability to intuit the next step.

Deeply imbedded in your psyche is the call to awaken. It does not sound like the call that anyone else hears. If you are listening to others, you will not hear the call.

But once you hear it, you recognize that others hear it too, in their own way. Blessing them, you bless yourself. Setting them free to travel their own path, you set yourself free to travel yours.

## THE WAY OF FORGIVENESS

*You are the only person you need to forgive.*

I have chosen the way of forgiveness, because it alone undoes the lock of time upon the wound. When there is no time, there is no wound. Let go of the past, and you will have no grievances

Time makes the wound seem real. It makes death seem real. It makes all the changes that happen in your life seem real. Yet none of these are real.

You are in heaven, but heaven is not acceptable to you. Heaven does not support your ego, your schemes and your dreams. Heaven does not support your power struggles, your lessons, or even your forgiveness process. There is no need for forgiveness in heaven because no one in heaven is guilty!

Heaven does not support your soap opera of crime and punishment. It does not support your drama of sin and salvation. In heaven, there is nothing that needs to be fixed.

You think you get to go to heaven by "being good." Yet no two of you can agree on what it means to be "good." Is it any wonder that the road map to heaven is a rather crooked affair?

Some of you believe that I hold the key to your salvation and that I am the one who will remove your guilt. But that idea just makes you dependent on me and unlikely to forgive yourself.

I'm afraid that none of this is helpful. Your guilt belongs to you and you are the only one who can release yourself from it.

There is only one person you need to forgive on your journey and that is you. You are the judge; you are the jury; and you are the prisoner. An unholy trinity, to be sure!

The more guilty you feel, the more you will beat yourself up. Projecting your guilt onto someone else and beating him up only adds to the guilt that you carry. The only way out of this labyrinth of fear is to practice forgiveness.

Look at every judgment you make with compassion for yourself and the person you are judging. Do not justify your judgments and you will not make your illusions real.

You mistakenly believe that you can hurt others and that others can hurt you. These beliefs run your world. Yet if a single one of you could be hurt, if your wholeness could be compromised or damaged by suffering or death, then your world would be beyond heaven's reach, and all your murderous thoughts would run rampant throughout eternity. Yours would be a dark and unredeemable world.

I know, at times, it seems as if this were true. But it is not true now, nor has it ever been true, even in the darkest of times. Your world, your life, your thoughts, have never been beyond the reach of heaven, for heaven is here, my brother, and heaven is now.

You see what you choose to see, because all perception is a choice. And when you cease to impose your meanings on what you see, your spiritual eyes will open, and you will see a world free of judgment and shining in its endless beauty.

The shackles of Earth will fall away, and you will be free to ascend to your place amongst the brightest stars. There you will look down on Earth, as I do now, and you will say with compassion: "There I walked too, when I was afraid, and learned to walk through all my fears. It is a holy place, where every enemy became a friend, and every friend a brother and a teacher. It is a HOLY LAND where the dream of death and separation came to an end. I feel privileged to have taken the journey and happy to be home at last."

Then you will know that you did not have to take the journey to be saved. You could have stayed home without any taint on your innocence. But had you not taken the journey, you would not have come to know your innocence as you now know it.

An angel who has not fallen from grace can never be a co-creator with God, for she is not capable of conscious creation. To create consciously you must understand your creation. And to understand your creation, you must join with them and experience their journey.

This you have done, my friend. And so we welcome you back home. Your journey through sin and death has left you surprisingly spotless and intact. Hallelujah!

Lucifer has been redeemed. The prodigal son has returned home. All the angels in heaven are rejoicing. But those who have taken the journey themselves are also shedding tears of joy.

## THE DEATH OF THE EGO

*Either you will die, or you will wake up,*
*which is a different kind of dying.*

Dwelling in peace requires that you see what links you to others, not what separates you from them. When you see what links you, you can learn to respect your differences. Differences are healthy when they are respected. They don't interfere with the potential for intimacy.

However, trespass occurs when you try to change others to fit your image of how you want them to be, or when they try to change you. This is the push/pull world of the ego.

The ego is always taking sides. It has no native confidence or generosity of spirit. Its nature is to divide and conquer. Where it cannot divide, it cannot conquer.

The ego is the part of you that doesn't know that you are loved. It can't give love, because it doesn't know it has love to give. How do the unloved and unlovable find love? That is the cry of every soul in exile in the world.

The ego must be taught that it has love. This is a threatening proposition, for as soon as ego recognizes it has love, it ceases to be ego. The ego must die as ego to be reborn as love.

Now you know why most of you resist enlightenment. The idea of waking up is scary to anyone who is still asleep. You keep thinking "When I wake up, I may not be there!"

That is why your fear of death and your fear of waking up are the same fear. The unlimited, universal Self is not born until the limited, temporal self dies.

So death will come, one way or the other. Either you will die, or you will wake up, which is a different kind of dying.

Once you are awake, dying is no big deal. You have no more prized identity to lose. Whether you stay in physical form or not isn't important.

Dying is one of the best ways to learn to be present. If you want to wake up quickly, try dying. When you are dying, you are aware of things in a way you never were before. You notice every breath, every nuance, every flower, every word or gesture of love.

Dying is like a crash course in waking up. Now that doesn't mean that everyone who dies wakes up. It just means they've taken the course. Those who graduate from the course are content to be wherever they are sent. If that means somewhere in a body, so be it. If that means assisting someone in a body, that's fine too.

It doesn't really matter where you go because you have nothing to prove. You are there simply to be helpful.

Disengaging from meaningless identity is an inevitable aspect of the path back home. The less you have to protect, the more help you can be. And the more help you give, the more blissful your experience becomes.

While I would not go so far as to say "dying is fun," I would say that dying is "not fun" only because you are still hanging onto some shred of self-definition.

Your whole experience on Earth is a process of learning to trust in yourself, in your brother, and in God. In the final moment of awakening, when trust blossoms fully, these three aspects of Self merge into one. That moment cannot be described in words, but I assure you that you will experience it. And until you experience it, nothing will ever make complete sense to you.

# THE GIFT

*This is not my gift, but God's gift to you.*
*Because I received the gift, I can give it to you.*

Forgiveness is a gift that was given to you for all time. It is not something that can be taken away. It is there always, and it is the only gift you will ever need to move beyond the experience of pain and suffering.

Forgiveness works in this world, but it is not of the world. It is of Spirit and cannot forget its origin. No matter how many times the gift is received and given, it can never be exhausted. For every sin or perception of sin, forgiveness waits with the answer.

You do not understand the immensity of the gift, because you have not accepted it into all areas of your life. You have not accepted it in all situations. When you do, you will know that there is nowhere it cannot go. There is no situation in which the gift cannot be given and received.

Forgiveness is the only gift that asks nothing in return. And so it is the only gift that can be given and received without guilt.

The all-encompassing love that lies beyond the door that forgiveness opens is incomprehensible to you now. Therefore, talking about it is not helpful.

Be then as you are. Stand before the door and knock. Be willing to look at every painful and unhelpful thought and let it go. Know that every thought releases or imprisons you and choose to be released.

When peace comes to your heart, the door will open. The veil will be lifted. Moses will enter the Promised Land. Until then, dwell where you are, in the heart of your practice.

God gave you one gift for your journey and one gift alone. He said "My son, remember, you can change your mind at any time."

He did not say "Do not leave, Son." He did not say "Son, you will be miserable until you return to Me." He just said "Remember, you can change your mind at any time."

You can change your mind about every painful and unforgiving thought that you think. You can question each unhappy thought and think another thought that releases you and brings joy into your heart.

God did not say "I will not let My Son make mistakes." He said "I trust in your return and I give you a gift to see you home."

All your mistakes mean nothing to God. To Him, you are but a child exploring your world and learning, through trial and error, the rules that govern it.

God did not make those rules. You made them when you made this playground. You forgot only one thing, and God gave that to you with his blessing. He said "No matter where your journey takes you, Son, remember, you can change your mind at any time."

With a single loving thought, He made temporal what you would make final. He made unreal what you would make real.

You created the ashes of death. He created the wings of the phoenix. To every unhappy thought you would think, God gave a single answer: "Remember, Son, you can change your mind at any time."

Like Prometheus, you tried to steal the fire of the gods. But He did not punish you for this. He did not chain you to the rock where you would live throughout all eternity with vultures as your only playmates. He said "Take the sacred fire, Son, but be careful, and remember you can change your mind at any time."

Like Adam and Eve, you stood in the garden and became curious about good and evil. When He knew your desire for knowledge would not pass, He sent the sacred snake to you with an apple and invited you to eat. Contrary to popular opinion, He did not trick you into sin and then banish you from the garden. He just said "Be careful, my Son. When you eat this fruit, your perception of the world will change. This garden may suddenly seem a dry desert where nothing grows at all. Your body with all its innocent grace and wholeness may seem to be separated into parts, some of which you accept and some of which you feel ashamed. Your mind, which now shares my every thought, may seem to think thoughts opposed to mine. Duality and feelings of separation may seem to enter your consciousness and experience. All this and more may arise from this tiny bite you would eat, but remember, Son, you can change your mind at any time."

Not only does God not condemn you for your mistakes, He is not concerned about them. He knows the child will burn itself with an open flame. He knows the apple will give indigestion. But He also knows the child will learn to keep the flame carefully and use it to warm himself and light his way. He knows the body will adjust to the acidic taste and use the apple for nourishment.

He knows that your decision "to know" will bring you into dangerous situations, situations when you think your happiness depends on the way another treats you, situations in which you forget you are not a vulnerable organism in an arid and hostile land.

He knows that you will forget your origin, and that there will be times in which the Garden seems but a distant memory, whose very existence is questionable. He knows that there will be times in which you blame Him for all of your troubles and forget that you were the one who chose "to know." But all this does not concern Him because, before you left hell-bent into your journey of separation, He said "Just a minute, Son. It may be a long time before we meet again. Won't you please accept this simple gift from me, and keep it wherever you go in remembrance of me?"

Most of you do not remember answering "Yes, Father." But I assure you that you did. And so the voice of God went with you as you went into exile and it is still with you now.

So, when you feel forlorn and lost, when you forget that you chose this journey, remember, "You can change your mind at any time." I am here to help you remember that.

This is not my gift, but God's gift to you. Because I received the gift from Him, I can give it to you. And if you receive it of me, you can give it to your brother.

But I caution you, do not be concerned with the identity of the giver. I am not important. I am not the gift, but the one who extends it, as indeed are you. Let us remember the origin of the gift so that we can give it and receive it freely.

Christ is the giver and receiver of God's gift. And Christ is born in you every time you give or receive the gift. It does not matter who offers the gift of forgiveness to you. It can be your child, your parent, your friend or your enemy. All that is important is that you receive it of him. And as you receive it, you become the Christ and so does he.

All who give the gift are the midwives of Spirit. Each one of you is Joseph and Mary, welcoming God's child into the world. And each of you is also the child who receives the gift of limitless love from mother and father.

God gave you the gift of forgiveness. This gift travels with you wherever you go. When you do not trust it, he sends His Son to you to remind you of the gift. And His Son tells you that you must give the gift if you would keep it.

Many beings of light have come as the Christ, bringing that simple reminder. All have the same purpose, for Christ is not a person, but a keeper of the flame, a giver of the gift, and a messenger of love. Light comes from him, because he has remembered light in the darkness of the world. Love comes from him, because he has received the gift and learned to give it unconditionally to all who would receive it.

What he has done, you too will do and more. For in your salvation is the salvation of every Son of God. You who see the Christ in your brother will help them see It in you. And so the light of truth will be lit in many hearts and the star will rise again in the sky above the Promised Land.

Many magi—men and women of open heart and mind—will come together to witness the birth of God's Son on Earth. And many others will oppose them, not understanding that He is them. All dreams of crucifixion, sacrifice, and loss will array themselves in vain against the forces of love, and once again love will triumph over fear.

Christ will reach out and take the wounded child in his arms and comfort him. And that child will arise in the light of his love and push the stone of death aside. Many men and women will walk safely across the waters of their fears and open the door that lies on the other side.

The Son of God will awaken from his slumber and his body will disappear from its tomb. All the exiles will return home to the heart of God, the Promised Land.

If you read this, know that this will happen to you. And take heart, for I am with you. Together, let us give thanks to God for His gift of love and forgiveness, for His eternal trust in us to find our way back home.

Father, we remember that You are with us in every circumstance and we rely on You to guide our thoughts and our footsteps. You did not let us leave comfortless, but gave us mighty companions to light our way.

In your name, we celebrate our journey here, and pray without ceasing for the end of guilt, the single cause of suffering. And toward that end, we embrace the gift You gave us, the only gift that we can give or receive without guilt. Thank you Father for the gift of forgiveness. We will use it wisely. We will use it in every circumstance. With it, we will bring light to all the dark places of our souls.

*Namaste.*

# BOOK 2

# The Silence of the Heart

*Silence is the essence of the heart.*
*You cannot be in the heart*
*unless you are in forgiveness*
*of yourself and others.*

# Introduction

*You are the one who learns to breathe the body and lift yourself
out of the pain of self-created conflicts.*

Silence is the essence of the heart. You cannot be in the heart
unless you are in forgiveness of yourself and others. You cannot
be in the heart if you are worried or angry. You cannot be in the
heart if your breathing is shallow or labored.

When the breath is shallow, thinking is superficial. If you want to
live a spiritual life, bring your awareness to your breath. Become aware
of the times when you are breathing in a shallow way and bring your
awareness to your thoughts. You will see that your mind is chattering.
None of these thoughts has depth or significance. If you relax and
breathe deeply, these thoughts will fly away like startled birds. And
then you will abide in the heart.

When the breath is labored, thinking is driven by fear and anxiety. Your mind-states are rooted in the past or future. You may be
focused on what other people are doing and how you can accommodate them or protect yourself from their actions. You are building a
fortress of thought around your heart. Take a deep breath and relax.
Now take another one. Breathe and return to the heart. Breathe and
return to your essential Self.

Unless you return to the heart, you cannot see with compassion.
And one who does not see with compassion does not see accurately.
All that is perceived is a fabrication, a hyperbole. It simply feeds your
boredom or anxiety.

Breathing is the key to living a spiritual life in physical embodiment. When the body dies, the breath leaves the body. Where does
it go?

Most of you think that the body is the creator of the breath. Actually, it is the other way around. The breath is the begetter of the body. When the breath goes, the body ceases to function. It disintegrates into nothing because, without the breath of spirit, the body is nothing.

If you want to lead a spiritual life breathe deeply and slowly. Take the air deep down into your abdomen and release it fully. The more air you bring into your body, the lighter it will feel, and the easier it will be for you to accomplish your responsibilities. One who breathes deeply is not afraid or overwhelmed by what life presents because she has the energy to meet all circumstances. Only one whose breathing is shallow or labored and irregular is de-energized and easily intimidated by the challenges of life.

Unless you breathe deeply and calmly, you cannot be in your heart. If you do not know what I am talking about, put this book down and begin to breathe into your abdomen, counting to five on the inhalation and counting again to five on the exhalation. Breathe in this way for five minutes, gradually extending your count to seven, or eight, or nine. Do not force. Just expand gradually, as your lungs comfortably allow.

Now you are in your heart. Notice that you are relaxed, yet surprisingly alert. Your consciousness extends to all the cells of your body. You are content where you are. You fully inhabit your body in the present moment. You feel warm and energetic. You feel safe and secure. Your thoughts have slowed down. You are no longer focusing on the "shoulds" and "what ifs" of your life. Tension and anxiety are absent. Past and future have receded from your awareness. Your thinking is centered and dignified. You can stay with your thoughts because they are fewer and further between. Now bring your awareness to your heart, as you continue to breathe gently but deeply into your abdomen.

Can you feel the presence of understanding and compassion in your heart center? Can you see that you hold yourself and others in gentle acceptance? Can you feel the love that dwells in your heart and freely extends to others?

Now you are in your heart. Now you are in the silence from which all sound comes. Like a boat on the ocean you feel the waves swell beneath you. And you move with the waves, yet you know you are not the waves. Thoughts come and go, yet you know you are not the thoughts. Some thoughts propel you further out than others, yet still you can return to your center. Like a large wave, a particular thought may be charged with emotion, yet if you remain where you are, the emotion will subside. Now you know you can abide the ebb and flow of the tide, moving out and moving in, feeling the contraction and expansion of thought.

Beneath the thinking mind is a pure, non-judgmental awareness. As soon as you discover that awareness, the heart opens, and giving and receiving are effortless.

Observing silence and breathing deeply and gently is the easiest way to open the heart. You can also open it through sacred dancing and movements which incorporate the breath and encourage gratitude and presence in the moment. The method you use to fall into the heart is just a tool. Do not make it important. What is important is that you find a way to access the deeper aspect of your being which is at peace.

There is no human being who is incapable of reaching this state of open awareness and compassion. However, very few people know that this capacity for peace exists in them. Most human beings live a stressful life in which they struggle to make ends meet. Their minds are consumed with thinking, planning, and worrying. Their bodies are constantly in fight or flight, weakening the immune system and creating the conditions in which disease can take hold.

Few human beings take direct responsibility for their physical and emotional well-being. It is no wonder that they lack a spiritual perspective on life. When people do not care for themselves, they blame others for their problems. They feel like victims. They feel trapped in their jobs, their relationships, their physical location, their roles and responsibilities. They appear to live inside a pressure cooker. Either they stay in their external situation and feel victimized and resentful, or they leave that situation inappropriately before it is healed, leaving a wake of broken hearts.

If any of this sounds familiar, then you know only too well how easy it is to get caught in the struggle of existence. Your life has speeded up—you are busier than ever before—but to what avail? Your money and possessions cannot buy you peace. Your name, fame and status in society cannot bring you happiness. Be honest with yourself. Do you feel good about yourself and the people closest to you? Are you optimistic about life? Do you look forward to each day? If not, you are living a life empty of spiritual nourishment, a life that has lost its rootedness in the breath, the body and the earth.

Speeding up life does not make it better. Traveling across the planet in cars and planes does not create closer relationships. Many of you feel that your lives are speeding up, but you do not realize that you are the one pouring the gas in the tank. I suppose it is easier for you to believe in the destruction of the planet through earthquakes and floods than to take responsibility for your desecration of the planet through your own anxiety, boredom, and carelessness.

Don't you see that the Earth is simply reflecting back to you the quality of your own consciousness? Its pollution is none other than the pollution of your own heart-mind. The more you turn away from yourself, the more you abuse the Earth and each other. The more you forget to breathe, the unhealthier the air gets, and the more interpersonal conflicts arise. If you keep forgetting to breathe, the planet is doomed.

"Well," you say, "I can do something about that. I can learn to breathe." Okay so try it for a while. Breathe deeply for one day and see what happens. Then, try it for another day. In time, if you commit to this practice, all that is artificial in your life will begin to fall away. And you may be surprised how much of your life begins to unpeel.

Consider this. Is your job safe? Not if you go to work out of sacrifice. What about your marriage? Are you with your partner out of duty or love? What about your values and religious beliefs...are they safe? Or have they been fashioned out of guilt and fear? If so, they will not stand the ebb and flow as the breath comes down into the belly and out through the mouth, the nose, and the skin.

Do you really want to detoxify? Do you really want to slow down? Are you ready to let the excess stimulation go?

"But," you ask, "can't I still read my paper and watch the news on TV? "

"Yes," I will tell you, "but only if you can keep breathing deeply and gently."

Most of you will find that this is impossible. To seek your peace means for the moment that you must forgo false stimulation in your life. Anything that is trivial or overly labored takes you away from the essence of who you are.

Don't ask me to spell everything out. I'm not going to give you a new set of commandments. Use your common sense. See what brings you peace and what disturbs your peace. Take responsibility for what you consume, who you are with, and what you do. You have choices in life. One set of choices brings you struggle and pain. The other brings you quietude and healing.

Can you live without overstimulation? Can you slow down, breathe and live in the moment? It may not be as difficult as you think. Since you can only begin now, not in the past or future, it is a simple challenge. Try it now. Be in the present and breathe for a few minutes. The more you do it, the easier it will become. This practice will gather momentum, like a stream coming down from a mountain, taking with it all the blocks that stand in its way.

When you commit to the practice of silence, your relationship to the entire universe changes. There is no more difference between inner and outer. Earth and heaven meet where your heart and mind join in silent bliss.

Only your fear keeps you in resistance to life. Move through the fear by breathing and the resistance dissolves. Now you are flowing with the current of life and so it can support you.

Every indigenous people that has lived on the planet knows what I am teaching to you. And somewhere, deep in your heart, you know it too. For once, before your ego tried to take charge of the journey, you were the patient captain of your own ship, moving to a destination intuited but unknown. And it is the same now, even though you think you must work at being in charge.

Breathe and in time the river of life will find you and adopt you. Then you will be its spokesman and its confidant. The one who listens and the one who tells the truth. The one who serves without saving. and loves without asking in return.

All this you will do, because the Messiah has come and the Messiah is you. You are the one who learns to breathe the body and lift yourself out of the pain of self-created conflicts. You are the one, dear brother or sister. Only you.

## CHAPTER 7

# Integrity

*The potter is not defined by the clay,*
*but by what he chooses to do with it.*

Integrity is defined as the "quality or state of being complete or undivided." While you aspire to have integrity, many of you do not feel either complete or undivided. You feel discouraged when you look within and your search for happiness with others exacerbates your deepest wounds.

There are no magical fixes for this condition. It is the raw material of life which has been given to you to transform. You must mold it and craft it into a work of art.

It would be easy for the potter to reject the clay as inferior and unworthy of him. But were he to do so, his life would have no meaning. He is not defined by the clay, but by what he chooses to do with it.

What do you choose to do with the hand you have been dealt? How can you work with the challenges of life to come to peace in your heart and in your relationships?

The answer is a simple one, but it may not be the one you expect. The answer is that you don't have to do anything.

"Well," you ask, "how does the clay get molded if I don't have to do anything?"

The clay gets molded by your willingness to stay with and in your process. In your struggle, and in your surrender, the clay gets molded. The work of art is offered, torn apart, and offered once again. At some point, you know it is finished and you can work on it no more. Then you walk away from it and, before you realize it, more clay is given into your hands. It has a different consistency, a different potential. It brings new challenges.

Just being in your life is the molding process. Even when it seems that you are resisting or denying what is happening, the clay is still being worked.

"What about the criminal?" you ask. "Has he created a work of art with his life?"

Yes, he has. His life is the record of his journey through his fears, just as your life is your record. Each of you has told your story. If you look into his heart, you will see that his story is not that different from your own.

There are no failures on this planet. Even the homeless, the prostitutes, the drug dealers, are molding the clay that was given to them.

Because you do not like a particular piece of artwork does not mean that it ceases to be a work of art. There are no boring stories out there. Each tale is a gem. Each sculpture has genius.

Integrity is a universal gift. Everyone has it. It is part of the clay itself. Whatever you build with your life will stand up. It will be there for you to reflect on and for others to see.

You may choose to leave it standing or to tear it down. That is your choice. Others may gawk and say unkind things. That is their choice. None of it means anything.

There is no right and wrong in this process. If there were, those of you who are "right" would be wearing permanent halos.

You cannot say that what one person builds with his life is less valuable than what another person builds. All you can say in truth is that you prefer what one person has built to what another has built. You have your preferences.

Fortunately God does not share them. Not yours nor anyone else's. God listens to everyone's story. His ear is to each person's heart. Nobody has pushed Him away by making a mistake. All He ever wants to know is: "Did you learn from your mistake?"

Integrity is not something you have to earn. It is essential to who you are. There is no one here who does not have integrity, just as there is no one here who does not deserve love.

Of course, there are plenty of people who don't think they have integrity. And they have the unfortunate habit of trying to find their wholeness by demanding the time, attention, or possessions of others. These people are not evil. They are just confused. They don't know that their life is a work of art. They don't know that they are master sculptors. They think that they got a lousy hand.

One day they will realize that they got the perfect hand. And then they will start to work with it consciously and energetically. Until then, they are playing at being victims. They are playing at being broken, unhealed, unwhole.

A black person confined to a wheel chair may not feel whole, but he has no less integrity than anyone else. He has not been given inferior clay. There are no accidents in this life. Nobody got anybody else's clay.

You see the problem is not existential. Integrity is there in each one of you. The problem is that you believe you are not whole. You believe that you need to be fixed or that you can fix someone else. You feel a false sense of responsibility for others and you do not take enough responsibility for yourself. You are driven by desire, greed, guilt and fear. You attack, defend, and then try to repair the damage. Of course, it doesn't work.

In truth, nothing is broken and nothing needs to be fixed. If you could dwell in this awareness, all your wounds would heal by themselves. Miracles would happen, because the ego structure blocking the miracle would dissolve.

This human drama seems to be about abuse, but it is really about learning to take responsibility. All suffering is a temporary construction created for your learning. And all the tools that you need to end your suffering have been given into your hands.

When you are not blaming each other for your problems, you are blaming God. You think it's His fault that you are unhappy. You don't like being put to the test. Neither did Job. It's not fun to have your magical beliefs smashed.

But you need to realize that no magical incantation is going to open the door to the prison. It doesn't work that way. Freedom is much more simple and close at hand.

"Well," you say, "if I only had a helicopter or a 747 I could get out of this hole!" You don't realize how absurd that sounds.

Forget about that 747, brother. Just use the ladder.

"That old cruddy thing? That can't possibly get me out of here!"

You know the dialogue. We've had this conversation before.

Others keep pointing to the ladder, but you keep looking away. You have a certain attachment to being a victim.

The problem is that the victim will never acknowledge the ladder. He will never admit that he has the tools he needs to extricate himself from his suffering. For, as soon as he admits that he has these tools, he ceases to be a victim. Nobody feels sorry for him anymore. The game of being a handicapped creator comes to an end.

So if you want to discover your integrity you need to stop pretending to be a victim. You need to stop pretending that you weren't given the right tools. You need to take the clay and work with it.

Anyone who does this stops complaining and gets on with his life. He learns to take care of himself and he gives others the space to take care of themselves. Indeed, he releases all sense of obligation to and from others so that he is free to follow the promptings of his mind and heart. For him, there are no excuses and so there is no need to procrastinate. Nothing stands between him and his joy.

His life is his work of art and he is busy about it even as a bee is busy pollinating flowers. If you speak to him of sacrifice, he will laugh and say, "Work that is not joyful accomplishes nothing of value in the world." And, of course, he will be right.

One artist does not work for another unless he is learning something of value to his craft. When he stops learning, he moves to another teacher, or begins working on his own. Nobody can keep him from his craft. No one can take him out of his life. For his life and his craft are one.

In a world where everyone is a genius, there are no bosses and no employees. There are only teachers and students in voluntary association.

If you do not like where you are, you must leave that place or you do not honor yourself. Do not force yourself to stay in any environment in which you cease to remember that you are a creator of your life.

I once told you, "Leave your nets." Do not struggle to be worthy when you already are. Leave that job or relationship in which you are unable to be yourself. Let go of your neurotic bargain for love and acceptance. And walk through your fears. You will never find your wings until you learn to use your arms and your legs. Don't ask God to do for you what you must learn to do for yourself.

In honoring yourself, you needn't make anyone else wrong. Just do what is good for you and express your gratitude to others. When you are stepping into your life, you do not leave others hastily or in anger. You say your goodbyes. You bless the person whose life you have shared and the place where you have lived. Because you can bless the past, you are free to leave it.

You cannot "leave your nets" and take the fish with you. In time, the fish will rot and leave a terrible stench. For miles around, people will anticipate your arrival. "The Fisherman is coming." Your past walks in front of you. This is not the way to freedom.

Be strong in your conviction about your own life, but gentle with others. Do not judge their needs just because you cannot meet them. Just be honest about what you can and cannot do, and wish them well. Remember, the one whom you reject follows you. Only acceptance brings completion.

When you are ready to leave the entanglements of your life and step out on the simple path of love and forgiveness, you will know it in your heart and mind. There will be no struggle, no deliberation.

In your clarity and generosity, others will relax and release you. And you will hold them in your heart wherever you go.

The only prisons in the world are the ones of your own making. And only one who is ignorant of his own genius could hold another hostage against his will.

Remember, dear brother and sister: for every prison you create in your mind, there is a key that unlocks the door. If you can't erase the prison, at least claim the key to the door.

You are not a victim of the world, but the one who holds the key to freedom. In your eyes is the spark of divine light that leads all beings out of the darkness of fear and mistrust. And in your heart is the love that gives birth to all the myriad beings in the universe. Your essence is unbroken, whole, dynamic and creative. It but awaits your trust.

## THE FUTILITY OF CONTROL

*Outwardly, life seems safe and predictable.*
*Inwardly, the dynamite has been lit.*

The key to living in peace is the ability to stay in the present moment. You cannot live in the present moment if you think you are the one "doing" your life.

If you think you are the "doer," you will feel justified in making endless plans. But watch carefully what happens to your plans. See how they inevitably change, reverse themselves, or even dissolve into thin air as you begin to live out your experience. No matter how hard you try to pin your life down, there are inevitable surprises, and you should be grateful for them. Without these surprises, your existence would be one-dimensional, routine and boring.

Your ego is terrified of the unknown. No matter how terrible the known past is, the ego prefers it to the unknown present. All of its energy goes into trying to make the present into the past. It thinks that this creates safety, but in truth it creates continued terror, and a constant aggravation of the wound. Eventually, the pain is so intense that it must be dealt with. You see, everything, even your ego, conspires toward your awakening!

So living the past over and over again creates the ultimate terror. Outwardly, life seems safe and predictable. Inwardly, the dynamite has been lit.

You think you are the doer of your life and that you have created safety, when in fact your life is about to explode and you are about to realize that you have no conscious control over what happens. You believe that you are powerful, yet you demonstrate again and again your utter powerlessness.

This is an interesting paradox, is it not? No matter how hard it tries, the ego cannot create safety. No matter how many times the ego tries to push you out of the present moment, it inevitably brings you into it full force, because the price of denial is pain.

The more you seek to control life the more life will give you the message that it cannot be controlled. And then you may try even harder to control. You see? It is a silly game. You cannot win the game, yet you can't stop playing it either. This is the one supreme addiction. It has many forms.

When you begin to realize that you are not the doer, you drop the subconscious attachment to playing to lose. You cease to be the victim. And when you are no longer the victim, you don't attract a victimizer. The karmic contract is broken.

The wheel of the past stops turning, and you enter the unknown present with a new freedom. Now you can walk with confidence, putting one foot in front of the other. You can walk your unique path and discover the gifts that lie on the other side of your fear.

## THREE STAGES OF CONSCIOUSNESS

*When a stage-three teaching is heard by stage-two ears,*
*the result is a stage-two interpretation of that teaching.*

There are three stages in the development of human consciousness. The first stage is Subconscious Knowledge. Driven by instinct and emotions, this is the state of ancient man.

The second stage is Conscious Knowledge. It is characterized by the quest for knowledge and information. This is the state of modern man.

The third stage is Super-Conscious Knowledge. It is the state of intuition, surrender, present-moment awareness. This is the state of human consciousness now evolving.

You are living at a time when stage two is coming to closure and stage three is being born. The entrance into stage three calls for a different way of living individually and collectively. It calls for a repudiation of the controlling mind and an understanding of the utter futility of its creations.

Living in fear, the ego-mind seeks safety, but never finds it.

Because it never investigates its own fear, it is unconsciously driven by it. It projects its fear on every person or situation it encounters. All relationship dramas stem from the mutual projection of fear.

If you want to awaken, fear must be faced. It must be made conscious. Facing your fears brings the darkness to the light and ends the split between ego and spirit. The light that comes when darkness has been fully explored is not the same light that was there when darkness was pushed away.

In stage one, you reject the darkness because you are afraid of it. In stage two, you push it away by trying to explain it. And in stage three, you embrace the darkness and integrate it.

In stage one, man is ignorant of God. The Old Testament is the teaching for stage-one man. It says: "Do this or God will punish you!" It is fear based at the deepest emotional level. That is why God destroys whole cities in his wrath. The message to man is "become aware of God outside of you."

In stage two, man is aware of God but still separate from him. The New Testament is the teaching for stage two man. It says: "God is not vengeful. He loves you and asks you to come and embrace his teaching. Your life will be happier if you make room for God in your life." Stage two teachings focus on what you will miss if you keep God out of your life. It is the teaching of persuasion, still based on fear and separation.

My teaching was always a stage three teaching. I told you "The kingdom of heaven is within" and you must find God in your own heart. However, when the stage-three teaching is heard by stage two-ears, the result is a stage-two interpretation of that teaching.

Now this is changing. You are beginning to hear the teaching as it was originally intended. You are in communion with me in your daily lives. You are coming to the realization that a great deal of what you have been taught about me and my teaching is false and must be rejected. You know now that you must find me in your heart and in the uniqueness of your own experience.

## GRACE & BETRAYAL

*What you love prospers. It unfolds. It gets roots and wings.*

Your need to think about the next moment is an attachment to the past. It is keeping you in fear. Recognize this. Have no illusions about your plans.

Yet also be compassionate with yourself. Your responsibility is to love and be gentle with yourself at all times. Don't beat yourself up because you can't help making plans, but watch what happens. See if the external structure you create for your life continues to match the internal reality as it unfolds. See how you limit yourself by taking what is true in one moment and legislating the next with it.

The nature of mind with its thought/feeling states is changeable. Your goal in watching the mind is to recognize what is eternal and what is temporal. If you build your life on the temporal, you will live in constant upheaval, because the temporal is always changing.

The mind is not bad and it need not be condemned. Be present without judgment to the ebb and flow of your thoughts and feelings. Only the attachment to mind-states creates suffering, not the mind-states themselves.

Learn not to build upon shaky ground. Place your faith where it alone is safe, on the bedrock of your experience. Act from a place of peace, not one of desire. For desires come and go, but peace is eternal.

Relationships that support your joy and peace and ongoing healing deserve your commitment. All others are lesson-learning devices designed to wake you up by showing you your own self-betrayal.

Opportunities for abusive interactions abound. Ninety percent of the psycho-emotional terrain you will encounter in this life is unsuitable for building. Some of it is harsh unforgiving rock, some of it seductive quicksand. If you value yourself, do not build your nest in these places. The betrayal you experience will not be someone else's fault, for all betrayal is self-betrayal.

Be kind to yourself. No one else can fix your life or bring to you a joy you don't already feel within your heart. Build on what you have, not on what you want, for want is an illusion that comes and goes.

As soon as the desire is fulfilled, another desire replaces it. The chain of desire is endless. It always takes you away from yourself.

The best relationships unfold without struggle because each person is honest. Without secrets, communication prospers and intimacy grows. Consistency and continuity are established. This is solid ground. This is where the foundation of your life must rest.

You have heard the expression "haste makes waste." It is true. What is deeply valued has your full loving intention and attention. It is nurtured, watered, and brought into fullness and truth. It does not happen overnight. It does not happen exactly how or when you want it. It flourishes through your commitment, your constancy, and your devotion. What you love prospers. It unfolds. It gets roots and wings. This is the movement of grace in your life.

First, find what is real, what is true, what is consistent and dependable in yourself. Then you can offer it to another.

Do not look for solidity in others. It will never come to you from the outside. If your life is anchored in the truth of your experience, then that truth can be shared. But if you are looking for truth, or love, or salvation outside yourself, you will be disappointed again and again.

Grace rests on a tenacious commitment to yourself, a commitment that says "no" gently but firmly to all who would tempt you to trade their dream for your own. Only by honoring yourself does the beloved come. Those who twist themselves into pretzels in the search for love simply push the beloved away.

## MAPS AND SIGNS

*When you go on a journey, a map can be helpful.*
*But once you embark, signs are a necessity.*

When you are embarking on a journey it is helpful to look at a road map. A road map is an intellectual construction that helps you get a general sense of how to proceed. Yet it is not, and can never be, an actual description of the road. No one can tell you what the road will be like. Only your experience can do that.

There comes a point in every situation when preparations end and the experience begins. Knowing that you have prepared well may give you confidence, but only trust in yourself enables you to excel. Trust is a big let-go into the experience. It is a leap of faith.

Eventually, everyone must put the road map down and be present in the experience. Perhaps one encounters unexpected construction, a detour, or a change in weather. Driving a car is different than looking at a map.

The best that linear, sequential thinking can give you is a map of your potential experience, but it cannot guide you through that experience. When you are in the midst of the experience, there are signs that help you out. The detour sign tells you when there is a need for a change of direction. Highway signs tell you to get in the right lane or the left. There are signs telling you where there are places to eat, to sleep or to get gas. Without reading these signs you could not have a successful experience.

Signs come from the interface between outer and inner reality. They are created through our intuitive connection with life. Signs happen only in the present moment. You don't get a sign that says "go right tomorrow or sometime next month." Signs show you how to navigate in the here and now. They are extremely useful and important. Unfortunately, they are almost totally neglected by the left brain, linear mind.

When you go on a journey, a map can be very helpful. Left brain information can help you to prepare. But once you embark, signs are a necessity. Are you paying attention to the signs that arise in your life? Or are you trying to do your life with a map alone?

Each of you has access to guidance at a deep emotional level. If you will be present in your experience, you will see the signs that are posted there. The sign may simply tell you "this feels right" or "this doesn't feel good," but that is often the only information you need. You don't need to have a vision of a saint in order to receive guidance.

Guidance is your greatest ally in life. When you rely on your guidance, you can get by with a minimum of planning. But when you ignore your guidance, no amount of planning can guide you home.

If you know where you want to go, you can rely on your guidance to help you get there. Trying to figure out how you will get there intellectually is an exercise in futility. You simply can't know in advance. But when you are in process, the signs will appear, and you will know what turns to take.

The more you trust your guidance, the more spontaneous your life becomes. Your plans are flexible, allowing for unanticipated circumstances, yet you remain committed to your goals. Indeed, you are able to make commitments from a deeper place and when you fulfill these commitments you do so without sacrifice.

## RE-NEGOTIATING COMMITMENTS

*What matters is not whether you come together or apart,*
*but whether you do so in mutual honesty and respect.*

Often, in the course of living, commitments need to be revised. A plan is made for the future that is not materializing. No matter how hard you try to follow the plan, it just won't come together. This is a sign to tune in, release past expectations, and be open to what wants to happen in the moment.

Re-negotiating commitments is not a sign of weakness or inconstancy unless it happens chronically. When something doesn't seem to be working for you, the best thing you can do is tell the truth to the other people involved. More often than not you will find that others have their own reservations about the plan. Revising the plan is therefore in the interest of all parties.

Sometimes you may ask for a change in commitment that won't be reciprocated by the others involved. Then, you will need to tune in and decide if this change is really important to you. Is your fulfillment of the plan really important to the other person? Can you fulfill the commitment and still honor yourself? Usually, if your intention is to honor yourself and the other people, a mutually acceptable solution can be found. Holding fast to the possibility that your highest good is not in conflict with the highest good of others facilitates the discovery of solutions that honor everyone equally.

Abuse and betrayal happen when plans are held rigidly or agreements are broken in fear. If you make a commitment and don't feel comfortable keeping it, you need to communicate this to the people involved. The important thing here is not whether a promise is kept but whether a change in heart or commitment is communicated. At all times, you best honor others by telling the truth about your experience.

Betrayal happens through reactivity. Fear comes up and it is not acknowledged or communicated. The fear-driven behavior that results is an attack against others. The alternative to this is honest communication. When you say to another "I am experiencing fear and I'm not sure I can keep my commitment to you," you have honored both the other person and yourself. But if you say nothing and withdraw in fear or act in a hostile manner, you simply deepen the fear that you (and probably the other person) are experiencing.

The issue of commitment is one of the most charged issues that comes up for human beings. Fears of being controlled, abandoned or betrayed are universal. Those who demand love from others or capitulate to those demands are ultimately abandoned or betrayed. That's because they are betraying themselves.

To say "yes" or "no" to another person is a clear communication. But to say "no" and mean "yes" or to say "yes" and mean "no" creates the conditions for abuse. You will save yourself and the other person a lot of grief by being honest with each other.

Ultimately, no one must hold another person to a commitment made in the past which no longer feels good in the present. If you cannot release another person from the past, how can you release yourself?

What matters is not whether you come together or apart, but whether you do so in mutual honesty and respect. That is the key to it all.

## NEEDS

*The attempt to give or get what you do not have is futile.*
*It can end only in disappointment and sorrow.*

Your major disconnect with the rhythm of love is the belief that there is something you can give or take from another. This belief and the manipulations that spring from it render your life painful beyond measure.

Consider why you are always disappointed in your relationships with others. Whatever you seek from another always floats up in front of you like a balloon filled with water. As soon as you prod it, demanding the love you feel you deserve, the balloon pops and you get soaked. Be honest: have you ever received from another what you wanted that person to give you? Of course not! The only reason that person came into your life was to remind you of the nurturing you need to give to yourself.

Consider why you always hit bottom whenever you try to give to, help or fix anyone else. The very need to fix someone else betrays your belief that you are not acceptable as you are.

Whenever there is "need" or compulsion in giving or receiving, you can be sure love is a long way away. When love is present, one gives and receives freely, without attachment.

That is because you can give and receive only what you have, not what you don't have. The attempt to give or get what you do not have is futile. It can end only in disappointment and sorrow.

If you are loving to someone, you will receive love, because love always returns to itself. If you demand love, you will receive demands for love. As you sow, so shall you reap.

The law of energy is circular. What goes out comes back and what comes back goes out. So how can you "get" something you do not have? It is impossible!

The truth is that you have everything that you need. Nothing that you need has been withheld from you. In this sense you can only "need" what you don't need.

Please stay with this paradox. I am not trying to confuse you.

If you "need" something, then you believe that it is not yours to give. If it is not yours to give, then how can you give it or receive it?

If, on the other hand, you know that it is yours to give, you will give and receive it readily. And in this case you will not "need" it.

The perception of lack blocks abundance. In truth lack is not real, but the belief in lack is real.

If you wish to demonstrate abundance, question every "need" you have. As long as you "need" something, you cannot have it. As soon as you no longer "need" it, it appears in front of you.

Nobody needs love. Nobody needs money. Nobody needs anything. But those who believe that they need seek without finding.

This is a simple law. You cannot receive what you are unable to give, and you can't give what you are unable to receive.

Giving and receiving are the same thing. Giving is receiving. Receiving is giving. When you know this, the whole chess game falls apart. The mystery is over.

## THE PERCEPTION OF EQUALITY

*The perception of equality leads to the transcendence*
*of the body and the physical world.*

Being in a body gives you the opportunity to explore the mistaken belief that your needs are different from the needs of others. As soon as you begin to see that your needs are the same as the needs of others, the veil begins to lift. You stop needing special treatment. You stop giving others special treatment.

What you want for one, you want for all. You do not make one person more important than others. The perception of equality leads to the transcendence of the body and the physical world. When you no longer need to hold yourself separate from others, you can serve without being attached. You can give without needing to know how the gift is being received or whether it will be returned. Service is an opportunity, not a job description. In serving, you are not the server. You cannot serve and have an identity.

You can only be helpful to the extent that you don't have an agenda. When you need to "help" others, you're just cleverly disguising your own need for help.

The goal, you see, is not to move beyond the body, or out of this dimension. The goal is to undo the belief in separation that gives rise to the perception of one body as different from others.

All bodies are essentially the same. All bodily needs are essentially the same. All emotional needs are essentially the same. All beliefs in separation are essentially the same.

When you help another, you help yourself. You help your mother and father. You help your third cousin. You help the drunk on the street corner. Your help goes to all who need it.

Help is for one and for all. You cannot offer it to one without offering it to all. Nor can you offer it to all unless you offer it to one.

There is no time or distance between the one and the many. Each is contained in the other.

## TWO PATHS OF LIBERATION

*Either method works,*
*but you cannot practice both at the same time.*

Time and space are mutually dependent. Without one, you cannot have the other. The same is true for male and female, parent and child, black and white. All things exist in relationship to their opposites and are indeed defined by them.

The analytical mind is essentially dualistic. To know it must compare one thing to another. Separation is essential to analysis. That is why it is impossible to "know" God. As soon as you "know" God, you lose the experience of unity.

Much of the frustration you feel on your spiritual path comes from the fact that you cannot experience something and study it at the same time. If you stand back and observe, you will not have the experience the participant does. And if you participate, you will not have the same experience as the observer.

One spiritual method asks you to become an observer. Another asks you to be a participant. Either method works, but you cannot practice both at the same time. If you want to "know," you must learn to stand back and observe. If you want to "be," you must dive into the experience.

One method requires detachment. The other requires immersion. My own teaching is oriented to those who would dive in. It is an experiential journey into the roots of abuse. You learn by making mistakes and practicing forgiveness.

## BLESSING THE BODY

*Physical love is no less beautiful than other forms of love.*

Whenever I point out the inherent limitations of the physical body, someone inevitably interprets my statements to mean "the body is bad, inferior, or evil." This need to reject the body is a form of attachment to it. Where there is resistance to desire, desire itself is made stronger.

The body is not bad or inferior in any way. It is simply temporal. You will never find ultimate meaning by satisfying its needs. Nor might I add will you find ultimate meaning by denying its needs. Taking care of the body is an act of grace. Preoccupation with bodily pleasures or pains is anything but graceful.

If you wish to follow the path I have laid out for you, accept your body fully and care for it diligently. When the body is loved, it does what you need it to do. It becomes a willing servant to the goals of Spirit.

Austerities are counterproductive. You cannot transcend the needs of the body by neglecting it or punishing it. Only caring and love lead to transcendence.

Each body is a sheath or a veil that holds the soul in some degree of ignorance/limitation. You are attracted to the bodily form that allows you to fully experience your current level of fear. The more volatile your fears, the denser the body must be to contain them.

That is why it is futile to try to escape the body you are in. You chose it because you needed it. Accepting your body is one of the lessons of this life. And this, my friends, includes your sexuality.

Physical love is no less beautiful than other forms of love, nor can it be separated from them. Those who view physical love as unholy will experience it that way, not because it is, but because they perceive it that way.

If a child is born to you and your partner, he or she becomes part of the fabric of your embodiment. There is no way to escape responsibility for this relationship. It will continue throughout your lifetime. And you will use this relationship, as you use all your intimate relationships, to lessen your guilt or to intensify it.

Dogmatic rules about marriage and children are not helpful if you would walk this path. I have asked you to "love all equally." That includes your spouse and your children. If you walk away from your spouse and children without full forgiveness and completion, you are simply postponing what must inevitably happen if you are to find peace.

Does it matter how long it takes? No, not to me, but I would not be honest with you if I did not tell you that the longer you wait, the more pain you will experience.

"Is it ever right," you ask, "to take the life of an unborn child?" I must tell you that it is never right to take a life, under any circumstances. Does that mean that it will not happen? No, that is for sure. And when it does happen, one needs to have compassion for all those involved.

## RELIGIOUS RIGHTEOUSNESS

*Your job is not to condemn, but to understand and to bless.*

Only those who are full of pride think that they have exclusive understanding of the truth and the right to judge or teach others. The Christian religion—the religion that purports to be inspired by me—is riddled with countless cases of spiritual pride.

It is inevitable, I suppose, that someone will always be looking for a soapbox to stand on. And others who are uncertain in their own faith will listen to him and call him Messiah. Proclaiming his teaching, they will neglect the wisdom that lies within their own hearts. But such idols inevitably fall, and when they do the fears of the followers come to light for healing.

The one who stands on the soapbox may be foolish, but the one who listens to him is more foolish still. And more foolish than both is the one who condemns either one.

You need to learn to let others live and learn. The only help that you can offer them comes through your acceptance and love and not through your judgment.

I am not one to condemn adultery, or divorce, or abortion. For if I were to condemn these situations, those involved in them would be

112

crucified. You would have yet another inquisition, another holy war pitting good against evil, just against unjust.

Your job is not to condemn, but to understand and to bless. Your job is to see the fear in people's eyes and remind them that they are loved. Why would you beat, burn or excommunicate those who are most in need of your love?

Please do not try to bring me to the level of your fear and attribute your fearful, misguided words to me. Stop your insanity. You have misunderstood. You are mistaken. My teaching is about love, not about judgment, condemnation, or punishment.

I have given you only two rules: to love God and to love each other. Those are the only rules you need. Do not ask me for more. Do not ask me to take sides in your soap opera battles. Am I pro-life or pro-choice? How could I be one without also being the other? It is not possible.

When the truth comes to you, you will no longer need to attack your brother. Even if you think you are right and he is wrong, you will not attack him with "the truth," but offer him your understanding and your support. And together you will move closer to the truth because of the love and gentleness you share.

Every time I give a teaching, someone makes it into a stick to beat people with. Please, my friends, words that are used to beat people up cannot come from me.

I have offered you the key to door within. Please use it, and do not worry about the thoughts and actions of others. Work on yourself. When you have established the truth in your own heart, then you can go out and share that truth with others.

Do not be a mouthpiece for words and beliefs you have not brought fully into the rhythms of your life. All who extend my teaching do so from the same level of consciousness as me. Otherwise what they extend cannot be my teaching.

CHAPTER EIGHT

# Right Relationship

*Your own pain is enough to work on.*
*Don't exacerbate it by taking on another's suffering.*

There is only one way that you will find genuine fulfillment in your life and that is to learn to love and accept yourself. With that as a foundation, relationships cease to be traumatic. Perhaps that is because one does not bring such intense expectations to them. When you know how to "be with" yourself, it is not so difficult to "be with" another.

However, if your life is a flight from self, how can you expect any relationship to be grounded? It just is not possible. All you have are a clash of wings in a crowded sky. In your time, with the break up of both extended and nuclear family structures, more people are struggling to make contact with the ground. Existential rhythms of acceptance and love have been destroyed. Trust is barely alive in the hearts of the majority of people. This happens whenever the old dies and the new is born. It is a time of trauma and transition.

Recognize this. Do not seek outside yourself for happiness in a time of great trauma. What you catch in the net of your seeking will be more than you bargained for. Your own pain is enough to work on. Don't exacerbate it by taking on another's suffering.

If you want to dance with another, root yourself first. Learn to hear your own guidance. Dialogue with the hurt child and the divine host within. Practice forgiveness and compassion for yourself. Be with your experience and learn from it. Stay in the rhythm of your life. Be open to others, but do not go out of your way to find them. Those who know how to dance will meet you halfway. It will not be a struggle.

This is how it should be. If you are at peace with your partner, you are in right relationship. If you are not at peace, then your relationship is inappropriate or premature.

Inappropriate relationships exacerbate the abuse patterns of the past. Learning in such meetings is painful. A better choice can and should be made. But in order to make that better choice, one must be able to ask unabashedly for what one wants. If you let another dictate the terms of the relationship, don't be surprised if you don't feel honored.

You know what feels good to you and what does not. Say what you need, speak your truth, and be firm in your commitment to your own healing. Only through your commitment to honor yourself can you attract a partner willing to do the same.

These are simple truths. But they are not practiced. Over and over again, you compromise, play by other people's rules, and betray yourself. By now, you should be tired of repeating the lesson and exacerbating the wound.

I will say this to you as clearly as I can: If you do not know how to take care of yourself, and if you are not willing to do so, nobody else will take care of you. Your lack of love and commitment to yourself attracts people with similar lessons into your vibrational field. Then you will simply mirror back to each other that lack of self-understanding and self-commitment.

Commitment to another is impossible without commitment first to self. This is important. Those who try to act in a selfless way are putting the cart before the horse. Embrace the self first and then you can go beyond it. What I am suggesting is not selfishness. It is the ultimate surrender to the divine within.

The beloved comes into being with the commitment to self. S/He manifests outwardly as soon as that commitment is trustworthy. Then the outer commitment and the inner one go together.

In worshipping the beloved, one worships the divine Self that lives in many bodies. This is sacred relationship.

Few meet the beloved in this life, for few have learned to honor themselves and heal from the inside out. However, you can be one of these few if you are willing to commit to your own healing. Make that commitment and the beloved is put on notice.

Take this simple vow: "I pledge that I will no longer betray or violate myself in any relationship. I will communicate how I think and feel honestly, with compassion for the other, but without attachment to how he or she receives my communication. I trust that by telling the truth and honoring myself, I am in communion with the beloved. I will no longer try to make a relationship work by sacrificing myself to try to meet my partner's needs."

## MARRIAGE

*Marriage is not a tie that binds but one that releases.*

Marriage begins first in the hearts of both partners. In all loving relationships, one wishes the best for the other person. One is willing even to give the partner up if s/he could thereby find a greater happiness. Contrary to popular belief, marriage is not a tie that binds but one that releases.

One wants the greatest happiness for the partner in the same way that one wants the greatest happiness for oneself. One loves the partner as one loves oneself, with an equal love.

Marriage extends to the partner the same caring, loving intention with which one embraces oneself. It is not a new gesture, but an extension of a familiar one.

Marriage is not a promise to be together throughout all eternity, for no one can promise that. It is a promise to be present "now." It is a vow that must be renewed in each moment if it is to have meaning.

In truth, you can be married in one moment and not in the next. Marriage is therefore a process, a journey of becoming fully present to oneself and the other.

All couples would do well to remember frequently what their commitment is. To lose sight of the commitment is to desecrate the marriage. Adulterous affairs are just the unfortunate outcome of a lack of intimacy between the partners. They are not the problem, but the symptom of the problem.

When you are truly committed to your partner, it is impossible to betray him or her. For to betray the partner is like betraying the self. You just cannot do it.

You may experience an attraction to another person, but you do not have a desire to be with that other person. You do not fantasize about what it would be like to take that person to bed.

When you are married, the urge to sexual union is an important part of the sacrament. Marriage is meant to be a full-chakra embrace. Sexual passion is part of a greater attraction to be with the person. Whenever it splits off, sex becomes an attack.

Many married people engage in non-devotional sex. This is the beginning of a process of fragmentation that often culminates in infidelity. However, this could not happen unless one first desecrated the relationship with the partner by engaging in non-loving, non-surrendered sex.

When love is mutual and the partners are surrendered to one another emotionally, sexuality is completely uplifting and sacred. Nothing outside could threaten the relationship.

However, when communication in the relationship becomes careless and shoddy, when time is not taken for one-to-one intimacy, the relationship becomes a shell in which one hides. Energy and commitment disappear from the relationship. And sex becomes an act of physical betrayal.

Communion can be restored if there is mutual willingness and trust. For the goal of full-chakra union is realized entirely through love, energy and attention.

## DIVORCE

*It is unethical to try to hold others against their will.*

Relationships ultimately end themselves. The energy and interest is simply not there anymore. The road to divorce begins with the recognition that there is no longer a shared purpose and a mutual energetic attraction.

Not all relationships are meant to be marriages. Some are temporary learning experiences lasting a few months or a few years. Unfortunately, people marry before they know in their hearts they have found a lifetime partner. But, as long as the mistake is mutually acknowledged, no harm is done.

Shame about making a mistake in marriage does not serve anyone. Lots of people make these mistakes. Some people suffer with their mistakes, staying in their relationships long after they have lost their sacredness. Others bail out of their relationships too soon, before they have learned their lessons and come to completion with their partners.

This is not a new story.

Divorce, like marriage, begins first in the hearts of the partners. It is an organic process of dis-entanglement. When people have gone as far together as they are capable of or willing to go, divorce is the only humane solution. It is unethical to try to hold another person against his or her will. At best, the divorce happens in the context of gratitude toward the partner for the time shared. As such, it is not a separation, but a completion.

It would be dishonest to suggest that children are not wounded by the divorce of their parents. On the other hand, they are also wounded by the unwillingness of their parents to love and respect each other. If the detachment of divorce helps the partners to come back into mutual respect, then it can be progressive for the children. Children benefit whenever they see adults acting in a loving and respectful manner to one another. However, in a healing divorce situation, parents must focus intently on providing consistent attention to the children so that they do not feel abandoned or blamed. The importance of this cannot be overemphasized.

## PROCESS AND BOUNDARIES

*Honest, heart-to-heart communication restores
the feeling of love and connection.*

Learning to be in a relationship requires an understanding of boundaries. You need to be responsible for your own thoughts, feelings, words and actions so that you don't project your fears and insecurities onto your partner. Nothing is more confusing in a relationship than the cycle of mutual, reactive projection. While the pain of interpersonal conflict may eventually lead to greater consciousness, there are gentler ways to learn.

To learn gently, choose a partner who desires a conscious relationship and is willing to take responsibility for facing his or her fears. Choose a partner you like and respect, a partner who can hold a safe, loving space for you. Do not settle for less.

Then begin to practice the following simple process whenever you and your partner are not experiencing peace together:

1. Identify your fear. Fear is at the root of all negative, stressful emotions, including anger and hurt. Be with your feelings long enough to identify the root fear. Exaggerate the fear if necessary.

2. Identify how you see yourself as a victim. Peace leaves our hearts only when we think it is possible for someone else to do something to us against our will. How specifically do you feel powerless in this situation?

3. Own the fear and the feelings of victimhood and state them to the other person in a way that takes total responsibility for your experience. (eg. When you didn't call, I felt afraid that I was going to be abandoned. I feel weak and powerless when I depend on you to love me in a particular way.) Ask the person to listen to what you say without judging it or responding to it.

4. Check to see if the person understood you, so that you can feel completely heard.

5. Ask the person if he or she has any feelings (not judgments or defenses) about what you have communicated.

6. Listen without judgment or interpretation to what the person shares with you and acknowledge that you heard it.

7. Thank each other for making the space to listen.

8. Don't try to resolve anything now. Just feel good about hearing each other. Agree to talk again if either of you has more feelings or some insight into what happened.

This process works because it helps both of you take total responsibility for your feelings in any situation. When you "own" what you are feeling and communicate it, the other person does not feel attacked, because you are disclosing information about yourself rather than blaming him or her for your experience. This keeps appropriate boundaries intact and does not invite mutual trespass.

The process also succeeds because it does not focus on "fixing" either the other person or yourself. The only outcome that is desired here is increased communication (in a non-threatening way) of what each person is feeling. Honest, heart-to-heart communication restores the feeling of love and connection. When that happens, problems—which are merely symptoms of separation and disconnection—disappear.

Trying to focus on the problem merely reinforces it. The energy goes to "fixing" the separation rather than understanding its cause. All need to fix comes from an assumption that something is wrong and, if something is wrong, usually "someone" is made wrong. It is more healing to start with the assumption that nothing is wrong. You just have a feeling you are holding which you need to communicate.

Holding back feelings is the beginning of separation. Sharing them is the ending of it. This is the ebb and flow of all relationships.

The key is to own your feelings first and then communicate them to your partner. Don't try to communicate your feelings until you have taken responsibility for them or you will be moving into shame and blame. But once you own your fear, your hurt or your anger, communicating it helps you to be more honest and authentic with your partner, and that leads to greater intimacy.

## DAILY RITUALS OF INTIMACY AND PEACE

*Practice softening the hard shell of your life*
*and letting your partner's love in.*

Just as the quality of your relationship with yourself can be measured by the amount of time you consciously give to "being" with yourself, so the quality of your relationship with another can be measured by the amount of time you consciously give to "being" together.

Find ways to honor and take care of yourself while being with your partner. Communicate to your partner what is peaceful and nurturing for you. Choose certain rituals which sustain you both to practice together on a daily and weekly basis.

Each day, celebrate your commitment to each other by spending at least five minutes of quiet time looking silently into each other's eyes. Practice softening the hard shell of your life and letting your partner's love in. Remember why you chose to walk with this being at your side and reconfirm your commitment to his or her highest good. Start the day with the gift of your love for each other. And then offer it to God. Pray for a day of learning, loving, and self-disclosure. Pray to open your heart to each person who comes into your life. Pray to walk through your fears. Pray to be of help. Pray to listen for your guidance.

Each day remember each other and remember God. In this way, the spiritual purpose of your partnership is renewed.

Each night before you go to bed repeat this ritual. Give thanks for all that happened that day to help you open your heart and walk through your fears. Give any unresolved issues back to God with your willingness to do what is for the highest good of all concerned. Let any uneasiness with your partner be cleared. Looking into each other's eyes, let your hearts be open. Move into making love with gratitude and celebration.

## SEX AS BODILY COMMUNION

*Making love is a sacred act.*

The enjoyment of your sensuality is essential for the full unfolding of your relationship. It is nothing to be afraid of or ashamed of. It is to be celebrated as a gift from God.

Some people have trouble accepting their own sexuality and seek to impose their dysfunctions on others. Pay them no mind. They have their own difficult lessons in this life.

The only sexual expression that is reprehensible is sex without love. Some people are addicted to this kind of object-oriented sex. They try to find their satisfaction through the pleasure of orgasm. This never works, because after the peak of every orgasm is the trough of existential contact with the partner. If you love the person you are with, the trough will be a peaceful, comforting space. If you do not love the person, the trough will feel hollow and uncomfortable.

Sex without love is ultimately unsatisfactory and addictive. More will always be needed. More sex, more partners, more stimulation. But more is never enough. When you engage in sexual activity with someone you do not love, you dishonor yourself and the other person.

Sex without love lays the foundation for abuse. If you wish to save yourself much grief, do not engage in sexual behavior with someone you don't love. Even if you are in a loving partnership, do not engage in sexual behavior when your heart is not open to your partner. Sex without love, under any guise, fragments the energy of your union and exacerbates your emotional wounds.

This is common sense, yet how many of you practice it? Don't be sloppy in your behavior with your partner. Don't close your eyes and go unconscious. The beloved deserves your full attention.

## WEEKLY RITUALS

*In our tradition, the Sabbath has always been a holy time.*

Once per week, gather together with others in fellowship to remember the divine within each of you. In our tradition, the Sabbath has always been a holy time. It is a time when the whole community assembles to remember its vow to take its direction from God.

On the Sabbath, you take a break from the ebb and flow of worldly affairs. You give thanks to God for all the joys in your life and you ask for His help in meeting the challenges. Together you pray for understanding and peace. Together you create a safe space where people may open their hearts and move through their fears.

Honesty and self-disclosure are welcomed in a non-judgmental, mutually supportive atmosphere. Suffering is acknowledged, shared, and released. No block or dis-ease standing between you and another is allowed to remain heavy on your heart or his. This is a place of confession and atonement. It is a place where the misfortunes and misunderstandings of your worldly experience can be righted in the forgiving light of unconditional acceptance and love.

Here the couple and the nuclear family find the extended family —the community—containing a diversity of human beings: black and white, old and young, male and female, rich and poor, educated and untaught. Here the individual's heart is open to all her brothers and sisters. Here she declares her equality and her solidarity with other women and men.

In every community, there should be a safe, loving, non-judging space open to all. If there is no such space in your city or town, perhaps this is where your ministry begins. The simple pre-requisite is your willingness to join with another human being in the goal of loving and supporting each other unconditionally.

There is no soapbox here, no podium for teachers to preach their self-serving gospels. This is not a place where beliefs are espoused, but where the principles of love and equality are practiced. It is a place of forgiveness, a place where you are safe to leave the past behind and open up to the miracle of the present moment.

Leave all idols behind when you enter the door of this sanctuary.

Leave behind all your struggles for self-worth, approval, money, or fame. Here recognition is given to you freely and without conditions. Here you are an equal child of God, a brother or a sister to each one who gathers with you.

Support the community with your time, your energy, the money you earn using your skills and talents. When every member gives according to his or her ability, sufficient resources are gathered to support the sanctuary and its program of service to the community.

Remember, keep it small and simple. To maintain intimacy and integrity, spiritual communities should not exceed one hundred active adult members. Anything larger than this becomes an institution and ceases to be responsive to the needs of its members.

The simplest form of spiritual community is the *Affinity Group*, a group of eight to ten people who are committed to practicing forgiveness and learning to love each other unconditionally. The *Affinity Group* is a new-paradigm spiritual community that has a facilitator rather than a leader or teacher.

In the *Affinity Group* no one is allowed to try to change, fix, or heal anyone else. Self-forgiveness and healing happen in the group when the individual is willing to stop playing the role of victim and begins to take responsibility for his thoughts, feelings and actions.

The group does not pretend to have the answer for any of its members. It simply extends to each individual again and again the recognition of his innocence.

Members freely and abundantly offer their love and receive it in return. Often, they feel connected to each other in a profoundly intimate way that cannot be put into words. Indeed, each person gathered there is experienced as the beloved. As members of the group learn to perceive each other's innocence, they hold it not just for themselves, but for all of God's children.

## UNDOING SHAME

*Every evil you perceive in the world points
to an unforgiving place in your own heart.*

Shame leads to an upside-down perception of the world. You believe that you are "bad, damaged, or unworthy," and you project that belief onto all your brothers and sisters. Every time you make a judgment of another human being, you are reinforcing your own shame.

Peace cannot come to the world until it comes into your own heart. And it cannot come into your heart as long as you see enemies or "evil" people outside of you. Every evil you perceive in the world points to an unforgiving place in your own heart that is calling out for healing.

So please stop judging others. Stop the game of shame and blame. Every judgment you make eventually returns home. It is not others you are condemning, but yourself.

The whole drama of salvation is played out in your own mind. Apart from your judgments there is no hell. Apart from your love, there is no heaven.

You like to pretend that there is an "evil" not connected to your shame and your judgments, but it is not true. Every evil and every devil you perceive is a projection of your shame. Do not see the drama happening outside of you or you will lose the key to the kingdom.

The drama of shame and blame must be shifted in your mind. It cannot be resolved externally. You are the one who holds the key to the kingdom. I invite you to use it.

By shifting your own conscious from fear to love, the drama of shame and blame comes to an end. Bridges of forgiveness are built between you and your enemies.

This is a circular world. What you are willing to give to others you give to yourself. If you offer committed love, love that overlooks faults and soars above judgments, how can any less be returned to you?

In truth, thought and action are simultaneous. As soon as you have the thought "I am not worthy" an experience comes in to confirm that thought. This is not a punishment from God, but a testimony to the power of your mind.

Do not blame God for the apparent misfortune you receive. Do not blame your parents, your neighbor, your spouse or your children. Do not even blame yourself. Simply ask to see everything in your life free of judgment. See how you called for it and it faithfully answered your call. See this without beating yourself up. See this without beating the stranger who came to your door to deliver the message. Just see it in surrender, in reconciliation with your self, your brother and your God.

Everything that happens in your life is part of your experience of God. If your experience feels painful, ask "What can I learn from this pain?" Do not ask the pain to go away. Do not reject the lesson. For every lesson turned away comes again in another guise. Ask instead "What would you have me learn here, Lord?"

The Father and Mother of Creation ask only for what contributes to your awakening. Their love for you is both gentle and fierce. One type of love is not enough. The love of both father and mother are necessary.

Pray to Father for courage and to Mother for gentleness. With courage, walk through your fears. With gentleness, open your heart.

## FORGIVING YOUR PARENTS

*You cannot extend forgiveness to another*
*until you have claimed it for yourself.*

Your success in your career and intimate relationships depends to a large extent upon your willingness to heal with your parents and get on with your life. If you are still blaming your parents for the difficulties of your life, your connection to love and your own creative power will remain blocked.

Is your problem with the male or female principle, with the father or the mother, or both? Problems with the male principle translate into an inability to understand and fulfill one's creative life purpose. Problems with the female principle translate into an inability to develop loving, intimate relationships. Generally, when there is a problem on one side of the equation, there is an overcompensation on the other. Balance can only be restored by honoring both parents and their contribution to your awakening, no matter how difficult that contribution seemed.

Since all unconscious behavior is abusive, and all humans are to some degree unconscious, there is no human being on the planet who has not abused others or been abused. When you pick up a stone to throw at someone you judge harshly, ask "How can I judge? How can I know the painful place from which this act has arisen?" Be in touch with your own pain, your own reactive behavior and feel compassion for this brother or sister who is also in pain.

Whatever abuse you experience in your life must ultimately be forgiven. When it is forgiven, you no longer hold onto the violation. You release the shame. First you forgive yourself. Then you forgive your abuser. Do not try to do it the other way around. You cannot extend forgiveness to another until you have claimed it for yourself.

When you come to peace with your parents and accept them as equals, then your healing of the past is complete. You no longer wish them to change to meet your expectations, nor do you feel any need to change to meet theirs. You rest in mutual acceptance. As equals, you bless them. You respect their achievements and have compassion for their challenges and mistakes.

When you are complete with your parents, you stop creating parental lessons in your intimate relationships. You end the cycle of unconscious, reactive behavior and attract a partner who challenges you to take the next step in your growth.

The soul mate or life partner comes into your life when your parental lessons are resolved. Then the man stops finding his mother in his wife and trying to be her husband, and the woman stops finding her father in her husband and trying to be his wife. Unconscious, abusive relationships come to an end or transform themselves and the stage is set for the journey of conscious, committed intimacy.

## SPIRITUAL MARRIAGE

*Once you meet the beloved in form,*
*your life cannot continue on as it was.*

A soul mate relationship is an exploration of the dynamics of equality, mutual trust and respect. It is a mature relationship that requires good communication skills, generally learned through the forgiveness process in previous relationships. In a sense, all of your past relationships prepare you for full participation in this one.

The soul mate cannot manifest until there is honesty and clarity in all of your relationships. If you are abandoning a previous marriage partner or your children in order to be with a new lover, you might as well face facts. You cannot find the soul mate by abandoning any other human being.

Genuine love never results in cruel behavior toward another. This does not mean that you cannot revise your commitments. But it does mean that you do so with respect and concern for others.

Your soul mate cannot enter your life until you honor yourself and others fully. As you become ready for this relationship, you are internally directed toward him or her.

In the acknowledgement of your life partner comes a shift in the ground of being. No longer do you live just for your own peace and happiness. Your partner's peace and happiness is as important as your own. You enter a new stage in your life journey. One becomes externalized as two, and two become inner directed as one.

Out of your union comes a work that could not be accomplished till now. Together, you accept your spiritual purpose, and fulfill it gracefully as your relationship unfolds and radiates love to all the people in your experience.

Once you meet the beloved in form, your life cannot continue on as it was. All that is separately held must be released. The isolated self must die so that the self as partner can be born.

## SPIRITUAL COMMUNITIES

*When you offer love, those who need that love will find you.*

Committed love extends without effort to others who are ready to receive it. Gradually, those who join in sacred union are guided into small affinity communities of people committed to holding a safe, loving space for each other.

The extension of the safe, loving space happens naturally. There is never any urgency about it. It is not a "doing," but an allowing. If there is ever any need to proselytize, convert, or build membership in the spiritual community, the space will no longer be safe.

Growth happens because there is a natural tendency for that which is loving and healing to attract that which needs healing and love. Since this happens magnetically, there is no need to go seeking outside. The environments in which this is needed are endless: schools, hospitals, shelters, prisons, you name them.

Through this simple ministry, a space of emotional safety is established in communities around the world. People begin to create the love they want and a spiritual renaissance begins on the planet.

Consciousness is shifting now. The age of the individual is coming to an end. Once the needs of the individual are met through the commitment to self-care, the capacity for genuine intimacy unfolds. Sacred relationships are formed and abusive relationships are transformed.

As you open to love, you become a channel through which God's love can flow to others. There is no mystery in this. As soon as you make space for God in your heart, He brings the stranger to your doorstep. As soon as you make space for God in your community, he brings the outcasts and the disenfranchised into the sanctuary of your church.

That is the way of Spirit. When you offer love, those who are in need of that love will find you. Your job is simply to maintain the integrity of what you offer. Keep the space safe for yourself and others. Practice forgiveness and be compassionate with each other.

Do not interpret another's experience or pretend to know what is good for her. Accept and honor each person as she is. Make a space for her in your heart. That is how she is brought to God. Through your loving presence.

CHAPTER NINE

# No Other Gods

*God is a living presence in your life.*

The door to the Divine Presence opens through your heart. It opens through your kindness to yourself. It opens through your gentle acceptance of yourself in any moment. It opens through your embrace of your experience, through your willingness to be with whatever is happening in this moment.

The door to the Divine Presence opens through your kindness and gentle acceptance of others as they are in this moment. It opens through your willingness to be with them whatever they are thinking and feeling, without judging them or trying to fix them. It opens through the attention and the blessings you freely extend toward others.

The door to the Divine Presence opens through your simple remembrance of God in any moment. It opens when you know that you are not alone, that every decision you make can be given over to God. The door opens when you no longer need to be in charge of your life, when you no longer need to make reality fit your pictures of how it should be. It opens when you can surrender everything you think you know and come to each moment empty of expectations.

If you want to find God, stop looking for Her in sacred books and religious practices. That is not where you will find Her. If you want to find Her, open your heart. Be gentle with yourself and others. See your judgments for what they are: the obstacle to peace.

Stop resisting your experience. Stop withholding your love and pushing the love of others away. Stop playing the victim. Stop blaming others for your grief or your pain. Open to it all. Tell the truth about your pain. Let yourself feel the pain of others without trying to fix them. Be with it all and God will be with you.

Be in the silence of your own heart. Let your thoughts come and go until the space between them opens. Let your feelings of anxiety, boredom, frustration come and go until a softness comes into your heart, a patience with yourself, a forgiveness that rides in and out on each breath.

Let peace come into your heart, all by itself. As you allow space to be there without needing to fill it, feel the presence that comes in. That is the Spirit of God, Grace, call it what you will. It abides in you and with you now, for you have left striving behind. You have left your judgments and wounds like empty shoes at the threshold of this sacred space. In your heart now, there is only love, only blessings. This is the divine embrace.

Once you have tasted the absolute joy of this communion, you will not want to be without it. You will find a few moments every day to breathe and be, to let the world spill out from your mind, to let peace come into your heart. You will do this not out of duty or the search for approval but because it is sheer bliss.

God is a living presence in your life, not an abstraction. She offers you an ongoing relationship, a companionship that goes beyond the limits of form. When everything else dissolves, Her presence remains with you.

# THE ONLY AUTHORITY

*Accept no other teaching than the one of your heart.*
*That alone is God's teaching.*

Do not expect your relationship with God to look like anyone else's or you will sabotage the relationship. God's presence in your life is totally unique. Don't try to measure your spirituality by comparing what happens for you with what happens for others.

Don't accept any intermediary between you and God. Reject all gurus and teachers. Do not make the mistake of thinking that someone else has more spiritual knowledge than you do. That is preposterous. Anyone who is close to God knows that it is you who gives God permission to be present in your life, only you. The attachment to the ideas and concepts of others interferes with the clarity of your direct connection to Spirit.

Reject magical thinking. Let go of potions and formulas. Forget what you think you know. Forget what you have been taught. Come to God empty and surrendered. This is a time when all the idols must be rejected. All forms of external authority must be stripped of their power.

Cultivate your relationship with God directly. Enter the silence of your own heart. Talk to God. Pray and ask for guidance. Open the dialogue and listen for God's answers within and in the signs that She sends into your life.

Get to know God in your own experience. Accept no substitutes. Forget the priests, the psychics, the shamans who would give you answers. They are the blind leading the blind.

And know absolutely that any message of fear does not come from God or from me. Any message that disempowers you or puts you down comes from a false prophet, a manipulator, an avenger. Turn away from such teachings, but send love and compassion to those who profess them, for they are in great pain.

Neither take a teacher nor be one. Be a brother or a sister instead. Prescribe not for others nor let them prescribe for you, but listen to the voice of God and be guided by it. For you do not know. Your brother and sister do not know. Only God knows.

Accept no substitutes. Forget your esoteric teachings, your psychologies and your holy books. None of them can lead you to peace. Accept no other teaching than the one of your heart. That alone is God's teaching.

Do not take communion in a hall where fools preside and the flock is mentally and spiritually asleep. Those who wish to be told what to do will find out soon enough that no one has the answers for them. Do not give your power to impostors. Accept only God's teaching into your life and take communion in the silence where you meet Her.

You, my friend, are enough. You are sufficient. All the jewels of knowledge can be found within your own mind. All the joys of spirit can be discovered in your own heart.

Gather with others in mutual appreciation and gratitude to God, but do not take direction from one another. Instead, honor each other's experience. It is sacred. It is beyond comment or evaluation.

Celebrate your common experience. Meditate and pray together. Break bread together. Give, receive, serve together. But accept no other authority in your life but God's.

Each of you is guided in a unique way and has unique gifts to offer. Celebrate that guidance and those gifts. But do not try to give your guidance to another and do not accept another's guidance if he offers it to you. That is a false gift. For what works for one will not necessarily work for another.

The only advice you can give to the seeker is this: seek for truth within your own heart, for there alone can you find it.

Share your experience—your story can inspire others—but the boundaries of such an offering are clear. It is YOUR experience, not a prescription for others. Whatever truth someone else sees in it is the truth he is meant to receive. This, of course, will be different for each person.

Ultimately, you alone are responsible for the beliefs you accept. Someone can tell you terrible lies, but it will never be his responsibility that you believed them. So do not waste your time blaming the guru, the cult or the church. Thank them instead. Tell them how grateful you are to them for pointing you on the true path. Without seeing their weakness and hypocrisy, you would have continued to idolize them and give your power away. Now you can reclaim your power and resume your path to peace.

Whether they realized it or not, they have done you a great service. Any abuser is a great teacher. He or she teaches you clearly what you are to avoid. Indeed, negative and positive teachings go hand in hand in building the character of the seeker. If you doubt this, think of the ones who sit in mesmerized bliss idolizing a teacher who takes their money, their sexual favors and their power and be thankful you have awakened from that kind of sleep.

Everybody at one time or another gives his power away, only to learn to take it back. That is an important and profound lesson on the spiritual path. Be grateful if you have learned this lesson. It means you are closer to your own truth, and if you are closer to your own truth, you are closer to God, the universal truth.

You come to oneness not through conformity, but through authenticity. When you have the courage to be yourself, you find the highest truth you are capable of receiving. Then, you are not threatened by others. You interact with them honestly and work to support the common good.

An authentic person does not capitulate to any form of authority. He knows that people suffer when they give up their power to others. But those who usurp the power of others also pay a high price. Those who hold hostages must house and feed them. They spend most of their time building prisons. They will not find freedom, for they do not give it.

Freedom comes to the self when one rejects all forms of external authority and when one refuses to be an authority for anyone else. Paradoxically, that is also the moment in which the self becomes Self.

I urge you to claim what is yours. Empower yourself. Empower others. Be a brother, a sister, a friend, but accept no other teacher than the one who lives inside your heart.

## THE CATERPILLAR DREAMING OF WINGS

*Finding your true inner authority is the work of a lifetime.*

Your true inner authority does not submit to the wants and needs of other people, however cleverly disguised. Nor does it submit to your own wants and needs, which are inevitably perceived in fear. The true authority of your heart blesses you and knows that you are completely loved and completely safe. It does not want. It does not need. It does not seek approval from others.

True inner authority is rock solid and self-nurtured. It moves perpetually toward its greatest joy without harming others. It knows without hesitation that its joy is not at odds with the joy of others. It serves others not out of sacrifice but through the extension of an inner joy that is constantly bubbling up and spilling over. It is totally committed to its own truth and totally welcoming of others. It seeks not to convert others to its own experience, nor to push them away. It merely rests in its experience, content, full, willing to share.

Finding your true inner authority is the work of a lifetime. You begin by understanding what it is not. It is not the desire to please others and obtain their approval, nor is it the desire to please self at the expense of others. It is not drawn outward into other people's dramas, nor inward into personal wants and needs.

Call it God. Call it your Higher Self. Call it your Christ Mind or your Buddha Mind. Names do not matter.

You access it through your own stillness, by sinking through the superficial dichotomies of mind into the depths of the heart. And there, not surprisingly, you encounter God not as other, but as Self. In the silence, there is just a single heartbeat.

You see, if you were not already living in God's heart, you could not find your way there. Yet you do. Each of you, in some moment, stumbles on your absolute atonement and bliss. It comes so quickly you wonder if it was real. But, in fact, it was always real, always present, always awaiting your visitation, your openness of mind and heart.

Sit for a moment in profound forgiveness of yourself and everything in your experience and you will dissolve the walls which appear to hold you apart from God's grace. Moving into that grace, the world as you know it disappears with your judgments of it. This is revelation. It is parting of the veil.

Do not make the mistake of thinking that this experience happens only to the chosen few. It happens to everyone. It is your destiny. You will awaken, because you cannot sleep forever. You cannot be in resistance forever. You cannot be in pain forever.

Sooner or later there is a letting go of resistance and withdrawal. There is nothing to defend and nowhere to hide. You become visible and vulnerable. You accept the experience of others without judging it or trying to change it. You stop reacting, defending yourself or running away. You no longer withhold your love or push away the love of others.

This is the birth of the Christ consciousness within you. It is the indwelling Spirit of God come to rest in your heart. Now you and God are not separate but are One.

You talk about the trinity, but you do not understand it. Who is the Holy Spirit but the indwelling Christ, the Spirit of God that dwells in the heart of the Son? And who is the Son but you or me, or any other human being who knows his divine origin?

I will tell you this plainly. The human must die that the divine be born. Not because it is bad. But because it is the shell that holds the spirit. It is the cocoon that holds the wings of the butterfly.

But you do not have to wait until the moment of your physical death for the human to die into the divine. You can make this transition now if you are willing to stop resisting, defending, hiding, projecting shame and blame.

Right now you are like the caterpillar in the cocoon. You can't run away, because your legs have disappeared. You are afraid to push through, but you really have no choice. It is not possible to go back to being a caterpillar. You will emerge from the dark shadows of your fear one wing at a time. It is only a matter of time before you claim your wings and learn to fly.

## SALVATION

*You are the way, the truth, and the life, just as I was.*

It is you not me that brings your salvation. For you are the only one who can own your experience and lift it up. You are the one who brings the love you have sought from others. You are the one who rescues yourself from abusive relationships.

Only when you know that you are the light bearer does the darkness disappear. But before you can become the light bearer you must walk through your own darkness.

When there is nothing about yourself or anyone else that you are afraid to look at, the darkness has no more hold over you. Then you can walk through the darkness and be the light.

To pretend to be the light bearer before you have faced your own fear is to be a pretender, an unhealed healer, a sham. All unhealed healers eventually come off their pedestals. Where there is only the pretension to light, the darkness still prevails.

To be the light you must embrace the darkness. You must come to terms with the ego mind and see its absolute futility. You must learn to look at fear with love in your heart.

You must know that all fear is alike and all fear betrays a lack of love. And you must learn to answer fear with love. Love is the answer to your deepest sense of separation.

Once you take the torch of truth up for yourself and bring love to the wounded parts of your mind, you take back your power. You surrender your victimhood. You can no longer be unfairly treated.

Where does love come from? It comes from you. You are the way, the truth, and the life, just as I was. Don't look for the divine outside yourself, for it cannot be found there. It can be found only in your own heart.

## WHEN HEAVEN COMES TO EARTH

*When you trust the gifts that have been given you,*
*the purpose of your life becomes clear.*

When does the kingdom of Heaven come to Earth? As soon as you accept the light, own it and become it. As soon as you open your heart and walk through your fears. As soon as you are willing to see yourself reflected in your brother's eyes.

When does the Messiah come? No, not later, not even at the end of time. But now. Now is the end of time. The end of separation. Now is the end of self-crucifixion. The end of projection. The final death knell of fear. Now.

Do not place salvation in the future or it will never come. Ask for it now. Accept it now.

God's kingdom manifests in this moment only. In this place only.

It does not require a special time. Every time is special. It does not require a special place. Every place is special.

When does Heaven come? When this moment is enough. When this place is enough. When this friend is enough. When these events and circumstances are acceptable. When you no longer crave something other than what stands before you in this moment.

When you come to peace with what is, there is no more separation. No more wanting. No more striving. No more resisting. No more withdrawal.

You are what is and it is you. You inhabit the cosmic body even as you move your physical arms and feet. You are freedom manifest in bodily form.

Even if you have a physical illness or disability, there is no resentment. There is no presumption of attack. There is no guilt or perception of punishment. There is just the experience and your simple acceptance of it. There is just your innocence, however ungainly or compromised your position may look.

You cannot be compromised if you are in acceptance of your life. You cannot be resentful or wracked by grievances. Whatever your life is becomes the vehicle. Whatever the body looks like is acceptable. Whatever gifts you have to give are the perfect ones. It does not matter if they are not the ones you thought you would have or the ones you wanted.

When you are in acceptance of your life, you do not refuse to give your gifts because they do not meet your expectations. You give them because they are there to be given, because the opportunity to give presents itself and because, in the giving of those gifts, your destiny is revealed.

When you begin to trust the gifts that have been given you, the purpose of your life becomes clear. You may not be able to put it into words, but you understand. You see how every lesson, every constriction, every problem, every moment of suffering was absolutely necessary for the gift to be revealed, trusted, given and received.

When you are in acceptance of your life, you are profoundly grateful, because you see and feel that a greater intelligence is operating in your life. That intelligence rests inside your heart and the heart of all beings. Its serves your good and the good of others simultaneously.

# FAITH

*Faith is the recognition of a higher good, a higher order.*

Faith is the perception of goodness in that which appears to be evil. It is the perception of abundance in what appears to be lacking. It is the perception of justice in that which seems unfair.

Faith is the bringing of love to the unlovable. It is the bringing of compassion to the unmerciful. It is the bringing of God's presence to the places where It seems to be absent.

Faith is the recognition of a higher good, a higher order, a higher truth than the one the frightened child would see. And faith is always won in the trenches.

Where do you find God's presence? In the moments when you feel totally abandoned and rejected!

This seems to be unfair, but it is hardly so. As long as you believe that you can be attacked, the Christ child will be perceived as an abused child.

Small and defenseless, he does not fight back. He does not resist evil, because he knows evil is simply the perceived absence of love. And the perceived absence of love can be transformed only by love's presence.

The strongest power in the universe seems to be so weak, so easily overpowered, crucified and forgotten. But it is not so. All who attack the Christ must return to serve Him. And they will keep coming back until they learn that He is them and therefore He cannot be destroyed.

Only in the deepest pain of existence is faith in God discovered. This is no mystery. It is the moment in which you realize that everything outside you is merely a reflection of an attitude you have toward yourself. In that moment, you stop being a victim. In that moment, you know your life has been perfect just as it is and has been.

When you awaken, my job will be complete. In truth, it is already complete, but you will keep returning until you know this in your heart, once and for all.

## THE LIGHT BEARER

*When Lucifer is redeemed, the light comes to man.*

A false prophet is one who makes his ego into a god. He claims to be self-realized, free of suffering and fear, but sooner or later his behavior betrays him and he is exposed as an imposter.

I have said before and I will say again: "By your fruits, you will know them." Do not listen to the clever, persuasive words of those who claim spiritual authority. Look to their actions. See if what they do is at odds with what they say.

If you are wise, you will not follow anyone. Then you will not be misled. But if you must find a teacher or a leader, look for one who empowers you to hear the truth in your own heart. Look for one who loves you without seeking to control you, one who is able to tell you his or her truth without expecting you to agree with it. Find a teacher who honors you and treats you with dignity and respect.

Anyone who claims a special knowledge and sells it for a price is a false prophet. Anyone who needs you to bow down, agree with his opinions, or carry out his agenda is a false prophet. Anyone who withholds love to gain money or sexual favors is a false prophet. Anyone who encourages you to give away your power, your self-respect or your dignity is a false prophet. Do not abide with such people. They do not have your good at heart. They are still abusing themselves and others.

Do not seek the company of one who smothers you and does not give you the freedom to be yourself. Do not accept a teacher who tries to make decisions for you. Do not accept the teachings or the friendship of one who criticizes you or blames you for his problems. Do not let anyone dictate to you or control your life.

On the other hand, do not dictate to someone else. Any need you have to control another person or make decisions for that person is abusive. Do not trespass on others or seek to take away their freedom to decide for what they want. Any attempt to do so simply binds you to the wheel of suffering.

What you give to others is what you get back. Do not be a victimizer or a victim. Be yourself and allow others to be themselves.

The Antichrist seeks salvation and peace by controlling others. It is the attempt to force reconciliation. It never works. What lives by the sword dies by the sword. Wrong means always lead to wrong ends.

However, even the Antichrist is not evil. He is simply starved for love. Being starved for love, he tries to buy it, demand it, control it. And by so doing he pushes love further away. The more love eludes him the more vicious he gets.

Often the Antichrist impersonates the Christ. The wolf appears in sheep's clothing. She seems to be gentle, compassionate and wise, but it is all an act. As soon as she has your allegiance, her true colors appear. That is why you must be very careful. You think you are worshipping Christ, but it is not Christ you are worshipping. It is the ego in disguise.

It is the scared, unhappy, angry little kid inside of you who feels unfairly treated. The wounded child is formidable only because you resist him. You are ashamed of him and push him away. All his shenanigans stem from the belief he has that he is not lovable.

When you have embraced the wounded child within, his angelic presence is revealed. Lucifer is not a sinful human, but a fallen angel. When he reconnects to love, his fall is broken and he finds his wings.

Lucifer means light bearer. He is the wounded child transformed into a shining being. When Lucifer is redeemed, the light comes to man. Victim and victimizer meet face to face. Equality and justice are realized.

Then Antichrist's work on Earth is done. The long detour is over. The long journey into fear and back is finally complete. Now you come home at last. Now you know that your innocence cannot be taken away from you. Once loved by God, you can never be abandoned by him, even though you stray far away from the fold. The prodigal son always returns home.

## DARK WINGS TO LIGHT

*You cannot awaken if your heart is closed.*

The greatest block to spiritual awakening is the pretension that you have no pain. If you don't feel pain in your life, you are either awakened or you are in denial.

There are few awakened beings on the planet and chances are you are not among them. I say this so that you can be realistic about your spiritual life.

The defenses you have built to protect yourself from attack or abandonment are blocks to love's presence. They may have helped dull the pain, but they have also closed down your heart. And you cannot awaken with a closed heart.

Of course, as soon as your heart opens, you feel all the pain and shame you have intellectualized or repressed. It is inevitable. So let the pain come up and be released. Be cleansed and purified.

If you continue to live with the pain, you will live a terribly limited life. By feeling the pain, you begin to work it through. You see that it is not overwhelming. You see you can be with it without being destroyed. You can feel the hurt, the anger, and the betrayal you never allowed yourself to feel as a child.

You cannot cease being a victim until you get in touch with why you became one in the first place. Get in touch with the self-betrayal and own it. No, don't beat yourself for it. Just own it and grieve it fully.

It is a spiritual law that no one can betray you but you. Don't settle for the victim role. It keeps you from experiencing all the pain of your self-betrayal. Let the pain be released. You have carried all this too long.

Very few people have done their own healing process. Even the ones who are out there trying to help others have not healed their own victim drama. How can they help you?

If you need a coach, choose one who has traveled the road him or herself. And be careful; there are not many who have. If you look carefully, you can see if the darkness in them has been integrated or if they are still pushing it away.

Anyone who is afraid of his own darkness cannot move toward the light. Do not accept a wounded healer, even if he has an angelic name. Find a coach without an agenda who can support in going through your dark night of the soul. Find a guide who has successfully taken the journey and has learned to be humble.

Don't trust those that make big claims. They are good salesmen but lousy mentors. Find a real mentor who can tell you the truth.

One who has made the journey to hell and back does not have sky fever. She is practical and grounded. She knows the dangers of blasting off into the heavens without a safe way to get back to Earth.

Your ego mind is the creator of your earthly experience with all its manifest pain and beauty. And you must find a way to come face to face with your ego and the fear that stands behind it.

You cannot move outside your own creation. You must move in it, be with it, and learn how to shift it. God will not come as a savior to free you from a world of your own making. That is an old paradigm idea. It does not empower you. Even if it were possible, it would not be in your best interest.

God comes through your own gesture of acceptance toward your ego mind. He comes in the love and compassion you bring to the wounded one within and without. He comes when you reach down to embrace the dark wings that hover in front of the doorway of your fear.

These wings will not hurt you. No one is defiled no matter how great the hurt. No one is robbed of his innocence, no matter how much abuse has been given or received.

You cannot come to God if you don't go through the dark night of the soul. All your fear and shame must be raised. All your feelings of separation must come up for healing. How can you rise from the ashes of your pain unless you will acknowledge the pain?

Those who pretend that there is no wound cannot begin to awaken. Those who mercilessly prod the wound will find an identity there and their growth will be arrested.

If you want to heal, feel the pain. Find the wound and the shame around it. Forgive yourself and the one who hurt you. Then, stand up for yourself and refuse to be a victim again. Refuse to accept what does not feel good. Say no to what you do not want and yes to what you do want. Tell the truth, even if others leave. Be firm. Be clear. Get on with your life.

When you are willing to heal, your pain automatically comes up to be released. The pieces of the puzzle emerge and begin to fit together. But this doesn't happen all at once. It is a process that unfolds at its own pace and can't be rushed.

You may try to run away from your pain, taking refuge in a drink, a pill, a meditation method, or a mountain cave. But your pain will follow you wherever you go. If you ignore it long enough, it will grab you when you least expect it.

Pain is a wake up call. Your awakening can be voluntary or forced, gentle or abrupt. If you receive the messenger, he will deliver the message and go away. If you refuse to open the door to him, he will come back with the sheriff and his deputies.

## ENDING ABUSE

*Once you become aware of the violation,*
*your journey to healing begins.*

If you did not make the wound, you could not unmake it. So be glad that your suffering is no one else's fault. Celebrate the fact that redemption is possible, that you can undo what you have done. But do not beat yourself with the knowledge that you are the creator of your suffering.

Your creations happen unconsciously, so in truth you do not know what you are doing. If you knew, you wouldn't do it. Becoming conscious of the way in which you abuse yourself or give others permission to abuse you is essential to undoing the abuse.

Until you become aware of the dynamic, you cannot change it. You can never be held responsible for what you do not understand. Your responsibility begins with your awareness of the abuse.

Once you become aware of the violation, your journey to healing begins. So pain is not bad. It is not a punishment. It is a call to awaken.

Don't beat yourself with the knowledge that you made a mistake, that you acted irresponsibly. Instead, correct your errors. Atone for the mistake. Take responsibility for your behavior so that the pattern of abuse can be undone.

Pain is a call to consciousness. Do not try to anesthetize the pain to dull it or make it go away. Feel the pain and find out what caused it. Become aware of your wound and bring love to it.

Until understanding dawns and responsibility is taken, new abusive situations will be created. Each of them conspires to wake you up. None of them carries the necessity of pain if you are a willing learner.

Each relationship offers you the opportunity to say no to what does not honor you. If you can say no before the violation occurs, you can avoid additional suffering. But if you accept cruel, controlling or unfair treatment in exchange for the security and approval you want, you will create the conditions in which abuse continues to happen.

Understand that it will not work. Love cannot be bargained for. You must wait for the real thing.

When love is given to you without conditions you know it, because it honors you. It doesn't manipulate you or demand more than you can give.

Learn to love and value yourself and you will draw others into your life who do the same. You cannot receive from others what you are unable to give to yourself.

## LOVE'S PRESENCE

*It is a gentle, forgiving dance, not a rigid one.*

When you love and honor yourself, there is harmony and peace in your life. Things unfold naturally, without struggle.

Grace becomes the guiding light of your life. It is the compass by which you navigate. Whenever you experience disharmony or conflict, you know you have lost your alignment with love. You know it is time to stop, breathe, and re-center.

Grace is not continuous for anyone. New lessons emerge that must be learned. No matter how far the heart has opened, there will be times when it still contracts in fear. That is to be expected.

Perfection is not possible. As long as you are here in a body you cannot be mistake-free. You see how alignment happens and is lost. You see how you lose the flow of grace in your life and how you need to adjust to regain your rhythm and reconnect with the flow of life.

The rhythm of the dance continues with you or without you. The breath comes in and goes out. Attention comes and goes. Self is forgotten and remembered. It is a gentle, forgiving dance, not a rigid one.

This is the best life has to offer. If you are looking for more than this, you search in vain. If you are looking for absolute enlightenment, absolute certainty, you will not find it.

Grace happens in the flow of life, not apart from it. And life is like a river moving from the mountains toward the sea. When it leaves the mountains, it rushes downward, impetuous and intent to reach its goal. Then it levels out and moves for what seems like an eternity through fields and plains, separating into different streams, joining with other bodies of water. By the time it reaches the ocean, it no longer has any urgency. Instead, it has a confidence born of experience. By the time it reaches the ocean, it no longer sees itself as anything other than ocean. It rests completely in itself, without beginning or end.

It will be that way with you too. When you enter fully into your life, all obstacles to love will be gently washed away. Breathing in, you will open to embrace what comes. Breathing out, you will gently release it.

CHAPTER TEN

# Right Livelihood

*Your gift brings joy to yourself and joy to others.*

The gifts you have been given in this life do not belong to you alone. They belong to everyone. Do not be selfish and withhold them. Do not imprison yourself in a lifestyle that holds your spirit hostage and provides no spontaneity or grace in your life.

Risk being yourself fully. Let go of the expectations others have for you. Let go of all the "shoulds" and "have tos" and consider what thoughts and actions bring you the greatest joy. Live from the inside out, not from the outside in.

To move toward your joy is not selfish. It is the magnanimous action you can perform. That is because your gift is needed. The spirit of others cannot be lifted up unless you trust your gift and give it unconditionally to the world.

Consider how empty life would be if others around you chose to abandon their gifts. All that you find wonderful in life—the music, the poetry, the films, the sports, the laughter—would vanish if others withheld their gifts from you.

Do not withhold your gift from others. Do not make the mistake of thinking that you have no gift to give. Everyone has a gift. But don't compare your gift to the gifts of others, or you may not value it sufficiently.

Your gift brings joy to yourself and joy to others. If there is no joy in your life, it is very likely because you are withholding your gift or not sufficiently trusting it.

All gifts are creative expressions of self. They reveal the self. They break down the barriers of separation and allow others to know who you are.

To create is to bring an inner awareness into form. That awareness does not exist in the world in the way you would express it. Your expression of it is unique and authentic. It is fresh, honest, manifested out of your own experience.

A creative person does not take direction from the outside. She does not imitate established forms. She listens within.

Now she may survey the world. She may even study and scrutinize it. But then she internalizes what she sees. She takes it in and digests it. She considers it in the light of her own experience. She feels it. She owns it. She makes it hers. And then she gives it back. And what she gives back is her vision, her unique perspective, her story.

And if she is honest, others will respond to her, because they hear their story in hers. They will share her vision and support her creative work. And their support will make it easier for her. The energy that she puts out will begin to come back to her. She will feel appreciated emotionally and financially. It is a beautiful process.

Perhaps you have tried this and it hasn't come to fruition. Perhaps you are still struggling to manifest your gift. "What am I doing wrong?" you ask. "Why isn't the universe supporting me?"

The answer is a simple one. Either what you are trying to manifest isn't your gift or you don't believe in your gift sufficiently.

"Well, how do I know?" you inquire.

Ask yourself "Am I doing this because it brings me great joy or because I am seeking the approval of others?" If your action is not joyful, it will not bring happiness to yourself or others. You may succeed or you may fail, but happiness will be missing. Only that which comes from your heart with great enthusiasm will prosper on all levels. Only that which you love will touch others and bring true appreciation your way.

Appreciation and approval are two entirely different things. Appreciation is the natural, spontaneous flow of energy back to you when others feel connected to you and your story. There is nothing you can do to precipitate appreciation other than to be yourself and tell the truth. You simply cannot be in control of what comes back. When you have shared authentically, something essential always comes back. It may not look like what you expect, because what your ego is looking for is not appreciation, but approval.

The search for approval is based on the consciousness that you are not enough. You want others to give you the love that feels missing in your life. This search is a futile one. If you feel empty and seek to be filled from the outside, others will experience your request for appreciation as an expectation or demand. They may feel manipulated and turn away from you. And then you will feel even more empty, rejected, or abused.

Energy cannot return to you unless and until you put energy out. Putting out a demand is not putting out energy. It is putting out a vacuum that sucks other people's energy. It shouts out to the world "I need you to value me because I don't value myself." Unless and until you love and appreciate yourself, other people won't receive your gift no matter how hard you try to give it to them.

Putting out energy means taking yourself seriously, but not too seriously. It means valuing yourself enough to be willing to share with others. It does not mean attacking people with your gifts. When you have a lot of expectations about how people should receive your gifts, you make it impossible for them to receive them.

If you value your gift, it won't matter so much how others respond to it. Even if they don't give you positive feedback, you won't be dissuaded from offering your gift again and again.

Happiness and personal fulfillment flow from the commitment you make to yourself. This commitment will be tested again and again. Over and over, you will be asked by the universe to offer your gift in the face of criticism, skepticism or apparent lack of appreciation. And each time rejection comes, you will be faced with the decision: "Do I do this again?"

If the gift is false, sooner or later you will stop offering it. It will become apparent to you that your expectations are not going to be met and that continuing to offer your services is a way of beating yourself up. So you will stop attacking yourself by offering a gift that no one wants.

On the other hand, if the gift is true, you will learn from apparent failure and rejection. You will learn to value the gift more deeply and to offer it more authentically. You will gradually stop attacking people with your gift and start creating a more loving space in which the gift can be offered and received.

An authentic gift will develop as you trust it. A false gift will not. The former is the gift of Spirit and it is your responsibility to nurture it into existence. The latter is the expectation of your ego, which must be surrendered if your true gifts are to emerge.

## NURTURING THE GIFT

*You can't hold onto your gift and give it away at the same time.*

Your gift always lies where your joy and enthusiasm run deepest. The only difficulty you will have in recognizing your gift is that it may not fit your pictures of what a gift is supposed to be. Suppose, for example, you have excellent listening skills. People come to you with their life dramas and leave happier and more peaceful. Over and over again, others tell you they like being around you. They feel that you accept them as they are. They feel empowered by you. You don't seem to take on their problems. And your presence has an uplifting effect on people.

You don't do anything in particular, so you can't understand there is a gift involved here. You keep looking for the gift outside of your experience. You think: "Maybe I should go back to school and be a librarian?" But you already have two master's degrees. You've already had all the training you need. Training is not the issue. Changing careers is not the issue.

The issue is that the gift is staring you in the face and you refuse to see it. You think the gift is "a doing," but it's not. The gift is "a way of being" that is effortless and exultant. It comes naturally to you. It immediately and palpably brings joy to others.

"Well," you think, "maybe I should go back to school and get a degree in counseling. Nobody will want to come to me and pay me money unless I have a degree." But you miss the point. It doesn't matter what you do. We are not talking about a doing, but a way of being. Whatever you do, you can express your gift. You don't need a special role, a special platform.

Seeking a special role is a way of pushing the gift away. It's saying: "This gift doesn't really meet my expectations. It can't support me. Why can't I have a real gift? Others do. What's wrong with me?"

If you could take the same unconditional love and acceptance that you offer to others and offer it to yourself, you would turn your entire life around, because you would begin trusting your gift. Until you value and trust your gift, how can the universe support you?

Many of your gifts go unacknowledged because they don't match your pictures of what a gift should be. Or you devalue the gift and push it away by comparing it to that of others. You envy their gift. You would rather have their gift than your own.

Every time you judge your gift or place a condition on giving it, you push it further away. You say "I will sing only if I have an audience of 1,000 people and I make at least $5,000!" Supposing not that many people have heard of you, how many offers to sing are going to come your way? How is your lifework to evolve if you do not take the first step to bring it into existence?

If you are not willing to start with small projects and modest expectations, you are programming yourself for failure. If you want to succeed, take the time to develop your gift and to learn to trust it.

You lifework is like a baby. It needs to be nurtured both in and out of the womb. When you first become aware of what your gift is, don't go around announcing it to the rooftops. Keep your own counsel. Begin singing in the shower. Find a teacher. Practice every day.

Then when your gift is ready to be shared with others, find an informal, low-key environment that does not put a lot of pressure on you to perform or on others to respond. Be easy with your gift the way you would be if you were six years old and wanted to share a song with your best friend. No matter how anxious you are to grow up with your gift, you must take the time to be a child first.

Learn, grow, and let your gift be nurtured into manifestation. Take small risks, then bigger ones. Sing to small audiences and gain your confidence. Then, without pushing or putting pressure on yourself or others, the audiences will grow.

Those who refuse to start small never accomplish anything. They shoot for the moon and never learn to stand on the Earth.

Don't be afraid to be an apprentice. If you admire someone who has a gift that resembles yours, don't be afraid to ask for lessons. That is one of the ways you learn to trust the gift.

On the other hand, you can't be a student forever. There comes a time when the student is ready to leave the teacher behind. When that moment comes, step forward. Trust the gift. Trust all the hours you have practiced. Step forth. Have faith in yourself. You are ready.

The way you relate to your gift says a lot about whether you are happy or not. Happy people are expressing their gifts in any venue life offers them. Unhappy people are holding onto their gifts until life gives them the perfect venue.

I can tell you now, the perfect venue never comes. Usually life does not match your picture of it, and real opportunities to express your gift will be squandered if you don't let go of your pictures and see what stands before you.

It's quite simple, really. All your pictures have to go. Part of trusting the gift is letting go of the way you think the gift should be received. That is not your affair. It is none of your business. No matter how great you become, you will never know who will be touched by your work and who will turn away.

To give the gift, you must release it. You must not be attached to who receives it and who doesn't. Nobody speaks to everyone. Some share their gifts with an audience of a few people. Some share with a few million. It is not for you to judge.

Don't judge the gift. Embrace it, value it and give it. And don't judge the way it is received. Give it without attachment to results, without expectations of return.

You can't hold onto your gift and give it away at the same time. When you see the absurdity of trying to do this, you will give your gift the wings it deserves. You will take the risks that you are ready to take, your gift will reach out to others, and the energy it invokes will return to you. The cycle of creativity, of giving and receiving, will be set in motion in your life.

## CREATIVITY AND TRANSFORMATION

*When one person moves toward individuation,*
*it gives everyone permission to do the same.*

Your commitment to the expression of your gift will transform your life. All the structures in your life that hold you in limitation begin to fall apart as soon as you make this inner commitment to yourself. Trying to change these structures from the outside in is futile. That is not how change occurs.

Change occurs from the inside out. As you embrace your gift and move through your fear of expressing it, old, outdated lifestyle structures are de-energized. Without receiving new energy from you, these structures dissolve. You don't have to do anything. As they dissolve, they create a more open space within your consciousness for the gift to be recognized, affirmed and nurtured into expression.

Your work situation, your family life, your sleeping and eating patterns all begin to shift as you get about the business of honoring yourself and moving toward your joy. Without struggle, you unhook from roles and relationships that no longer serve your continued growth. This happens spontaneously. There is no forcing or violation involved.

When faced with your uncompromising commitment to yourself, others either join you or move swiftly out of your way. Grey spaces created by your ambivalence—your desire to have something and give it up at the same time—move toward yea or nay. Clarity emerges as the clouds of self-doubt and attachment are burned away by the committed, radiant self.

When one person moves toward individuation, it gives everyone permission to do the same. Dysfunctional family structures are dismantled and new structures that honor the individuals involved are put in their place.

This is what commitment to self does. It destroys sloppiness, codependency, neurotic bargaining for love, boredom, apathy and critical behavior. It frees each individual to be himself and find alignment with others in a more honest and authentic way.

One person's fidelity to self and willingness to live her dream explodes the entire edifice of fear that surrounds her. It is that simple. And it all happens as gently as the first "yes" said in the silence of the heart.

No one can be abandoned by your "yes" to yourself. If you think otherwise, you will build a prison of fear and guilt around you. Your "yes" to your essential self and life purpose is also a "yes" to others who care about you. You cannot love another by abandoning yourself.

Neurotic bargains for love in which boundaries are constantly compromised cannot stand in the light of self-affirmation. In setting yourself free, you call others to their freedom. Whether they answer the call or not is up to them.

The call to self-actualization is not a call to abandon others. It is not a call to separate or avoid responsibility. The call to honor self is also a call to honor others. It comes to fruition only when the heart remains open.

Sometimes—in order to be honest and authentic—you may have to act in a way that others cannot understand or support. That may be difficult for you, but you must learn to stand firm in your commitment to what is best for you. Please don't capitulate to those who would make you feel guilty for following your heart. But remain open to them. Love them, bless them, talk with them, and they will come to understand and respect your decision.

Your commitment to other people must be an extension of your commitment to yourself, not at odds with it. How can you choose between your good and that of another? It is not possible. No one asks you to make such a choice.

There is a choice that honors you and also honors others. Find that choice. Make that decision. Don't abandon yourself. Don't abandon others.

Let the old form of your life go and allow the new form to emerge at its own pace. Go willingly into the open space of "not knowing." Whenever you release the past, you must enter this space. Don't be afraid. Don't be embarrassed. It is okay not to know. It is okay to let things evolve.

Just be present and tell the truth. Be patient. Growing is a process. Be gentle with yourself and others.

## THE ONLY WORK THERE IS

**_Only work that is joyful will bring happiness to you or to others._**

Spiritual work involves expressing the self joyously and uplifting others. If your work is not joyous, if it doesn't express your talents and abilities, and if it doesn't uplift others, it is not spiritual work. It is the world's work.

Many times I have asked you to be in the world but not of it. What does this mean? It means that you can do the tasks that other men and women do, but you do them joyfully in the spirit of love. You give your labor as a gift. There is no sacrifice involved.

If there is sacrifice involved, there will be no joy. And so there will be no gift. Do not work out of duty, even if you serve others. Do what you do joyfully or do not do it.

Do not do something you don't enjoy just to earn money. Even if that money supports a family of people, they will not prosper through your sacrifice.

Nothing prospers that does not come from love.

There are hundreds, if not thousands of ways, in which you can cheat yourself and work out of sacrifice or duty. There are just as many ways in which you can cheat others and work out of impatience and greed. Be aware of the many subtle ways in which you can betray yourself or others. Do not settle for the rewards the world would give you. Material wealth, name and fame will not bring you happiness.

Only work that is joyful will bring you happiness. Only work that is joyful will bring happiness to others. Do not think that happiness can come from sacrifice or struggle. The means must be consistent with the ends. The goal unfolds through the process itself.

Be wary of work motivated by guilt or spiritual pride. Do not try to save yourself by helping others. Do not try to save others when it is you yourself who needs to be saved.

First, put things right in your own heart and mind. Learn to forgive the past and honor yourself here and now. Learn to trust your gifts. When you are fully expressing who you are joyfully, your work will naturally extend to those who will benefit from it.

Having found your lifework, the greatest obstacle to its fulfillment lies in your attempt to "direct" it. You cannot make your spiritual work happen. If you try, you will fail. You will see the loftiest work be tainted by spiritual pride and undermined by your ego expectations.

You cannot do your spiritual work the same way you did your worldly work. The former requires surrender. The latter requires the illusion of control.

As soon as you give up the need to control, any work can become spiritual. As soon as you try to take charge, the most spiritual projects begin to fall apart.

What is spiritual is not what you do, but how you do it. What you do joyfully is spiritual work. What is worldly is not what you do, but how you do it. What you do out of duty, sacrifice, or the search for approval is worldly work. It is not the outer shell that matters, but the inner motivation.

Do not try to discover your life purpose by listening to the ideas and opinions of others. It is not possible. You discover your life work by listening to the voice of your heart. There is no other way.

It seems to be a lonely journey and, in a way, it is, because no one else can do it for you. You must run the first few miles by yourself. You must demonstrate your commitment. You must show that you will not be drawn off course by others.

In time, others come forward who share your path. This is inevitable. You do not have to go looking for them. You meet them in the natural course of honoring yourself and being open to your experience.


## THE MYTH OF MATERIAL PROSPERITY

*You cannot measure spiritual riches with a worldly yardstick.*

Few people are genuinely committed to God's work. That is because the world does not support your journey to authenticity.

The world supports only what it understands. And right now all it understands is duty and sacrifice. That will change in time, but don't expect it to happen soon. Don't go into your lifework with the hope of worldly support and approval.

Those who understand my teachings and try to live them are often treated with disdain by the world. Don't be surprised if this happens to you. It is not a sign of divine disapproval that other men and women feel envious of or threatened by you.

If this happens, bear it patiently and send love and acceptance to others. When they see that you have their highest good at heart, they will soften to you. If you are committed to the journey, your patience will be rewarded. But, if you are seeking approval or recognition, you will not find it.

Pay no mind to the religion of abundance. That is no more true or helpful than the religion of sacrifice. God does not necessarily reward spiritual work with material success. All rewards are spiritual. Happiness, joy, compassion, peace, sensitivity: these are the rewards for a life lived in integrity.

If material success does not come, it is not important. If it seems important and resentment develops, then more ego expectations need to be stripped away. You must learn, once and for all, to stop measuring spiritual riches with a worldly yardstick.

If material success comes, it is often a test to see if you can transcend self-interest and greed. Material wealth, like all other gifts, is given that it may be shared with others. If you are holding onto wealth, you will not reap the reward of true prosperity, which is happiness and peace.

Don't make the mistake of thinking that your lifework must bring in a large paycheck or meet with worldly success. On the other hand, don't make the mistake of thinking that you must be poor to serve God. A rich person can serve God as well as one of humble means if he is willing to share his riches. It matters not how much you hold in your hands. What matters is whether or not your hands are extended outward to your brother.

All men and women are entrusted with a gift. It does not matter how one person's gift compares to that of another. What matters is that each person comes to embrace the gift he or she has been given.

CHAPTER ELEVEN

# Healing the Divided Self

*For healing to result, the split off aspects of self*
*must be retrieved and integrated into conscious awareness.*

Neither self-indulgence nor self-denial brings peace or happiness. Those who indulge themselves eventually see that their substance of choice is addictive and satisfies less and less. And those who deny themselves eventually find that they become brittle, rigid, without sensitivity or compassion.

Both addictive and repressive behaviors are ways of pushing your experience away. They enable you to override the experience, instead of being with it and feeling all the feelings you have about it. By detaching from the experience and not feeling the feelings, you create a dual consciousness. Part of the self becomes hidden, inaccessible, split off from the whole.

For healing to result, the split off aspects of self must eventually be retrieved, along with their traumatic memories, and integrated into conscious awareness. All fearful experiences cause some form of dissociation that disconnects the individual from his feelings.

When parents, teachers and other significant adults do not validate their experiences, children stuff their feelings and begin to develop a false, socially accepted persona which enables them to cope with the demands around them. This persona is a sham. It is constructed out of fear, covers over shame, and presents to the world a thin veneer of "normalcy."

All human beings have this false self, this thin veneer, worn as a mask to protect themselves from perceived judgment and attack. All human beings have the shame of self-betrayal, which they hide from even their closest family members and friends.

Eventually, the thin shell of the false self begins to crack. The person may lose his job or his primary relationship, or someone close to him may die. He may get a serious physical illness or his addictions may spiral out of control, landing him in a hospital or treatment center. Once the shell is cracked, the buried material can surface through the cracks.

Since all experiences are recorded in the body, all repressed experiences of violation have the potential to manifest as physical or emotional illnesses. As such, illness is a wake up call, a call to awareness and healing. As the psyche of the individual becomes more attuned to love, repressed memories are more likely to come up because the individual is ready to face them, feel the feelings and integrate the experience.

## THE FLOWER OF ACCEPTANCE

*No strings attached. No judgments. No rules. Just be.*

Often, the most difficult and challenging circumstances foster the greatest spiritual growth. Sometimes only the most obvious self-betrayal creates the awareness in which the self will no longer be betrayed.

In the end, you must stop judging your experience and comparing it to that of others. Your experience, with all of its ups and downs, is perfect for you. It brings the lessons you need to learn to move beyond fear and guilt.

To live a surrendered life is to be present moment to moment with your experience and to accept it without judging it. Of course, at times you space out and disconnect emotionally, but you learn to be aware of this and gently bring yourself back.

"Bringing yourself back" is the essence of meditation. You become aware of your thoughts and see how they take you out of the silence.

Waking up happens when you become aware that you are asleep. There is nothing special about it. You are awake right now, and then you forget and go to sleep.

Pain, discomfort, and conflict wake you from your sleep. Stop resisting your greatest teachers. Thank them for coming. Thank them for bringing you back to the present moment. They have given you the most profound gift.

In the present, you may just be. You needn't be there for someone else. Just be. No strings attached. No judgments. No rules. Just be. That is the flower of acceptance. Christ is a being, not a becoming.

## NEW PARADIGM TEACHING

*New paradigm teachers do not try to heal others.*
*They know the light itself will heal all wounds.*

New paradigm spiritual teachers claim no authority over others. They do not pretend to have the answers for others. They speak only of their own experience. They invite others to share in what they have learned from their experience, and to draw whatever conclusions they will. They do not take responsibility for what others choose to see.

They do not preach. They do not try to fix. They simply accept others as they are and encourage others to find their own truth.

They empower. They see the light in others and encourage it. They don't close their eyes to the darkness, but they know it is ultimately of no significance. When love is present, the darkness is illuminated.

They do not deny the darkness or go to battle against it. They know there is nothing wrong, no evil to oppose, no battles to fight. They just gently encourage the light. They know the light itself will heal all wounds.

New paradigm teachers do not try to heal others. They encourage others to heal themselves through self-acceptance and self-love. They model unconditional love by listening compassionately, without judging or trying to fix.

The old paradigm teacher wants to heal others and save the world.

The new paradigm teacher knows that others are fine the way they are and the world is just a reflection of their beliefs.

Has the new paradigm teacher closed her eyes? Doesn't she see the suffering in the world, the environmental catastrophe, the endemic violence? Oh yes, she sees the struggle and the pain, but she has a different interpretation of them. She doesn't believe that people are guilty or that the world is doomed. She hears the vast call for love, the universal cry for acceptance and understanding. And that is what she gives.

Does she give food and medical supplies if they are needed? Of course, but she remembers to whom she is giving them. She remembers the call and she answers it. She knows that food is helpful, but it is not the solution to the problem. It is not what is being asked for. What is asked for is love.

As soon as you see a problem that needs fixing, you have disempowered the person standing before you. Do not do this. Do not accept the pose of powerlessness. There are no victims in the world.

If you see a beggar, don't be taken in. Ask him instead "Why are you standing here begging on this street corner, Oh great one?" Let him know that you see who he really is. Look into his eyes and see his divinity with your own.

You see, powerlessness is a great disguise. Look behind the veil. Don't give the beggar money and walk on without acknowledging him. If you wish to give him money, do so. But do not pass by without acknowledging him. For it is not money he needs, but your love, your blessing, your acknowledgment. You are not here to fix his life, but to honor him.

The new paradigm spiritual teacher is content to be a brother or a sister, or a friend. He has met the inner teacher and put all outer authorities aside. And so he does not come to you offering help or asking for it. He comes to you as an equal partner. He treats you as he would like to be treated. And he treats the person next to you the same. There is no pecking order, no preferences.

He does not ask you to follow him. He doesn't trade his knowledge for sexual favors. He does not judge you, isolate you or invalidate your experience. He remains always an equal brother or sister and, in that equality, the seeds of redemption are sown.

## DANCING IN YOUR OWN TRUTH

*Do not become lost in the world before you know who you are
or your chances of waking up are not strong.*

Few people are alone with their experience. Most people are afraid to
be. The irony is that those who are alone do not feel that they are alone.
And those who are not alone, feel lonely.

The lonely seek companionship, yet companionship is not possible, for they have not yet discovered who they are.

The self is a wilderness. Leave it unexplored and cities are built
over it. Explore it courageously and intimacy becomes possible.

True equality requires individuation. Until you know the contours
of your own heart you can't learn those of another. If you leave home
before you are ready, you look for home without finding it. You find
mother instead of wife, father instead of husband.

When you have found your home, you take it with you wherever
you go. Find your home first, and then seek companionship.

Find out who you are, not according to someone else's definition,
but according to your own. Play with that definition before you
accept it. Let all of yourself become present. Explore the dunes that
swell up at the sea's edge. Feel the salt spray and walk along the beach
at low tide. See all the life-forms, all the possibilities revealed when
the tide is rolled back.

Know thyself. Do not become lost in the world before you know
who you are or your chances of waking up are not strong. The world
will be only too happy to give you a role and a responsibility. Other
people will be only too happy to assign you a role in their play.

Let's face it, some roles are seductive. They promise a lot. It's hard
to say no. "Leave your lonely wilderness and come and live with me.
I will love you and take care of you." These are the words the homeless child has been waiting to hear. At last direction has come. The
missing parent has materialized. All will be well. Or will it?

Hardly! Rather, this is how the self is betrayed. This is how the
wilderness is paved with asphalt, stifling its grasses and trees, invad-
ing its sky. Call it domestication, technology, progress. It is anything
but that.

The homeless person is always ruthless in making his home. He is without compassion for his environment or for the well-being of others. He simply externalizes his anger and his pain.

Try to live with someone before you have learned to live with yourself and you will make a mockery of relationship. It won't work.

Find home inside your heart first. Only one who knows and accepts himself can find equality with another. Anyone else gives himself away.

It is never the other person's fault when relationship doesn't work. All relationship endings can be attributed to a single cause: lack of fidelity to self.

If you were not faithful to yourself when you entered the relationship, how is it possible that you would be faithful to yourself while you were in it? You see, it can't be the other person's fault. You came together with him or her because you were lonely and tired of seeking and you went to sleep together.

Soon enough you discovered that sleeping together wasn't all it was cracked up to be. You woke up and asked: "Why did I trade one dream for another? The original dream was lonely, but it was also a simpler one."

You just took a detour, a delaying maneuver. You went from sleeping alone to sleeping with another. But the real challenge for you wasn't to sleep, but to wake up.

Unless you commit to your own awakening, others can offer you only detours, side-trips, running in place. Time goes by, but nothing changes. The pain doesn't lift. The old dissatisfaction is still there.

The sheets have been changed, but the bed still sags. The problem is not a cosmetic one. The problem is in the foundation itself. That is what must be addressed. That is what must be shored up.

Your dissatisfaction says one thing and one thing only: "You are not honoring yourself." If you were honoring yourself, there would be energy and commitment to a vision in your life. You would not be bored. You would not be lonely. You would not be anxious to trade your dream for someone else's.

You are the one who opts for the detour. Don't blame the companion who accompanies you. It was your choice. But don't beat yourself up over it. Make a different choice.

Make the courageous choice to be alone. Being alone means to be yourself fully. It means to be fully individuated, yet connected to the whole. It means to be "all one."

When you fully inhabit your life, you will be drawn to others who are doing the same thing. Then, you will not have to give up your life for another. That is the beginning of a more beautiful and challenging dance. But it is a dance that cannot happen unless you are already dancing in your own truth.

## MOVING TO A SHARED VISION

*All important decisions in a partnership
are made through intuitive consensus.*

As the self becomes congruent and learns to manifest its own vision, people come in who share that vision. Yet, notwithstanding the shared sense of purpose, ego struggles inevitably arise. One person wants a certain configuration or outcome. Another person wants another outcome. Then there is a jousting of egos and the potential of trespass. However, if the sense of self runs deeply enough, there will be a communication of wants and expectations and a willingness to stay open to a solution that honors both sides.

Partnership can be built only on shared vision and the willingness of the partners to let go of their rigid pictures of the way things should be. Hearing the deep need of each person, the two enter the silence together, asking for the highest good of all concerned. In the silence, sometimes both hear the same thing, or one hears something that the other feels good about. All important decisions in a partnership are made through intuitive consensus.

Often the two do not know why they are guided in a particular direction, but they decide to trust it anyway. Great strides are made in this way. Situations that seem etched in stone are transformed. Obstacles dissolve. Possibilities previously discounted present themselves again at the right time. Miracles are experienced.

As partners learn to trust their intuitive consensus, their shared purpose is revealed to them. Then, they understand why they have met and what they are asked to accomplish together.

## NOT GIVING YOURSELF AWAY

*The romantic tradition is merely a socially acceptable,*
*institutionalized form of self-betrayal.*

There is a tendency when people go into relationship to "go limp," the way an animal goes limp when caught by a predator. There is a kind of "false surrender," a giving away of one's power to the other person. This sets the stage for later violation.

I urge you to go slowly and consciously into relationships so that you do not give yourself away. The desire to please the other, to be liked and accepted, to be loved and adored, easily and quickly crosses the line and becomes self-betrayal. You must realize that relationships can be addictive. They can offer you the opportunity to escape from self, to avoid feeling your feelings.

If you are unhappy with your life, a relationship may provide a temporary escape from your troubles, but sooner or later your problems will return. And they will be exacerbated by the demands and expectations of your partner. When your ego agendas emerge, both of you will feel disappointed, if not betrayed.

The emotional high of a new relationship promises more than it can ever deliver. If you experience "falling in love," you can be sure that you will experience "falling out of love." The very expression "falling in love" should tell you that this experience is about self-betrayal. In what other area of life would you allow yourself "to fall" and be whimsical about it? The whole romantic tradition is a socially acceptable, nearly institutionalized form of self-betrayal.

Just as the child creates a false self to cope with the unreasonable demands and expectations placed on him early in life, so does the adult create a "false surrender" to a lover to ease the pain of personal and social isolation. NO foundation for the relationship has been built and so it cannot withstand the eruption of the dark side. As soon as unconscious fears arise, the balloon bursts.

In true surrender, you do not choose the partner just because he or she makes you "feel good." You choose the partner because there is a shared vision and a mutual commitment to growth. The partner helps you to create a healing environment, in which both of you are nurtured and challenged to evolve. You have a mutual commitment to be present with each other throughout the ups and downs of experience.

Most relationships fall apart as soon as trouble comes along. The promise "to have and to hold, in sickness and in health" is for most people an exercise in absurdity, for many people go to the altar without having taken the time to get to know each other. For this reason, formal marriage should be discouraged until couples have lived together for at least three years.

Most relationships will not survive this three year period of mutual exploration because, for most people, they are a form of addiction. They are initiated by a mutual desire to seek pleasure and avoid pain.

However, when people fall out of love with each other their repressed pain surfaces with a vengeance. And then the person they once looked to as a savior becomes their arch enemy. The whole thing is a big set up.

Relationship can never be a panacea for the wounds and traumas of the individual psyche. At best, it is an incubation chamber. Hard as it is to admit, emotional safety is not to be found in most relationships.

How do you avoid falling in love and betraying yourself? Not by refusing to fall in love but by learning to "be present" with the one you love, even when his or her dark side rises up to meet you. You notice the judgments that come up, the desire to please or to be taken care of. You see when you feel accepted, rejected, trusted, or betrayed.

You don't go into the relationship wearing rose colored glasses, seeing only what you want to see. You look at everything and you communicate honestly.

If you can keep your eyes open as you explore an attraction with someone, you avoid the inflation and deflation of falling in and out of love. By staying awake through the process, you can avoid the disappointment of discovering after a month or two—when the hormones stop raging—that you and your partner have very little in common.

It all comes down to one question: "How honest are you willing to be?" As long as you have something to hide, there will be deceit operating in your life. Part of you will be visible but another part will be heavily disguised or missing in action. Where did it go? And who are you without it?

All masks must be peeled away if you are to stand face to face with each other. Until then, this is just a carnival, a public rite the meaning of which has been forgotten.

## SELF-EMPOWERMENT AND REALIZATION

*There is only one person who needs to wake up and that is you.*

I ask you to be rigorous in understanding that no one knows more than you do. No one has anything to give you that you do not already have.

Forget your teachers and gurus. Forget your cults of secular and parochial knowledge. Forget your dogmas, esoterica and metaphysics. None of this will bring you freedom from suffering. It will only add to the burden you carry.

Be realistic about your experience here. There is only one person who needs to wake up and that is you. Those who have a gift to give you will not withhold it. Those who withhold information or love from you, have no gift to give.

Beware of those who would make you jump through hoops or stand in line. They are just lining their pockets at your expense. Do not tolerate the idea that salvation lies somewhere else. It doesn't.

Either you hold the key or you don't. If you have it, you must begin to use it. If someone else has it, then you will have to pay dearly to get it. And by the time you get it back, the locks may have been changed.

Don't allow others to limit you or take your freedom away. Don't live by someone else's rules.

Hold the self in high regard. It is and must remain unassailable. Hold others in high regard. They must always be honored and set free. But clearly and with good humor let go of relationships with people or organizations who would tell you what to think or what to do.

Don't line the pockets of those who make empty promises to you. It doesn't matter what they promise: more security, more money, more sex, or more peace of mind.

My friend, the light and peace you seek is already within you. You already have the resources you need to fulfill your creative purpose. There is only one thing that you do not have. And that is the awareness that all this is true.

Nobody can give you that awareness. Not me, not some used car salesman, not some swami peddling Samadhi. If someone tells you he can, it's time for a belly laugh. Put your arm around him and tell him that's the best joke you've heard in fifty years.

Do you hear me? Awareness is not a gift from someone else, but a gesture of the self. It is an energetic movement to be present and to embrace life. Awareness comes and goes with the breath. If you want to be aware, breathe! Breathe in to embrace this moment. Breathe out to release it. Breathe, breathe, breathe. Each breath is an act of awareness.

Now if I came to your doorstep and told you I was selling breaths for $5 million a piece, you would think that was pretty funny, would you not? You would tell me, "that's very nice, brother, but I already have all the breaths I need."

Of course you do. But you keep forgetting that you have them. You keep buying the insurance policy, falling in love with prince or princess charming, chasing doctor *I can make you feel good* or swami *I've got it all come and get it for five bucks.* You know, they all have such long names, it's a wonder you can pronounce them!

Take a breath, my friend. That's right, a deep breath. Nobody has what you need. Did you hear me? Nobody!

You see, you really are all alone here. But it's not as problematic as you think because there is no part of you that's missing. If you just hang around yourself long enough without giving your power away to others, you will retrieve all the fragmented and dissociated aspects of yourself, for no other reason than they never went away. They just got covered over in your race for the exit.

"Just hang around and you'll get it." Great advice from a holy man, right? "I guess we better send this guy to entrepreneurship training or a spirituality and business workshop or he won't make a living."

I have news for you, friends. I don't need to make a living. I AM a living. And so are you.

Just hang around and you'll get it, because you never lost it. One moment you were fully present, and then the next moment your body was there, but your mind was on vacation in the Bahamas. Now, after thirty years or however long it's been, you can bring yourself back.

Can you believe that thirty years passed between one breath and another? It may seem strange, but I'm telling you it is a common experience. The next time someone asks how old you are, just tell the truth. "People say I'm forty-five, but I've only taken four breaths!"

I'm just kidding you. Or am I? How many breaths have you really taken? Don't worry about the past. Just begin now. Breathe and claim your life. Breathe and let go of all the mental and emotional crutches you have carried. Breathe and reject all the words ever said to you by authority figures. Breathe and soften. Breathe and strengthen. Breathe and be. You are authentic. You are intact. You are a child of the great Spirit that animates us all.

## BUDDHA'S WINDOW

*All that is transcendent comes from the lowly,*
*the light from the dark, the flower from the mud.*

The Buddha began in the same place where you begin. So did I. The nature of suffering does not change. You have not been given a special handicap, nor were you given fewer abilities. There is no difference between you and Buddha, or between Buddha and me.

You are pure being. The Buddha is pure being. You struggle with identification with form. So did the Buddha. So did I.

We are all tested. We all build on quicksand and get sucked down into the muck of conditioned existence. But we are not the conditioned.

All conditions come from us. As soon as we stop placing conditions on our embrace of life, relative existence falls away.

You are the lotus swimming on the murky surface of the pond. You are the awareness, the profound discovery that grows out of the darkness of the conditions. You are the white flower, nurtured by those murky waters.

If you are looking for beauty without sadness, you will not find it. If you are looking for celebration without the poignancy of pain, you will search in vain. All that is transcendent comes from the lowly, the light from the dark, the flower from the mud.

Give up linear thinking and rigid, left-brain expectations of what spirituality means. Life is not one-dimensional. If you are looking for the absolute, you will not find it in the conditional.

Don't choose one side of the argument. Learn to take both sides and work toward the middle. Both extremes reflect each other. Those who are in conflict share the same lesson.

There is only one way to freedom. Buddha called it the middle way, the way between all extremes.

You can't get there by taking sides. You can't get there by choosing the good over the bad, or the light over the dark. Your path goes through the place where good and evil cross, where the light is obstructed, casting long shadows.

There are no maps that take you to this place. If you ask one person, he says "Go to the right." If you ask another, he says "Go to the left." If you ask the pessimist where you can find truth, he will say "It was here yesterday. You missed it." If you ask the optimist, he will reply: "It will be here tomorrow."

Who gives the correct answer? Is there, in fact, a correct answer? Or is the expectation of a correct answer itself the illusion?

When you can observe the argument without taking sides, when you can be in the middle of the battleground without attacking anyone, then you have arrived in the place where the lotus blooms. Few will notice you, but it will not matter. You have come home.

You have slipped through the veil. You are no longer an object blocking the light, but the window through which it passes.

No longer imprisoned in a role, you are glad to be of help. No longer seeking, you are happy to point the way. When someone asks "Which way to the divine?" you answer "Any way will do."

You know now that the outcome doesn't matter. Only being present on the journey, moment-to-moment matters. Between now and then, between this and that, the Buddha dwells.

"What a dreamy man," you say. Yes, it is true, his existence spans centuries. Yet, there is no place where he has not been, no heart he has not touched. If you will allow him, he will touch your heart too. If you will allow him, he will open the window in your mind that separates all sentient beings.

CHAPTER TWELVE

# Communion and Community

*The door of my church is open to all who would enter.*

The community I am calling you to is a church without walls, a place where people of all faiths come together to love, support, and honor each other. My teaching has nothing to do with what you call Christianity, or with any dogma that separates people. It has nothing to do with any religious hierarchy or organizational structure.

All are welcome in my church—the poor and the rich, the sick and the healthy, those who call my name and those who call the name of other teachers. I do not stand against any man or woman, for each is God's child. I stand for the sanctity of all beings who in their innocence bless creation with their presence. I celebrate life in all its forms and in its quintessential formlessness.

When you enter my church, you do not need to take off your coat or your hat, but please leave your prejudices outside. They have no place here. Come to the altar not to hold onto your judgments, but to confess them, to release them to God before your brothers and sisters. You do not have to wear a special hat or robe to enter my sanctuary, but you do have to surround yourself with the awareness of your equality with all beings.

My church is a place of peace and reconciliation. It is a place where fears are acknowledged and trespass is forgiven. It welcomes all those who admit their mistakes. It casts no one out who seeks the safety of its loving arms.

Many congregations purport to be mine, yet they hold onto their fears and institutionalize their judgments. The stranger and the outcast are not welcome in their sanctuaries. They have built a prison and called it a church. I would rather be worshiped by murderers and thieves than by imposters who pretend to do my will by judging and excluding others.

I have never tolerated hypocrisy. Those who call themselves spiritual guides should set a sincere example for others. They do not have to be perfect, but they must have the courage to admit their mistakes. They must be honest about their humanness. They must step down from their pedestals and learn to empower others.

Do not have lofty, inflated expectations for yourself or for your spiritual advisors. To ask another person to be mistake-free is unrealistic and unkind. Instead, ask your teachers and guides to be honest and direct, to admit mistakes and to have compassion for the mistakes of others. Ask them to help you create a climate of understanding, safety and love.

That is what my church provides. It is a safe, loving place where each person can connect with his or her spiritual essence.

## UNDOING SMALL-MINDEDNESS

*Hierarchical, closed belief systems promise Shangri-la and deliver Alcatraz.*

Many people go to church or temple to be with people who believe the same thing they do. Given their homogeneity, such places often legitimize narrow-mindedness and prejudice. Anyone can find someone who agrees with his beliefs. Anyone can create a religion for insiders and exclude those who would challenge his beliefs. This has nothing to do with spirituality. It has more to do with the insecurities of the individual and his tendency to capitulate to the tyranny of the group mind.

Cults thrive on this kind of insecurity. They create a seductive environment that seems to be loving and then proceed to chop away at the ego structure of the individual until he is totally confused, self-doubting and helpless. In the name of spiritual surrender, initiates are asked to capitulate to the authority structure of the cult. In this way, brainwashing poses as enlightenment.

Hierarchical, closed belief systems promise Shangri-la and deliver Alcatraz. They offer freedom from suffering and deliver physical abuse and mind control. Those who are drawn into such situations have lessons around the abuse of power. You can't prevent them from enrolling in this classroom, but you can offer them a helping hand when they are ready to get out.

Some fundamentalist groups use the similar fear tactics to control their members. Even traditional churches and temples do not tolerate diversity well. As a result, they lose members who are exploring their spirituality in an authentic way.

Only by honoring the unique spiritual experiences of their membership, while emphasizing areas of commonality, can churches and temples speak to the deeper spiritual needs of their members. Dogma and religious hierarchies no longer make people feel safe and secure. Face to face interactions, simple participatory rituals of singing and dancing that help people open their hearts to each other are what establish the emotional bonds of community. Mutual respect and tolerance for differences are absolutely essential to the creation of a safe, loving space.

It is not necessary for people to have the same beliefs to experience spiritual communion. Communion happens in spite of the mind, not because of it. Communion happens through the extension of love and non-judgment. It can happen anywhere, with any group of people committed to inclusive, unconditional love.

The time has come for houses of worship to redefine themselves. They must cease to be places where minds cling to linear beliefs in fearful agreement and become places of self-exploration, where differences are welcome. Love, not agreement, must become the bond that holds the community together.

## LOVE & THE SWORD OF TRUTH

*It appears to be gentle and soft, but it is stronger than steel.*

Love challenges you to be flexible about your beliefs and let others into your heart. It pushes up against the boundaries of what you are used to and what you feel is acceptable.

This is a kind of love that you don't easily relate to. Your concept of love is tainted by your ego need for agreement. It is a milk-toast version, a soft version of what is the greatest awakening force in the universe.

Instead of milk-toast, I offer you the sword of truth. Use it to remove the soft, fatty tissues that surround your heart and make your breath labor unnecessarily. Use it to remove codependency and victim consciousness from your notion of love. Your version of love is weak, exclusive, and hypercritical. It isn't really love at all.

Love has within its essence a great purifying and awakening potential. It offers a kundalini experience that throws off past conditioning. It appears to be gentle and soft, but it is stronger than steel, more powerful than an earthquake.

Love is not only creator but destroyer. It destroys the past. It dissolves what is no longer needed, so that the new may be born. Love is not only the embrace of water that nurtures and sustains, but the fire of spirit that purifies.

John baptized with water and told you I would baptize with fire. When you first hear my words, they are like the crimson flame of dawn gently lifting itself above the horizon's edge. But when my words sink completely into your heart, they will burn like the desert sun.

I do not offer a milk-toast version of love or spirituality. My love for you was not soft 2000 years ago, and it is certainly not soft now.

You see my love as soft, because you are afraid of your anger. Yet anger at injustice is one of the highest forms of love.

When you stop projecting your anger and fear on the world, you can stand for truth without hurting others. You stand not against individuals, but against untruth. Even as you oppose falsehood, you feel compassion for those who cling to false beliefs. You do not criticize them. But you oppose their mistaken ideas with a firmness and clarity that reaches to the roots and exposes the fear and insecurity on which all illusion is based.

When love is broad, it embraces all things as itself. It is like water: feminine, accepting, without discrimination. When love is deep, it destroys all the obstacles in its way. It is like fire: masculine, discriminating, clinging only to truth.

Many of you know the soft, feminine Jesus. But how many of you know the strong, masculine one? The one who brings the sword of discrimination, the sword of truth?

Both are necessary.

If you would know me, you must bring both the feminine and masculine sides together in yourself. Without the masculine side, spirituality is soft, ineffective, without the potential for awakening.

## A LIVING CHURCH

*Without forgiveness, correction is impossible.*
*Without correction, forgiveness is incomplete.*

The church I call you to must embrace both the feminine and masculine sides. It must welcome everyone without conditions, yet be devoted to truth without compromise. In a living church, each person is free to determine her own spiritual path. She is granted total freedom in this pursuit, and in return grants this freedom to others. She agrees not to try to convert or to fix anyone else. She asks for unconditional acceptance and support for her journey and gives the same to others in return.

Anyone who violates this agreement is asked to publicly discuss her motives and behavior and hear the feedback of others. The goal is not to shame or embarrass, but to hear, to be of help, and ultimately to determine whether the individual embraces the spiritual guidelines that govern the community.

All violations of the public trust are dealt with in a loving and compassionate way. The desire is always for understanding and inclusion. But the guidelines must never be watered down or compromised. Spiritual truths should never be adjusted or revised to accommodate people's weaknesses or condone their mistakes.

Mistakes are to be acknowledged and forgiven. To understand what is wrong is to make it right. Such understanding happens spontaneously when individuals are willing to look at their behavior and see how they impact others and themselves. Correction and forgiveness go hand in hand. Without forgiveness, correction is impossible. And without correction, forgiveness is incomplete.

The living church or temple must be clear about and faithful to its process. Since the process is loving, forgiving, and supportive, many different types of people will be drawn in. The flexibility, tolerance and openness of the church/temple and its members will be continually tested. In all this, it must be firm within, and gentle without. All people must be treated fairly and with respect.

In the living church or temple, power always lies in the hands of the congregation. The role of the minister is to lead by example and to empower others to walk their own unique spiritual path. The more successful the minister is in empowering others, the more participatory the organization becomes. Then, it does not matter if the minister leaves, because the programs of the church or temple retain their energy and coherence.

Through empowering others skillfully, a good minister makes himself dispensable. His job is quite simply to help transform old paradigm congregations into new paradigm ones. As a skillful facilitator, he invites others to take responsibility, to share their gifts, and to co-create the organization with him. When the congregation is fully empowered, the minister's work in that place is complete and he will be drawn to a new environment which will challenge him further.

A fully empowered congregation does not need a minister, although it can certainly choose to have one if it wishes. A core group made up of the most committed members can guide the group to intuitive consensus. The core group must embody the principles of sharing and empowerment established by the founding minister. Its job is to secure the safety of the space in which people come together to practice acceptance and forgiveness. If the safety of the space is compromised, or if members cease to be actively involved in the church, the creative energy will dwindle and members will revert to an old paradigm energy of polarization, separation and struggle for control.

All social institutions can be transformed by following the Affinity Group Guidelines I have shared with you. Churches, schools, businesses, nursing homes, prisons, government agencies can all be called to a spiritual purpose through the implementation of these simple ideas.

Three things can be said about my teaching. First, it is simple. Second, it applies to all situations, circumstances and environments. Third, if you practice it, you will find peace in your heart and harmony in your relationships.

You would think these attributes would recommend the teaching, yet look around. Do you see anyone lining up at my doorstep?

Somehow people intuitively understand that if they take up this path, their lives will never be the same. They aren't sure they really want a revolution happening in their lives.

I understand that. Many people like to play at surrender, while retaining their addiction to control. They want to love others who are like them while retaining their judgments about others who are different. That way, they appear to be spiritual, without having to risk becoming vulnerable. They talk about love, but keep a hard shell around them which pushes love away.

They have the semblance of love, but not the real thing. Real love would crack their lives open.

## CONGRUENCE

*The more you know yourself,*
*the more clear you can be with others.*

Congruence comes through fidelity to self. It comes through the capacity to accept and be with your own experience, even when it is different from the experience of others.

Congruence is exhibited when your actions are consistent with your words. That means you can be trusted. You act in good faith. When you make a mistake, you admit it and try to learn from it. You make amends. You ask for forgiveness.

A congruent person is always becoming more honest with and faithful to herself. And the more honest and faithful she becomes to herself, the more honest and faithful she becomes to others. Inner congruence and outer trustworthiness go hand in hand.

The more you know yourself, the more clear you can be with others. You do not make promises or commitments you cannot keep. You say "no" when you mean no, and "yes" when you mean yes, and "I don't know" when you are not clear. The potential for misunderstanding is minimized by your willingness to tell the truth to yourself and others.

The safe, loving, non-judgmental space of spiritual community helps you become increasingly honest and transparent. And then all your relationships with others, even the most disturbed interactions, begin to shift and to heal.

Each of you is present for your own healing and others are merely witnesses to that. They do not come to analyze you, fix you, or enlighten you. They come simply to accept and bear witness to your healing process. They trust your process to lead you exactly where you need to go.

My work asks you to get out of the way and trust the Spirit to heal. When you try to become the healer, the minister, the teacher, the technician, you just add more confusion, fear and guilt to everybody's plate.

You don't have to have all the answers to grow, to walk through your fears, to inhabit your life more completely. As you tell your truth and witness to the truth of others, the alchemical process of transformation begins in your heart. And it, not you, is in charge of the journey.

I cannot tell you where that journey will take you. Indeed, it isn't important for you to know. But I can tell you to trust the process and know that it is bringing you home to yourself, home to your heart, and home to love.

## HEALTHY GROUP PROCESS

*Learn to communicate your feelings honestly*
*without shaming or blaming others.*

Genuine spiritual community happens only to the extent that it fosters an open mind and an open heart.

You cannot foster an open mind if you teach any dogma. Giving people answers is manipulative and controlling. Instead, help them articulate their questions and begin the search for their own answers. Empower them on their journeys of self-understanding. And let them know that the community is a place where they can share ideas without being judged or preached to. Respect the ability of each member to find her way and she will find it.

You cannot foster an open heart if you exclude anyone who is sincere from your community or give preferential treatment to any of the members. People open their hearts when they feel welcome and treated as equals. Nothing closes the heart down more quickly than competition for love and attention. Most people are wounded emotionally and react quickly and defensively to any semblance of inequality or injustice, even if it is not intended.

This is why the primary focus of the community must be on establishing clear boundaries and healthy group process. Each person must be given a chance to be heard and encouraged not to stuff feelings or hide them from others. He must also be encouraged to avoid shaming or blaming others, but to take responsibility for his own thoughts, feelings, words and actions.

When a safe space is created in which feelings can be expressed without attacking others, misunderstandings, judgments and projections can be dissolved. People can return to their hearts and their bodies. The breath can be restored. Trust can be reestablished.

It is absurd to assume that this kind of physical, emotional and mental reconciliation can happen without a loving environment to foster it. Leaving a group together without teaching them guidelines and process skills is like leaving a toddler alone in a house. He may be okay for the first fifteen minutes, but after that he'll find the chemicals under the sink and the drawer where the knives are stored. You don't want to see the outcome.

And yet you know it. You see it over and over again. As soon as egos rise to attack and defend, it isn't long before the battlefield is strewn with corpses. And then, of course, you have the walking wounded, the ones who have been hit and don't know it yet. You assume that they are normal until you do something to trigger their repressed rage.

No, you don't want to leave a group of wounded people alone to fend for themselves. You want to teach them how to communicate their feelings without blaming, shaming or attacking others.

Many people who join spiritual communities are desperate to find love and acceptance. They will say "yes" to the guidelines of the community without understanding them. When the time comes that their buttons are pushed, they may explode in rage, attacking all who get in their way. What do you do in such a case?

The only thing you can do is to practice the guidelines. Take responsibility for your thoughts and feelings. Don't project. Listen without interrupting. Don't allow yourself to be cut off or steam-rolled, but ask that you be heard in the same way that you listened. Do not attack. Do not defend. Just ask for equal time. By not making the other person wrong, but insisting on equality, anger is diffused, and the community receives a living demonstration of the guidelines at work.

A core group of community members must be skillful in practicing the guidelines. Through their ability to model the practice of the process, the entire community learns the process, and then even the most difficult situations can be resolved in a way that honors everyone.

Both the heart and the mind have a tendency to close down. If you join in community with others expecting everyone to be open all the time, you will have a rude awakening. You will see all these "loving, spiritual" people losing it, acting out their wounds in unmistakable ways. And you will wonder: "Why did I come here? This is just as bad as my nuclear family experience, maybe even worse!"

It's time for you to drop your fantasy about what community is. It's not a love-in, but a process of transformation that challenges the skill and resources of its members. It is not a bonfire on the beach that goes out when the wood has burned. It is a crucible that burns steadily and, unless process skills are learned early on, the elixir will be missing, and lead will not be turned into gold. The whole process will break down and it won't be pretty.

Transformation requires not just willingness from the members of the community. It also requires skillful leadership and modeling of a safe, interactive process free of projection.

Many people walk away from heart-centered, interactive spirituality because it is so rarely successful. They retreat from the fire, seeking an easier and less explosive path. They do not understand that it takes a lot longer to go around the fire than it does to go through it.

## OPEN HEART, OPEN MIND

*Through the practice of voluntary confession*
*a community of equals is born.*

When the mind is closed, the heart shuts down, and vice versa. It doesn't really matter which one closes first, the other one isn't far behind it.

Don't expect the mind to stay open. It won't. An open mind is a mind free of judgments. How long is it before a judgment arises in your mind? Be honest. Is it every two hours, every two minutes, or every two seconds?

In between those judgments, the mind is open. When judgments come up, the mind closes and stays closed for as long as the judgment is held.

Don't try to stop yourself from having judgments. That is a futile exercise. Instead, be aware of the judgments that come up in your mind, look at them, and let them go. If you do this, you will discover that there will be more space between your judgments.

Acknowledge your judgments to your friends and the members of your spiritual community. Help create an atmosphere in which no one beats himself up or attacks another person because he is having judgments.

Through the practice of voluntary confession a community of equals is born. No one is more spiritual than any other. All have judgments. All wish to release them and return to peace.

By acknowledging mistakes, there is no pretension to spirituality. There is no desire for perfection, nor shame about imperfection. There is just acceptance of the ego as it rises and falls. There is patience and compassion. This deepens the safety of the space.

When you establish a climate in which the ego is accepted and forgiven, life becomes much easier for everyone. Spirit now holds the ego in its loving embrace. Fear diminishes and the ego's tendency to split the mind is thwarted. As reactivity slows down, the wounds of the psyche have time to heal.

This is the work of a healing community. It is a place where forgiveness is practiced and each contraction of fear is held gently in the arms of love. It is a sanctuary where heart and mind close only to open more fully to the presence of love.

## ARROGANCE AND SPIRITUAL PRIDE

*You don't know what is in your brother's heart.*

It is spiritual pride to think that you are any further on the journey than anyone else. Even if this were true, it would not serve you to talk about it. What serves you is humility.

You do not have the capacity to make a correct determination of the spiritual progress of any other person. One who seems to be far behind can move ahead in a flash. And one who seems far ahead can be seriously disabled. The whole idea of ahead and behind is meaningless, since you don't know where the starting line is or the finish line.

Others do not necessarily start where you do. They don't necessarily end where you end. Some have a short journey packed with heartrending challenges. Others have a long journey composed of many uneventful lessons.

You can look at others and think you understand, but you will just be kidding yourself. You have no idea what anyone else's life is about. Nor is it really any of your business. You have enough on your plate to keep you busy. Just to embrace your own lessons is the work of a lifetime.

Be careful if you are a teacher, counselor, healer or other authority figure. Many people seek a helping role before they have done their own emotional healing work. They hide behind their role and so avoid any kind of self-scrutiny. However, they will not be able to hide behind their spiritual mask forever. Sooner or later, their own dirty laundry will be aired. It is inevitable.

This is a place where you become visible. Even if you play the game of hide and seek, it is only a matter of time before you are found and called to account for your thoughts, feelings, and actions.

Wearing clever disguises and pretending not to be home when the doorbell rings is just a delaying tactic. It cannot work in the end, because the entire planet is on a wake-up mission. This is not the place to be if you want to hide or stay asleep. If your goal is unconsciousness, you are in a dangerous place!

If you were in touch with everybody's intention to wake up and help you wake up, you could not take any trespass personally. When someone bumps into you, you would just say "Sorry, brother. I didn't see you. Thanks for the wake-up call. I'll be more alert now."

It's not just the trespass that wounds, but also the interpretation of it. You judge others for attacking you and you judge yourself for allowing them to do so. It is not just the wound that needs to heal, but also the shame around it.

You will not wake up as long as you insist on remaining a victim and holding grievances toward the one who victimized you. No one wakes up without forgiving self and other and learning to take personal responsibility for learning the lesson.

If you want to wake up together, stop interpreting what happens and learn to communicate honestly. Don't presume guilt. Don't presume to know the other person's motives. Tell the truth about your experience and ask for the truth in return.

You don't know what is in your brother's heart. The best you can do is to ask him openly. This is as close as you will ever come to knowing what he thinks and what he feels. If you never inquire of him what his experience is, how will you ever come to know what his intentions are toward you? All you will know are your own projections, your own judgments and interpretations. These say a lot about you and very little about him.

And, if you cannot presume his innocence, how will you ever be able to presume your own? You see, there is no way out. Every judgment you make about someone else returns to haunt you.

Better to give those judgments up and admit that you know nothing of other people's intentions or motives. Pretending that you know when you don't is arrogance and spiritual pride.

## CHAPTER THIRTEEN

# Opening to Miracles

*Miracle consciousness depends on your ability*
*to intuit the presence of God in your life.*

That you exist at all is a testimony to God's love. When you are in touch with God's love for you, everything that happens in your life is miraculous. All you see are extraordinary opportunities to love, learn, create and be fully present in your life.

When you are not in touch with God's love for you, everything that happens in your life seems to be insufficient or not good enough. You perpetually find fault with yourself, with others and with your experience.

Your relationship to yourself and your creator determines the quality of your life. When you feel worthy of God's love, you are connected to all that is and grateful for your life. When you feel that you are just a random, purposeless creation, you lead an isolated, aimless life. You do not know why you are here.

Miracle consciousness depends on your ability to feel or intuit the presence of God in your life. To do that, you must be willing to trust yourself, to trust others and to trust your life as it is moment to moment.

When you trust, you understand that you are here for a reason. You open to the unfolding of the divine plan in your life.

## LEARNING TO TRUST

*God can't be in charge as long as you think you are the boss.*

Experiment with being in your life without judgment. Be neutral about what happens. You don't have to see things in a positive light. Just stop seeing them in a negative light. Stop imposing your expectations on the events and circumstances of your life. Just let life unfold and see what happens.

Your judgments and interpretations of life do not bring you peace or fulfillment. So set them aside and let life be what it is. Experience life free of the limitation you place upon it.

When you live without judgment things go smoother. Problems resolve. Relationships move on course. Your life starts to work. Increasingly, you realize that you are not the one who makes your life work. So you stop trying. You stop trying to figure things out. And you just show up and do what you are asked to do in the moment.

You can't know God's plan as long as you insist on your own. God can't be in charge as long as you think you are the boss.

The primary obstacles to your relationship with God are your knowledge and your pride. Surrender these and you will make room for God's plan in your life. Giving up your agenda allows you to open to the divine plan.

Your ego's tendency is to keep things as they are, no matter how bad they may be. God says: "Let go of the past and make room for something that honors you more deeply."

You are afraid to do that because there is no guarantee that the new will be any better than the old. You'd rather hold onto the old and invite the new in at the same time. That is the inevitable Catch 22. The new cannot come in until the old is released. When you are attached to the past, you cannot move forward.

When you let go of the past and accept what is, the universe instantly moves to support you. The deeper your let-go is, the more resources rush to your side.

It is the nature of the ego to project the past forward into the future, to meet the new with conceptual nets that would tame it and make it conform to yesterday's experience. There is nothing new in this. It is simply the movement of fear which resists anything new.

It is important to see how that fear operates in your life. It is important to realize how you become attached to your previous experience and resist anything new that wants to come into your life.

When you hold onto your experience or use it to interpret the present experience, you push God away. When you surrender your ideas about the way things should be, let go of the past, and open to the future, you invite God back into your life.

Your ego's agenda is to keep you safe. And safety is perceived in what is familiar, so the ego will argue that you should do things as you have done in the past. The ego is basically uncomfortable with change. It wants continuity, predictability.

You have to demonstrate to your ego mind that you can take risks and be safe too. Each time you let go and have a positive experience, you will be mapping a different course for your life.

Growth requires change and new challenges. It disrupts the continuity in your life and asks you to go deeper.

If something is continuous, it is not miraculous. Miraculous events are not continuous with what happened before them. They represent a shift of energy, a movement out of past perception and limitation. They are unpredictable and unexpected. Sometimes they even shake things up. They take away what is no longer needed so that something new and exciting can emerge.

Without your surrender of the past, miracles cannot come into your life. You create the space in which the miraculous occurs.

## MIRACLES AND THE UNMIRACULOUS

*The real miracle is to be found*
*in the spiritual purpose behind the event.*

When you think of miracles, you no doubt think of people who are cured of serious illnesses, who are delivered unexpectedly from dangerous situations or who experience unanticipated good fortune. But what about the person who dies of an incurable illness, who is paralyzed in a serious accident, or is the victim of some terrible crime? Are we to view these apparently negative events as completely unmiraculous, as out of sync with God's laws? And, if so, can we say that those who experienced these negative events were people who were not spiritual or close to God?

Nothing could be further from the truth. All events cohere in a higher order, the meaning of which dawns on those who open their hearts and minds to their experience. No event, no matter how unfortunate, is devoid of purpose.

The cripple is no less holy than the man whose broken limbs are mysteriously healed. Don't be fooled by appearances. Job experienced intense suffering in his intimate encounter with God. Things often do not mean what you think they mean.

Linear thinking is always dangerous, but when applied to issues of spirituality, it becomes a tool for inappropriate self-criticism and false pride. You are not bad if you don't receive the miracle you ask for. You are not good if you do. Such thinking comes from looking only at the surface of life. And, if you want to understand the miraculous nature of life, you must look beneath the surface.

All events are miraculous in the sense that they have a higher purpose. Often, you don't see what that purpose is and you may feel betrayed by God. You may think you are being punished. But that is just a limitation on your part, an unwillingness to accept, to trust, to look more deeply for the meaning that eludes you.

The real miracle does not lie in the outer event, in the apparent good or bad fortune involved. The real miracle lies in the spiritual purpose behind the event. The purpose may be to strengthen your faith or to challenge it. It may be to strengthen your body so that you can better serve, or to weaken your body so that you can leave its limits behind.

You are not capable of deciding what anything means. All you can do is ask: "What is this for? What is the meaning of this?"

Miracles help you break through the limits of your own mind. They challenge your world view and urge you to let go of your interpretation of life so that you can see the possibilities that lie beyond it.

It is odd, perhaps, but sometimes an apparent tragedy turns out to be an unanticipated blessing. You have heard people say "Thank God for my cancer. Without it, I never would have transformed my life" or "Thank God for the lesson of my child's death. It helped me wake up to my purpose in this lifetime."

Sometimes what appears to be taken away is the greatest gift, because it calls you forward. It brings you out of our shell into your life purpose.

## MIRACLES & PHYSICAL LAWS

*Your job is not to try to alter physical reality*
*but to be fully present with it.*

The real Miracle is your joining with God and understanding His Will for you. External healing or other blessings are not required. They may happen or they may not. You may be cured of your illness or you may not. The real miracle comes in your surrender to life as it is. When you come to peace and acceptance of your life, the miracle of God's love dawns in your heart.

Some people feel that a miracle has not taken place unless a physical law is transcended. The ocean parts and lets the people pass or the body is raised from the dead.

I hate to disappoint you, but everything that happens on the physical plane happens according to physical laws. That does not mean that spiritual laws are not in operation. They certainly are. But spiritual laws work with and through physical laws. There is no contradiction.

Spiritual laws do not govern how things work, but what they mean. How you interpret your experience and give meaning to it determines your psychological experience of the event.

If I had superhuman physical powers, I could have stopped my crucifixion from happening. But my spiritual understanding did not make me a superman. It simply enabled me to see the truth of what was happening to me. So I did not take the crucifixion as an attack. I did not condemn my brothers, for I saw that their actions were motivated by fear. And I felt compassion for them.

Yes, I was crucified. But I did not close my heart. I did not cast blame on anyone. I surrendered to God's will in that moment, as I had done in every other moment of my life.

If you think your faith will stop the crucifixion, you are just as likely to be wrong as right. Perhaps your faith will help your executioners open their hearts and change their minds. Perhaps it will not. Perhaps your faith will simply allow you to suffer your fate without condemning others.

You see, you don't know what God is asking from you until He asks it. And then, your choice is either to resist or to surrender.

It is that way in any moment of your life. It is that way in any situation. You don't know what it means. You just need to come to it willing to let go, willing to allow, willing to surrender.

Those physical laws which appear to be vitiated in certain miraculous experiences are simply laws that are incompletely understood. If you understood the laws fully, you would see that the event occurred entirely in harmony with them.

Of course there is much that you do not understand about the laws that govern physical reality. As your understanding of physical reality matures, you will increasingly see how physical laws interact with spiritual laws to create the experience you need in each moment.

I strongly discourage magical thinking, or the attempt to alter physical reality through the concentration of the mind. It is not that such things are impossible, but they are improbable and represent an aspect of your experience which does not need to be tampered with. To stand in the middle of the train tracks with the train approaching, while visualizing the train disappearing, is not something I recommend.

Miracle-mindedness is not demonstrated through the attempt to manipulate physical reality with the mind. That is an activity of the ego. The attempt to produce miracles on demand is the activity of a clown, not a spiritual man or woman.

You demonstrate your miracle-mindedness by surrendering to your experience and connecting with God's will for you in each moment. Your job is not to try to alter physical reality but to be fully present with it. As you endeavor to do this, your fear, your addictions, your attachment to the past, will rise up before you. Your job is to meet that fear, those addictions and attachments in a loving and compassionate way.

Your job is to walk through your fear and your pain, to recover from your addictions, to drop your interpretations and judgments and to enter your experience with an open mind and undefended heart. Your job is to meet the wounded child within you with love and encouragement, to help him feel safe so that he can heal and grow into his strength and purpose.

## EVERYTHING CAN BE LIFTED UP

*The only thing which can bring freedom from violence*
*is that which is free of violence.*

God needs your cooperation. Your brother and sister need your cooperation. You are not alone and you cannot live as if you are the only one who matters. When you try to live depending on yourself alone, you stumble and fall. Only when you think and act beyond your immediate ego needs does your life become subject to the law of grace.

To honor and care for yourself is your responsibility. Anything that honors you cannot possibly hurt another. But to act in a selfish way, placing your good above another's, invites conflict and resentment. The ways of the world are harsh in this regard. One who takes advantage of others may be feared but he is not loved. When his fortune changes, which it invariably does, and he begins to self-destruct, others are more than happy to help pull him down.

The outside world inevitably reflects back to you the fruits of your thoughts and actions. "As you sow, so do you reap."

Every time you attack another, you have something to defend. You are always looking over your shoulder to see who or what might be sneaking up on you. This is not a particularly satisfying or dignified way to live. Your fearful thoughts and actions call forth the fearful thoughts and actions of others.

These fear-based interactions become institutionalized in your "eye for an eye" system of justice, which perpetuates the cycle of abuse. By punishing the perpetrator, you hope to discourage him from brutalizing others in the future. You don't understand that all of his rage comes from his perception of himself as a victim and it is that which you are reinforcing by punishing him.

If you want to change the criminal, you must stop punishing him and begin to love him. Nothing else will work.

Love is not a reward for his trespass. It is the redeemer of his soul. It recalls him to himself. It shifts him out of the reactive cycle in which he dehumanizes himself and others. In the face of genuine love and caring, even the hardened criminal softens.

You cannot stop hate by fighting it with revenge. Every act of violence begets a counteract. By now you should know this.

It would be so easy if all you needed to do to contain violence was to meet it with force. That would be a religion and world view you could easily understand. But were this the case, there would be no hope of spiritual awakening on the planet. So it cannot be the case. The "eye for an eye" system of justice is not built into the blueprint for healing on planet Earth. The only thing which can bring freedom from violence is that which is itself free of violence.

Only a spiritual solution works. Human solutions to human problems invariably fall short. You can't solve a problem on the level on which you perceive it. You must go to a higher level, see the big picture, see the cause of the problem and address that.

That is why you need God in your life. That is why you need a spiritual practice. That is why you need something that calls you out of the cycle of attack and defense in your life.

There is no peace without God.

You can't find peace in the world. You can find it only in your heart, when it is open.

An open heart invites the beloved in. It invites the stranger in, and yes, even the criminal. An open heart is a sanctuary where all are welcome. It is a temple where the laws of spirit are practiced and celebrated. It is the church you must enter again and again to find redemption.

Ask yourself "Am I thinking and acting for myself alone, or do I have the good of the other in my heart?" If you do have his good in your heart, you will lift him up and you will be lifted up with him. If you don't, you will retreat in fear, closing your heart, seeking more protection.

It is a simple choice. Crucifixion happens when your heart closes to your brother. Resurrection happens when you open your heart to him, when you stop blaming him for your problems, when you stop punishing him for his mistakes, when you learn to love him as you love yourself. Only this will bring release from the prison of fear. Only this!

Love is the only miracle. All other "miracles" are frosting on the cake. Look beneath the surface of every one of them and you will see a shift from fear to love, from self-protection to self-expansion, from judgment of others to acceptance of them.

Love says: "I accept you as you are. I will consider your good equally with my own." Do you have any idea how powerful this statement is? To every person you address in this way, you offer freedom from suffering. And by offering it to him, you offer it to yourself.

If you do not seek equality, then you will never learn how to give love without conditions. It you do not offer equality, you will never learn how to receive unconditional love.

What you seek, you will find. As you offer, so shall you receive. The law has not changed.

## A FREE LUNCH

*A free lunch costs more than the one you pay for.*

For some, it is a great challenge to consider the well-being of others. For others, it is far too easy. In fact, it is easier for them to meet the needs of others than it is for them to get in touch with their own needs. In this case, serving others can be a form of self-betrayal.

When one opens his heart, he includes others in his sense of well-being. He does not trade their well-being for his own. He doesn't try to please others at his own expense. He does not give himself away

197

and find an identity in someone else. He expands his territory of caring to include his family, his friends, and ultimately his enemies. He expands his sense of self continually, as he learns to open his heart and soften to his experience.

By contrast, one who tries to please others at the expense of self is not offering love, but sacrifice. And sacrifice has its price. Hidden in the apparent show of selflessness is the demand for recognition, the desperate search for approval, the need to insure acceptance and love at any price.

Because hidden demands eventually surface, the one who is the recipient of the sacrifice usually feels manipulated and controlled. He feels beholden to the other person and stays in the relationship not out of joy but because of guilt. "How can I leave her? Look at what she's done for me. And, if I did leave, she would not make it. She'd self-destruct. She'd commit suicide!"

Ironically, the very people who have been cared for "so selflessly" become custodians too. Roles reverse. Caretakers extract their side of the bargain. Or if they can't, there is great bitterness on their part.

Beware of those who would sacrifice their lives for you. They will insist that they are repaid for every self-effacing gesture. Anyone who offers to give himself away for you will expect you to do the same for him.

You have heard the expression "there is no free lunch." That is ultimately true. But there are lunches that appear to be free. You don't have to pay now, but you most definitely have to pay later. Generally speaking, you can assume that what you don't have to pay for now is given on credit. Eventually the bill collector will come and he will want interest too!

Better not to accept the deal when it is offered to you. Better to say: "No, sister. I would prefer that you honor yourself. Please do not ignore your needs because you wish to please me. Nothing good can come of it." I realize this is not the popular thing to say. Temptation comes in many guises. One of the most prevalent ones is some version of the free lunch. Watch out when food, money, sex or attention is offered to you "without strings attached." The longest strings are the ones that are invisible!

If you are responsible, if you have the ability to pay, a free lunch does not appeal to you. If you can go into an elegant restaurant, order a good bottle of Cabernet Sauvignon, and eat filet mignon and baked shrimp on the deck overlooking the water, why would you go to the local soup kitchen?

You would do it only if you were greedy. Greed does not bring a kind or happy future. A miser doesn't take the time to enjoy his wealth. And death comes before he has learned to seize the moment and live it fully.

If you are a responsible person, you pay your way up front. You support others by purchasing their services. You don't need a free lunch and you don't need to defraud others in order to make a living. You know that receiving without giving is out of harmony with nature and the divine will. You don't seek that which is unfair, no matter how seductive it may appear.

CHAPTER FOURTEEN

# Reconciliation

*Pain is the great equalizer. It brings you to your knees.*
*It makes you more humble and sensitive to the needs of others.*

If you look at the surface of people's lives, you would have to say that people aren't equal. One person is a great athlete making millions of dollars a year. Another person is a handicapped veteran living on disability. One person has several advanced degrees. Another has not even finished the eighth grade. This hardly seems equal or fair. Indeed, in the eyes of the world, there is very little equality.

Yet, in the eyes of Spirit, people are completely equal. The rich man has no more privilege than the poor man. The simple man is no less appreciated than the brilliant intellectual. When you see beyond appearances, when you see what is in people's hearts, you see the same struggle, the same pain. The wealthy doctor who has lost a son to AIDS has the same pain that the woman on welfare has when she loses her daughter.

Pain is the great equalizer. It brings all human beings to their knees. It makes them more humble and sensitive to the needs of others. Pain is the greatest teacher on planet Earth. It undermines all hierarchies, social status or material riches. It brings everything up for healing.

If you have touched your own pain deeply, you know this. And you feel great compassion when you see others in pain. You do not need to push them away, nor do you need to try to fix them.

You just hold them deeply in your heart. You offer them a hug and some words of encouragement. You know what they are going through.

The world builds people up and it tears people down. There is no permanence in the world. Fame and ignominy, poverty and riches, happiness and despair run hand in hand. You can't experience one side without experiencing the other. If you think you can, you are in denial.

Most of you are in some degree of denial. That is probably because you have hardly touched your pain. It is too scary for you to do so. You would rather pretend to be spiritual than admit that you are having a really rough time. You don't want people to see your dirty laundry: your judgments, your desires, your suicidal thoughts. It is easier for you to let people see the pasteboard mask than the contorted face behind it. You are proud of the spiritual adult, but you are still ashamed of the wounded child.

The worst thing about denial is that it creates a culture of pretense and shame. Because so many people are pretending to be well-adjusted spiritual beings, those who are in touch with their pain feel that they are social misfits. They do not feel worthy to associate with others. They are ashamed of their pain and they isolate themselves, afraid to be seen or heard by others who might judge or reject them.

A person who is in touch with her pain threatens others. Her very presence cuts through the pretense in human interaction. Others find it difficult to wear their masks around her. Her willingness to be emotionally present with what she is feeling tends to bring up feelings in others that they may not want to deal with.

Yet for those who have the courage to be with their pain, a sacred passageway opens. The closed heart stretches and opens, the body begins to breathe, and blocked energy is released. This is the first step in the healing process. In the acknowledgement of pain and the willingness to be with it, the sacred journey begins.

## THE JOURNEY OF AWAKENING

*Feeling your pain enables you to be honest and authentic.*
*It connects you with a healing community.*

One cannot find genuine intimacy with others without being deeply with one's experience and communicating honestly about it to others. Relationships based on mutual denial are emotional prisons. Since two people wearing masks cannot communicate easily or honestly, partners in such relationships have no tools to open the prison door.

Enter an awakening crisis—the death of a loved one, a physical illness, or the loss of a job—and presto, the shell of denial is cracked. The prison door is blown open and the shell-shocked inhabitants are led out into the fresh air. Here they feel worse than they did when they were in prison, because now they are in touch with their pain.

Awakening events take chronic pain and make it acute. It hurts more. People get sicker. They can't function in the world as well. They have to make time and space to be with their pain.

To begin to "feel" your pain is the first great act of self-liberation. It is the end of unconscious sabotage and collusion. It is the birth of conscious awareness.

When you "feel" your pain you begin to move through it. It is a passageway, a means of shifting your life. It is not meant to arrest you. You are not meant to fall in love with your pain, hold onto it, or build a new identity around it. It is not a stationary train, but a moving one. Once you get on it, it takes you where you need to go.

Feeling your pain enables you to be honest and authentic. It empowers you to ask for unconditional love and support from others and to be willing to offer the same in return. It connects you with a healing community. You meet other human beings whose shells of denial are cracking and you begin to heal together.

The decision to heal is often a lonely one, yet no one ultimately needs to heal alone. Your healing is much quicker and much more profound when you are witnesses to the healing of others.

A healing community is very different from a hospital, where people go to get fixed or die isolated and alone. In a healing community, people connect with their feelings and discover greater intimacy with others. In a healing community, people may die, but they do not die alone. They die surrounded by loved ones. They die having stepped more fully into their lives. They die in forgiveness, in acceptance, and in peace.

It is time to stop building hospitals and start creating healing communities. Don't do this for other people. Do it for yourself, for your family, for your friends. You all need a safe, loving space in which to heal.

When pain is faced, people meet as equals. When pain is acknowledged, people learn to tell the truth about their experience. Then God's work can begin on planet Earth.

## ADDICTION TO PAIN

*Pain and suffering are not meant to be constant companions.*
*They are messengers, not roommates.*

Some people who begin to acknowledge their pain see that it gets them lots of attention. They build a whole identity around being wounded and they become addicted to telling their war stories.

When someone tells the same story over and over again, you know that person is not being authentic. The authentic person is not a professional storyteller. He is not a confession artist. He does not need to be the center of attention to feel good about himself.

The authentic person tells his story because the telling of it is an act of healing. As he tells it, he comes to a more profound insight into and acceptance of what happened. He embraces his experience more fully. He deepens his compassion for himself and others. As he tells his story, he heals, and so others heal with him.

The moment he has integrated his experience, he no longer needs to tell his story. If he insists on telling it, it becomes an impediment to his spiritual growth. It becomes a crutch that he leans on, even though his limbs have healed and he is ready to put all his weight on them. He becomes attached to his story, wedded to his pain. His story becomes an act. It no longer empowers people.

The acceptance of pain brings a shift away from dis-ease. It brings increased ease, self-acceptance and confidence. It allows you to take the next step on your journey.

Acknowledged pain is a door that opens, an invitation to expand, to trust more and take more risks. As you step into your fear and your pain, you move toward your joy. You leave old limits in your life behind. You shed your old skin.

As you share authentically, you empower others to heal. You move on. They move on. A life of pain is no longer called for.

Pain is necessary only when there is dissociation or denial. Suffering happens only when you are in resistance to life. While pain and suffering are universal phenomena, they are temporary ones. They touch every life at one time or another. But they are not constant companions. They are messengers, not roommates.

To say that the messenger is not present in your life when he is knocking at your door is utter foolishness. Please answer the door and hear what he has to say. But when you have heard the message the messenger can leave. His job is over.

## THERAPEUTIC ABUSE

*The compulsion to heal and the compulsion to wound*
*are different faces of the same coin.*

When it becomes "chic" to be a victim of childhood trauma or sexual abuse, therapists too easily get away with putting words in their clients' mouths. Memories of events that never happened are enshrined on the altar. Incidents of minor insensitivity or carelessness are exaggerated and painted with the language of fear and guilt. Everyone imagines that the worst must have happened. This is hysteria, not healing. It is a new form of abuse.

Instead of inquiring into what happened and allowing the inner child to speak, a professional label is placed on the wound. The victim's voice is squelched once again and she is given someone else's opinion of what happened to her. In order to gain approval, the wounded child tells the story the authority figure—now her therapist—asks her to tell. By capitulating to authority, she is told she is getting well.

The therapist projects her own unhealed wounds onto her client. Her subjectivity is taken for objectivity by the courts. Families are separated. More children are punished. The chain of abuse continues.

The attachment to pain is debilitating. The embellishment, exaggeration or fabrication of pain is insane.

Just as the creation of a priestly class of authority figures undermined the organic spirituality of the church, so the creation of a new class of therapist/healer authority figures undermines the ability of individuals to access the healing that is their birthright.

You can't make anyone heal any more than you can make people act in a moral way. Healing is a voluntary act. It happens as people are ready. Many people in therapy have no intention to heal. Many people dispensing therapeutic advice have no commitment to their own healing. For these people, therapists and clients alike, therapy is a form of denial.

Letting the wound heal by itself is just as important as ministering to the wound. We forget that the spiritual essence of the person does the healing. It is not the therapist or healer who heals.

Those who intervene or interfere in the natural healing process will ultimately be called to account for the damage they do. For attack is attack under any guise. And the compulsion to heal is just as vicious as the compulsion to wound. Indeed, they are different faces of the same coin.

The true healer respects the inner healing ability of her patient. She helps her patient make the connections that are ready to be made. She advocates integration, gentleness and patience. Thus, her clients get stronger. They heal and move on.

The unhealed healer is only too quick to make her patient into a victim, too quick to blame others. In the process, the patient is stripped of all dignity and self-confidence. She is made dependent on a steady diet of prescription drugs and doctor authority figures.

If you are not to make a mockery of the healing process, you must avoid the extremes of denial and fabrication of pain. Pain must be faced, not imagined. If it is there, it will express itself authentically. It will speak with its own voice. Your job is to invite the voice to speak, not to give it the words to say.

Blaming others does not lead to healing. Overcoming shame is more important than finding people to blame. Even when it is clear that violation has occurred, punishing the perpetrator is not the solution. For the perpetrator is already a victim and punishing him just reinforces his own shame and powerlessness.

The question you must learn to ask is not "how do we heal?" but "how do we create a safe space where healing can occur?" If you can learn how to do that, then healing will take care of itself and the conditions that cause abuse will be undone at their roots.

## AUTHENTICITY

*Guidance cannot be found in the opinions of others.*

Whatever your experience has been, your challenge is to learn to accept it without judgment and to embrace it unconditionally. When you can do that, you can integrate the experience and the lessons it brings into the fabric of your life.

The denial or fabrication of experience is inauthentic and results in greater fragmentation of consciousness and imbalance in the psyche. You must neither deny what happened, nor make it up. You must acknowledge what happened—however unpleasant or painful that may be—with the help of a therapist if you need it. That is what starts the shift from untruth to truth, from secrets to revelation, from hidden discomfort to the conscious awareness of pain.

Pain is a doorway you walk through when you are ready. Until then, you are the doorkeeper, the sentinel who stands guard and decides whom to exclude and whom to let in.

It is okay not to be ready. It's okay to exclude people or situations that feel unsafe. You are in charge of your own healing process. You decide how fast to go. Don't let anyone else dictate the pace of your healing process. If you work with a therapist/healer, make sure that s/he knows whenever you feel pushed or unsafe in any way.

Honoring your own process is essential to a life lived authentically.

Others will always have ideas, suggestions, and plans for you. Thank them for their concern, but be clear that you, not they, are making the decisions in your life.

Beware of those who criticize you "for your own good." And watch out when they play to your guilt. You don't owe anyone anything, except the truth.

"No" is not a bad thing to say when people invite you to betray yourself. Indeed, it is precisely what your experience is attempting to teach you. Say "no" to all bargains and trades for love and approval. They cannot make you happy. Don't give away your freedom in return for a few conditional strokes.

You need your freedom if you are to learn to be yourself fully. A genuine spiritual guide celebrates your freedom and encourages you to follow your own heart. A true teacher points you within, where you receive your guidance, and not without. For guidance cannot be found in the opinions of others.

## PERMISSION TO BETRAY

*All forms of manipulation are rooted in fear and insecurity.*
*They may promise love, but they cannot deliver it.*

The majority of people you give your power away to will abuse or betray you. That is especially true for anyone you accept as a savior. You may say "But I didn't know he would take advantage of me." I say to you, "Wise up. Take responsibility for your life. Realize that you bought the farm. Stop trying to blame another for the choices you made."

You gave permission. You gave your power away. Perhaps you did not know how bad it would be. The abuse came, as it frequently does, wrapped in sugar-coated promises. Friendship may have been offered, or financial security, or spiritual redemption, or sex, or love. You name it. It doesn't matter what the bait was. You swallowed it and you got hooked. Be wiser next time. See the offer for what it is. You gave your power away in order to gain acceptance and love. But love never comes from any form of manipulation. All forms of manipulation are rooted in fear and insecurity. They may promise love, but they cannot deliver it.

Don't believe those who say they would sacrifice their good for yours. Even if it were true, they would be committing a sin against themselves and nothing good could come of it.

Don't accept anyone else's authority over you and don't accept authority over anyone else. Claim your freedom and offer freedom to others.

Those who try to manipulate or bargain for love will spend their whole lives in an emotional labyrinth with little hope of egress. Conditional love is an endless prison. The only escape is to tell the truth to yourself and others. Then you can walk free.

Neither a borrower nor a lender be. Do not borrow approval from others. Do not offer it when others seek it from you. Get out of the approval business. Get out of the lending business. Give what you can give with your whole heart and let the rest lie where it is.

Too many of you get caught in the horizontal journey. I have tried to tell you that, no matter how far you go in the exploration of "other," you will return to self. Earth is round. After you travel the circumference of the planet, you return to the same place.

Why leave self at all? Why go astray seeking the other when there is no other? There is only the self. This you will discover sooner or later. The more you go out the more you will return home.

All others offer you a detour from the universe of self. The more you believe that you need others to be happy the more miserable you will be. Happiness cannot be given by others, for, contrary to appearances, there are no others out there. There is only the self.

What you perceive as "other" promises to love you, but as soon as you give your power to it, it attacks and betrays you. It commits murder, rape, child abuse, you name it. It does all this because it believes, as you do, that someone else can meet its needs or make it happy.

All this is but a mirror, showing you the vicious nature of the abandoned, separated self. Separation cannot be undone through force. The unloved cannot find love. Only the one whose heart is softening can find the love he wants, but he does not find it outside the self. And once he finds it, he cannot lose it.

Love yourself well and others move easily and naturally into your love. In truth, when two people meet who love themselves, there is no "other" present. There is just one being who dwells in the single heart of love.

There is only one person here who needs to give and receive love and that is you. Give love to yourself and include others in that love. If they do not wish to be included, let them go. It is no loss. You do not need another detour, another useless journey.

Be steadfast in your love for yourself. Let that be your absolute number one commitment. Grace will bring others in who are happy to be with themselves. They will not come in making demands of you. They will not come in trying to take control of your life.

When someone makes you an offer you can't refuse, you must learn to refuse it. Don't betray yourself, regardless of the price.

The tempter will always come to you offering extraordinary gifts. Don't be fooled. He seems to have supernatural powers, but they are not real. He is just your brother moving off course, trying to draw you into his drama of self-abuse.

Don't say yes to his offer. Listen to what God is telling you now and in each moment: "Your needs are completely met. You are whole. You lack nothing. Relax and breathe. This too will pass."

Yet even when you refuse him, the tempter will not yield. He will play to your insecurity and victim consciousness: "No," he will tell you, "you are not okay. You are lonely. You need companionship. You need a better job. You need a better relationship. You need more money, more sex, more notoriety; all of this will I give to you."

Surely, you have heard this pitch before! Some knight in shining armor or damsel in distress always appears when you are feeling low. Where has it gotten you in the past? How many knights or damsels have sped off on their steeds leaving behind them a trail of blood and tears?

Yet this one seems better than the last. He or she is more sincere, more sensitive, more grounded. You fill in the words. It is your drama, not mine.

If you look deeply enough, you will see that every pitch is the same. Every invitation to self-betrayal has the same sugar-coated promises and the same heart-wrenching core.

Those who seek salvation in another lose touch with self. They go off like Don Quixote on the great horizontal journey. And they always find damsels to rescue and windmills to fight. That's part of the terrain. But in the end, they return home tired, wounded, and lacking in faith. The horizontal journey defeats everyone who takes it. There is no salvation to be found in the world.

You can find peace only if you stay at home. Stay with the self. Bring love to the parts of the self that still feel unloved. Become rooted in the eternal blessing of God's abundance and grace.

Here there are no strings attached, no neurotic bargains for love and approval. Here there is authentic wholeness, the joy of being present alone and together. Here abuse is impossible, for there is no other to distract the self and take it from its purpose. Here freedom and love are intertwined for, without one, you cannot have the other.

## EMERGING FROM THE DREAM

*You are the shining one dreaming the dream of abuse.*

All apparent abuse is a game between phantoms or shadows. People emerge with gaping wounds. They appear to get hurt, but genuine hurt is impossible, because the self is unassailable. You cannot put holes in it. You can only pretend to hurt or be hurt.

Nobody can be separated from the source of love, but people believe that they can be, and their actions are based on this belief. As soon as this belief is challenged, love reveals itself. For it is always there behind the drama of attack and defense.

If you see only the surface of life, you will see through a glass darkly. You will see only dream images. But if you lift the curtain and look behind it, you will see the actors behind their masks. You will see how everything that happens to you is called for from the depths of your being. And all of it contributes to your awakening. It forces you to look behind the curtain. It forces you to drop your role of victim or victimizer. It exposes your secrets.

It lets you know that nothing can separate you from love, because you are love incarnate. You are the shining one dreaming the dream of abuse. You are the angel walking as wounded.

Denying your hurts doesn't take you home. Pretending to be an angel when you feel like an abused kid does not contribute to your awakening. But neither does holding onto the wound.

When the wound is addressed with love, it heals. That healing can be instantaneous or it can take a lifetime, depending on the degree of your surrender to love. But victimization does stop and healing does happen. The drama of suffering does comes to an end.

Awakening is not a wrenching process, but a gentle giving up of blame and shame. A gentle letting go of projection.

Suffering falls away and wounds dissolve in love's embrace. And in the end, it is as if the wound never happened. At best, you could say it was a dream of abuse, a dream from which you have gloriously awakened.

Who you are is inseparable from love. It is therefore inevitable that you will awaken from the dream of separation. Nothing that you can do will change this outcome. God made certain of this.

You cannot hurt yourself permanently. You cannot cut yourself off permanently from God's love. At best, you can take a circular journey away from yourself. At best, you can be seduced into thinking that happiness or unhappiness lies outside of you.

## SOLITUDE

*Caring for yourself is a full-time vocation.*

Your fear of being alone and your emotional dependency on others set you up for many disappointments. Constant failure in your relationships exacerbates old wounds, making it harder for you to heal. Your self-confidence is diminished and your anxiety about your self-worth is increased.

All this can be shifted if you are willing to accept your aloneness as a state of being. Make room for activities that you enjoy and relationships that honor you and respect your boundaries. Find a way to care for your body and express your creativity. Live in an inspirational place. Find quiet time to center yourself. Walk in the woods or by the ocean. Work at something you enjoy doing. Be joyful. Eat well. Sleep well. Care for yourself and refine the quality of your life.

Caring for yourself is a full-time vocation. Do not try to make it into a part-time activity. It must become the major focus of your life.

When you become established in the flow of your life, your days are full of joy, creativity, and caring relationships that honor your newfound energy, optimism, and tranquility. These relationships are different from any you have experienced so far, because they are built on a solid foundation.

When you know how to take care of yourself, there is no invitation to self-betrayal. Your behavior is not wound-driven and you do not attract abuse or codependent relationships.

Solitude is necessary for your emotional health, whether you are living alone or living with another. Solitude gives you the time and space to integrate your experience.

Without solitude, spiritual nourishment will be lacking. If you want a single cause for the amount of distress in the world, it is the fact that people do not take time to commune with self, nature and the divine. A spiritual life—a life free of needless tension and self-created suffering—requires such communion.

If you keep the Sabbath, you dedicate one day a week for self-nurturing and communion. That is enough to keep you centered in your life. If you meditate or take a long silent walk for an hour each day, you can achieve the same goal. It doesn't matter what ritual you choose, as long as it provides time for silent reflection.

The time you take to integrate your experience is as important as the time you take to have the experience itself. If you remember that, you will assimilate your lessons with greater depth and rapidity.

If you eat a meal and then take a half hour nap, you will wake up rejuvenated. You will have given your body uninterrupted time to work on digestion. Try to do the same thing with all of your experiences. Allow time for digestion and assimilation. Let your experience percolate within you. Be with it. Let it live inside you, before you try to respond or live out from it.

Every breath you take has three movements: an inhale, a pause, and an exhale. The inhale is for the taking in of experience. The pause is for its assimilation. And the exhale is for the release of extraneous material. While the pause is just a second or two, it is essential for the integrity of the breath.

Likewise, solitude is an essential aspect of a conscious, integrated life. The quality of life rests on it. Energy and spirituality require it.

If you drop out this part, your life will be an empty shell. A great deal may pass in and out of it, but nothing will stick. There will be no growth in consciousness.

## ROOTS AND WINGS

*Only your rootedness can help you bring heaven to Earth.*

The simple beauty and majesty of life is to be found in its cyclical rhythms: the rising and setting of the sun, the phases of the moon, the changes in the seasons, the beating of the heart, the rhythmic unfolding of the breath. Repetition provides continuity, familiarity, safety. Yet within every cycle, there are variations that provide challenges and opportunities for growth.

Many people are disconnected from the rhythms of nature and their own bodies. They do not have a safe, nurturing, environment in which to live and respond to the challenges that arise. This is one of the tragedies of contemporary life.

The connection with the earth, the body, the breath, is disrupted. The nuclear family is stressed out and attenuated. The extended family is virtually extinct. Life today is a shell of what it used to be.

Changes happen quickly without the time to reflect on them and integrate them. Relationships begin and end before people can establish trust or honest communication. Emotional demands crater the landscape of the heart, tearing into the soft tissue.

Many people today are walking wounded. Yet few people notice it. Life goes on, driven to perpetual distraction. As entertainment flourishes, awareness and communion wane. More and more stimuli intrude. Life becomes busyness. The only quiet time is during sleep, and even that is prey to restless dreams.

This is a travesty of life. It is life without breath, without energy, without intimacy. It is an attack on the senses, an overwhelming of the mind, and a violation of the spirit.

It is life without heart, without rhythm. It is ungrounded. It reaches for the heavens while ignoring the earth. It spins out, careening wildly thorough the sky, moving from one self-destructive adventure to another. It is unsafe and abusive to all concerned.

The more unsafe it seems, the more the wounded child inside seeks the security it believes an authority figure can provide. But that is just a trap. The greater your need for outside approval, the more devastating the betrayal of trust will be.

People marry authority figures. They elect them. They go to their churches and join their cults. Yet eventually all these authority figures are discredited. And, as they fall from their pedestals, those who worshiped them once move in for the kill. It is an old story.

You live in a time when all external authority is gradually being undermined. The more people look without, the more their lessons will force them to look within.

All who seek the sky without getting roots in the earth will be beat up by their experiences. In time they will return, shovels in hand, and begin the work of planting.

There are no wings without roots, except for birds. And they make sure to take shelter in trees with deep roots in the ground.

All that is spinning out to heaven will fall to Earth, abused, shattered, forsaken, licking its imagined wounds. That which is rootless will learn to grow roots. That which has sought authority without will learn to find it within.

And then, with feet firmly planted in the earth, the eyes will notice the procession of sun and the moon. The senses feel the rise of sap in the spring and the lifting of leaves in the fall. Blood and breath will be restored. Rhythm will return. Safety will be re-created where it authentically lies, in the heart of each person. And organic order will be re-established on Earth.

If you are not growing roots, you are asking for trouble. Only your own rootedness can help you bring heaven to earth. Not willfulness or spiritual pride. Not left-brained agendas.

Spirituality is a living with, not a living for. It is the poetry of being, the rhythm of life unfolding in each person, each relationship, each community.

CHAPTER FIFTEEN

# Embracing the Self

*You have only two choices in life.*
*You can be faithful to yourself or you can betray yourself.*

Most of you know what you want, but you do not wait for it. You compromise your needs and your values to fit the situations which present themselves to you. You take the job or the relationship not because it offers you what you desire, but because you are afraid a better offer won't come. You live your life afraid to take risks because you do not want to give up the security you have.

I have news for you. That security is your death knell. It prevents you from asking sincerely for what you want.

For a moment, stop looking for satisfaction or security outside yourself. Do what makes you happy. Do not question it or apologize for it. Care for yourself gently and generously. Eat what your body requires. Sleep as long as you need to. Energize yourself on all levels of your being. Do not compromise. Be committed to you.

Without a commitment to yourself, nothing worthwhile can be accomplished in life. Give yourself what you need to thrive.

You have only two choices in life. You can be faithful to yourself or you can betray yourself. And no one else is responsible for the choice that you make.

When you betray yourself, you eventually betray others. When you do not ask for what you want or accept what you do not want, you set others up for disappointment. Sooner or later, you will have to admit the truth: you don't really want what you asked for!

The cycle of abuse continues until you see your own self-betrayal for what it is. The only way out of the detour of codependent, mutually deceptive relationships is to befriend the self, honor the self, love and embrace the self. Then one can build relationship on the truth of self-coherence. This is the new paradigm relationship.

In the old paradigm relationship, the commitment to self is vitiated by the commitment to other. In seeking to please the other, self is abandoned. Since the abandoned self is incapable of love, this constitutes a vicious cycle of attraction and rejection. First the self is excluded, and then the other is excluded.

All genuine relationship must be built on the foundation of one's acceptance of and love for self. That is the primary spiritual gesture, the one that opens the door to the potential for intimacy.

When you know what you want, don't be afraid to ask for it. Stay focused on it and do not settle for less. Reject all the conditions with which love and attention are offered to you. Hold fast to the truth of your heart. Be patient and committed, wait for what you want, and know that you deserve it.

Be faithful to yourself, learn to bring love to yourself, answer the call within your own heart, and one day the Beloved appears at your doorstep. This is not a magical occurrence, but the fruit of a committed spiritual practice.

# ILLUMINATION

*When you have the courage to look within, the light will appear.*

The world you know is engendered by self-betrayal. It is a sad, defeated, spiritless world. Those who try to redeem it do so by focusing on the sins of others. They punish others for their mistakes and hope this will lead to a change of mind and heart. However, punishing others for doing something they don't know why they did rarely leads to a change in their consciousness or behavior.

Trespass against others comes from childhood wounds in the psyche and the fear and shame around them. For redemption to happen, these wounds must be uncovered and healed.

Both the victim and the victimizer are wounded. They use their relationship to re-enact the wound so that it can be seen and healed.

Society tends to have more compassion for the victim than it does for the victimizer, but that is because it does not understand that the victimizer was a victim first. Because he was hurt and traumatized, he attacks others. He has been taught to do this by his victimizer. Victim and victimizer are two sides of the same coin.

Victim and victimizer call out to each other. And when they answer the call, they do so with conviction. Thanks to the other, each is given a wake-up call. Each is given the opportunity to uncover the wound and the fear and shame around it. If he is willing to look courageously, he can see how the wound is passed down from generation to generation.

As a compassionate society, we should help both the victim and the victimizer uncover their wounds and begin to heal them. We must do this with profound gentleness and compassion. We do not want to "blame the victim" or "condone the actions of the perpetrator." We simply want each one to heal and stop projecting his pain onto others.

All forms of trespass are comprised of reactive behavior patterns that stem from core wounds in the psyche and the fear and shame around them. All reactive behavior patterns lead to self-betrayal, even those that result in the attack and betrayal of others.

One cannot meet one's needs by attacking others. The strategy does not work. There is only one person who can be betrayed in the end and that is the betrayer himself.

To heal, you must encounter your own wound. Healing requires a safe space. You cannot heal if you are involved in an abusive relationship. You cannot heal if you are actively projecting your pain or being the target of your partner's projections.

Sooner or later you will have to look within at the darkness. The wound may be stuffed down in the shadows, but it is not going to go away. Every encounter with an abuser just deepens the pain of the wound and confirms your apparent powerlessness.

Yet you are not powerless. When you have the courage to look within, the light will appear. And you can carry it with you into the dark places of your soul where your wounds fester and your shame lies like a dark blanket over your innocence.

As long as you are afraid to look at the darkness, the light cannot come. But when you are ready to face your fears and bring love to the wounded places in your heart and mind, then the light of awareness is finally lit. It is the beacon that illuminates the shadows. It is the lighthouse that guides the ships out of the stormy waters into the safety of the harbor.

As long as you feel unworthy, you will have trespass and abuse. But unworthiness is not an endless curse that cuts you off from the love that you want. It is a temporary obstacle that can be removed if you have the courage to face your fears and walk through your shame.

Many are afraid to take this journey through the dark night of the soul. That is understandable. But those who have taken the journey know that it looks much scarier than it is. They know that the light comes to those who ask for it, and in the end the darkness cannot hide from the light. In time, every hidden object is illumined. In the end awareness comes and the process of emotional healing is set into motion.

## ALONE, WITH HEART OPEN

*When you are content to be yourself,*
*you take your brothers and sisters off the hook.*

When you finally discover that no one else can betray you, your relationship to your brother changes profoundly. He is no longer someone who can hurt you or treat you unfairly. Nor is he someone who can save you or make you feel better about yourself.

Because you don't worship him or scapegoat him, his significance in your life greatly diminishes. He is simply a fellow traveler, a neighbor. You are willing to help him from time to time or receive his help. But you no longer wish to depend on him or have him become dependent on you.

A new and healthy sense of boundaries is established in all of your relationships. You become capable of being a friend and receiving the fruits of friendship from others. But your interest in your brother or sister is no longer intrusive. Your happiness does not depend on how he or she responds to you.

When you are content to be yourself, you take your brothers and sisters off the hook. They no longer have to be perfect in your eyes. You see their shortcomings and mistakes without judging them harshly. You see their beauty and integrity without envying them or placing them on a pedestal.

The more you claim your freedom to be yourself, the easier it becomes for you to grant others the same freedom. You do not demand attention from others, nor do you tolerate relationships with others who make artificial demands on your time or attention.

When you are alone, you remain open to others. When you are with others, you are not thrown off-center or drawn into their dramas of self-abuse.

## MARRIAGE VS CELIBACY

*Marriage is one spiritual path. Celibacy is another.*

Establishing in the self is the true meaning of celibacy. It may involve sexual abstinence, but this is not always the case.

When you are celibate, you do not promise anyone an exclusive partnership. Your vow is to honor yourself and tell the truth in each moment. A celibate person is not looking for marriage or partnership. S/he is committed to being single as a spiritual path.

Celibate people consciously choose a lifestyle of living alone. They are up front with others about their decision not to marry or cohabit. They choose to live alone because their creative pursuits and/or spiritual practices require the majority of their time and attention and make living full-time with another person an unwise and unwieldy proposition.

There is nothing wrong or right with celibacy. It is one spiritual path. Marriage is another. Both paths have their challenges and their rewards. Moreover, during the course of one's lifetime, one may choose to be married first, then celibate, or celibate first, then married. Society would do well to acknowledge the importance of different interpersonal models as people go through the inevitable lifecycle changes.

Of all the choices available, abstinence is the least likely to succeed. It is tragic that the church has demanded this sacrifice of its clergy. Very few people are capable of sexual abstinence. Those who try and find that they cannot do it must engage in secretive, deceptive, and sometimes abusive behavior in order to satisfy their desires. Witness the many cases of pedophilia and other sexual assaults by clergy that have been covered up by the church, thereby undermining its authority and credibility.

It is time that such abuses come to light. And it is time that all religions rethink their positions on both celibacy and abstinence. For a clergyperson may in good faith choose to be married—being a model to the congregation of what a successful marriage looks like —or to be single and celibate—being a model to the flock of the life of a solitary visionary or mystic.

In the end, the form chosen does not matter as much as the commitment to honesty and truth. An honest but unconventional life is to be greatly preferred to a traditional life twisted by secrets and lies.

## CREATIVITY AND CONFORMITY

*Authentic self-expression is neither offensive nor apologetic.*

In order to fully individuate, you may have to walk a different path than others walk. Your authenticity is often challenging to others who lead a more predictable, socially acceptable life.

When you move across the grain, you can expect more friction than when you don't. When you challenge the values, standards and perceptions of the dominant reality, you are unlikely to be supported financially or emotionally by it.

Original work breaks new ground. And the more faithful you are to your own creative vision, the more you will tend to move into uncharted territory. A true artist is ahead of her time. She does not act from the outside in. She does not make her work conform to the demands and expectations of the marketplace.

However, self-expression without feedback is solipsistic. It is not a dialogue with anyone. Without dialogue and feedback creative work does not grow. It turns in on itself. It becomes a private language.

The extremes of artistic license and artistic conformity are to be avoided. The former closes the audience out. The latter closes the artist in.

Don't expect your creative endeavors to speak to others if you don't use a vernacular language. It you want to engage others, you must speak in a language that people understand. If you are wise, you will speak plainly and directly, the way you would like to be spoken to.

Will authentic work support you? Perhaps it will. Perhaps it won't. In an enlightened society, all authentic work would be supported. But the world you live in has not reached that point of trust and investment in the creative process.

However, you cannot afford to deny the creative aspect of your being just because it does not support you financially. That is self-betrayal. So find a way to make time and space for your creative self-expression. Give yourself an hour a day, or a day a week. Make a consistent commitment to your own creative process. Let there be a rhythm with it. Make it a ritual of self-honoring.

Self-expression is essential to the honoring of self. Yet you must take time not only to create, but also to engage with others. That is the gesture that builds community.

The desire for approval prevents honest self-expression. It is soft and apologetic. But the need to shock can be harsh and offensive, pushing people away.

Authentic expression is neither offensive nor apologetic. It delivers its message and invites dialogue. It challenges you to grow, to question your values and beliefs, and to find a way to understand and appreciate others who have a different perspective and experience.

Without the full realization of the creativity of each person, social life becomes dull, humdrum, restrictive and boring. It caves in upon itself. There is no spark, no energy, no diversity or interchange.

A family or educational system that does not foster creativity and dialog is not doing its job. In an enlightened society, children are encouraged to honor their creative process and respect that of others. Time and space are provided for individual self-directed work, as well as for sharing and cooperative group activities.

A creative watershed does not happen overnight, but evolves over time as your commitment to your own creative process deepens and expresses. The most profound learning happens at the experiential level. And your children learn best by watching what you do and emulating you.

## CHAPTER SIXTEEN

# *Awareness*

*All experience contributes to reawaken the memory of the One Self:*
*absolute, all-inclusive and therefore unassailable.*

It is true that there is no ultimate reality in the wound. Yet your challenge is not to deny the wound, but to bring love to it. When awareness of the unwounded whole (love) is brought to the wounded part (unloved), the wound heals.

The self cannot be damaged by its experience. All experience contributes to reawaken the memory of the One Self: absolute, all-inclusive and therefore unassailable.

Ironically, the more you individuate, the closer you come to touching the universal experience. For it is only by walking through the door of self that you fall directly into the heart.

This should indicate to you the utter futility of following someone else's ideas or using their experience to validate your own. Only by accepting what comes directly and experientially to you will you find the door to the universal.

It is paradoxical perhaps. It is by honoring the self that you move beyond self-interest. All teachings of self-abnegation are false. To go beyond the small self, you must become it fully. You must inhabit it and break through it.

Denying your needs will just inhibit your progress. If you want to come into your true nature, you must learn to be completely human, authentic, and present to your experience.

You are a fallen angel who must become fully human to win back your wings. You come here not because you are forced to, but because you are anxious to complete your lessons. No one can hold you back from moving into embodiment. It is not possible to defray your hunger for experience. It will always have its way.

You come into this world thinking it would be easy but it is anything but that. What seemed to be a gentle walk up the hill of judgment turns into an intensely challenging climb. Sometimes you think you can't make it. So you bail out of the experience. But that doesn't help. Wherever you leave the path is where you will have to resume your journey. There are no shortcuts. There is no way to skip over the lessons you carefully fashioned for your awakening.

## FREEDOM FROM THE PAST

*Do not stir the pot unless you want to smell the stew.*
*Do not solicit the past unless you want to dance with it.*

All dreams of self are present in this dream. That is why it is not necessary to concern yourself with who you were in some past life, unless memories spontaneously come up for your attention.

Your preoccupation with the past is what limits your ability to be fully present in the moment. And that presence is necessary if you are to wake up from the dream of abuse.

In any moment you can be free of the past or enslaved by it. In any moment, you can justify your fear or walk through it.

Do not go in search of memories from the past. If they come up, acknowledge them, be with them and integrate them. Do this not to empower the past, but to complete it, so that you can be present now. Anything that takes you away from your immediate communion with life is not helpful. On the other hand, resisting something that wants to come up takes you even further away from being present in the moment.

Are there past lives? Only if you remember them. And if you remember them, you will continue to live them until you come to forgiveness of yourself and others.

The key to all of this is simple: do not gather wood unless you want to make a fire. Do not stir the pot unless you want to smell the stew. Do not solicit the past unless you want to dance with it.

But if there is a fire in your house, you must pick up your things and leave. If the stew is boiling, you can't help but smell it. If the past is dancing in your mirror, you can't pretend to be in samadhi.

Resistance of experience creates endless detours. But so does seeking. Do not resist. Do not seek. Just deal with what comes up.

Don't try to save the world. Don't try to save others. All that just adds to your job description. Just be with your experience the way it is and try to get your arms around all of it. There is plenty there for you to digest.

Nobody comes into embodiment with an empty plate. Everyone has at least a scrap or two to digest. Some have seven course meals!

Since each person must deal with what's on his plate, let him deal with it as happily as he can.

Don't interfere in the lives of others or you will have a much bigger meal to digest. Stay detached from what someone else does or does not do. Don't even have an opinion about it. Just let it be.

Don't borrow someone else's experience. Don't try to give someone else your experience. Don't be codependent.

Step into your life. Sleep in your own bed. Prepare your own food. Clean up after yourself. Practice taking care of yourself and let others do the same.


## OPEN HEART, EMPTY MIND

*The process of enlightenment unfolds by itself.*
*It requires no help from you.*

Nothing will crucify you faster than your own thoughts. Better not think at all, if you can do it. If you can't, think about simple things like washing the dishes or doing the laundry. And when these things are done, let the mind be empty.

Everything you believe about the nature of your existence keeps you limited to the past. If you want to experience the moment unconditionally, give up all your concepts of it. Just be present in your life as it unfolds.

Watch the tendency of the mind to try to figure everything out. Watch how it tries to structure and plan, plot and re-plot. Watch it try to hold onto mutual exclusive possibilities. Watch how easily it goes into opposition and conflict.

Mind is always looking for the thread of the story so it can continue to weave the plot, or at least maintain the illusion of the story. But the interesting thing is that there is no plot. And the story is just a story, something that has entertainment value at best.

Now if you know this, you might say some things that people would find disturbing. You might tell people, "It's all a sham. There is no world, no heaven, no birth, no death, no self, no other, no ego, no God, no nothing." Can you imagine how embarrassing that would be for the powers that be?

But you aren't ready to do that yet. You are still the living in the story. You are still limited by what you see. A radical practice is needed if you want to break through the limits of your perception. Begin seeing everything around you as a mirror showing you what you believe. Practice this every time you start to take your life or someone else's life too seriously. Practice it when you are in pain and feel you can't take another step forward. Prctice it when you are in love and can't wait another moment for your lover.

Practice this and keep your eyes open as you embrace your experience. Don't go to sleep. Don't pretend that you know what something means. Just remember everything that you see shows you what you believe and be willing to look into the mirror.

It is like watching a rock skipping over the surface of a pond. You see it skipping, but you don't know who threw it. You have to look for a long time before you see the trajectory of the rock and the one who threw it.

While you are watching you can consider these questions: If a tree falls in the forest and no one hears it, does it make a sound? What is the sound of one hand clapping?

Of course, you aren't going to figure any of this out, so just be present with the questions until they drop away. Then you can come to God with empty hands and an open heart.

The process of enlightenment unfolds by itself. It requires no help from you.

## SURRENDERING WHAT YOU KNOW

*Spiritual Knowledge is more an unknowing than a knowing, more an emptying out than a taking in.*

Since people have different beliefs and perceptions, they react to similar circumstances in very different ways. That is why you can never predict what anything will mean to another person. The event that one person responds to with compassion will stir up anger or resentment in another.

Of course not all beliefs and the choices resulting from them are conscious. Unconscious choices made in the past can determine present realities. Each person lives in the karmic flow of his life and while certain experiences may be perfect for the evolution of his soul, he may not consciously understand or appreciate them.

When you want to wake up, you learn to surrender to your experience. When events arise which challenge you, you listen for the message hidden behind the veil. You work to see the soul value and potential for learning in each encounter. Your effort is not focused on trying to manipulate your experience to achieve the outcomes desired by your ego, but rather to commune with your experience to learn the lessons that it brings.

Your life is a continual dialogue between experience and your interpretation of it. Increasingly, you learn that your suffering is not caused by what happens, but by the meaning that you give to it.

Nevertheless, there are times when you resist your experience and have difficulty taking responsibility for it. And those are the times when you are challenged to go deeper in your spiritual practice and expand your consciousness beyond what you know and anticipate.

The biggest obstruction in your relationship with the divine is the belief that you already know. That belief makes you a prisoner of your own subjective interpretation. What you think you know is just your fear asserting itself. Your description of reality is not reality. Instead, it limits reality to fit your bias, prejudice, judgments, and mistaken beliefs. In the end, you must surrender what you think you know in order to discover what you need to learn.

Spiritual knowledge does not help you control and manipulate your life or that of others. It does not enable you to predict events or interpret what they mean. It is a knowledge that enables you to look within, to see through the veil of your subjective reactions, to learn to appreciate the essence of life as it unfolds without attaching your own meaning to it.

Spiritual knowledge comes from giving up what you think you know and surrendering to what is. It is more an unknowing than a knowing, more an emptying out than a taking in.

Some of you have tried to gain knowledge of the past or future through a variety of esoteric systems, but all of these systems are limited. The desire for esoteric knowledge is one of the ego's last defenses against the truth. This defense must be surrendered before the truth can be placed in your hands.

## SPIRITUAL WORK

*This is a journey to full empowerment.*
*When the self is empowered fully, abuse will be impossible.*

Spiritual work asks you to look at yourself, not to look at others. You learn the most when you examine your own thoughts, feelings, and actions, not when you look at what other people think, feel, say or do.

When others trigger you, your reaction has nothing to do with the other person. Your reaction shows you where you are in conflict, not where the other person is.

Every fear or insecurity you have about yourself is a button waiting to be pushed. The fact that people push these buttons is not at all remarkable. What is remarkable is that you blame them for pushing them.

When you wear a sign that says "hit me," are you surprised that a few people come along and take you literally? People who attack you are doing what they, in their self-deluded way, think you want them to do. And you allow them to do it.

The abuse will stop when you learn to say "This is unacceptable. I will not permit it." Yet this is hard for you to do. Why?

Perhaps you are a child being abused by an adult. The adult is the authority figure. Often it is a parent whom you love. You want the abuser's love and approval, regardless of the costs to you, so you deny the pain, or dissociate from it

Adults who are victimized as children seek to recreate the pain of childhood trauma so that they can break through patterns of dissociation, recall the abuse and come to conscious grips with their wounds. That is why they frequently marry a person who is exactly like their abuser. Only by aggravating the wound can the shell of denial be cracked. The release of rage, guilt and self-hatred open the door to healing and integration.

There are many versions of abuse and betrayal. Understanding your version is important. However, blaming your abuser will not free you from the cycle of violence, because the pattern is a self-generating one. As long as you stay in it, you will pass the wound on to your children.

Until you have the courage to stand up for yourself fully, someone will always be around to abuse you. Indeed, you will keep calling abusers to you until you decide that you have had enough.

Don't blame the abuser. Ask instead, "Why did I allow myself once again to be drawn into a situation in which I am not respected and listened to?" See your low self-esteem. See how you accept love at any price. See how you keep recycling your fear of abandonment because you are afraid to face it head on.

Stand up and stop the game of abuse. Refuse to be an object, even though being an object seems to offer you the attention you desire. See the trail of broken promises and the tears of regret. Conditional love has given you nothing. It has just deepened your feelings of abandonment and your experience of betrayal.

Remind yourself that you decided to play the game. You gave permission. Acknowledge your mistake and learn from it so that you don't repeat it. Take responsibility. No one is a victim unless he decides to be one.

Until you see the pattern and take responsibility for breaking it, it will continue. It doesn't matter how much therapy you have or how many treatment programs you have been in.

Until you learn to say "yes" to yourself, you won't be able to say "no" to others. Others don't really betray you. They mirror your self-betrayal. Without their help, your awakening process would take considerably longer.

Your brother is your teacher. He shows you what you need to look at in yourself and you do the same for him. Yet he is not responsible for your experience, nor are you responsible for his.

Your fellow human beings are not meant to be either scapegoats or demigods. They are not the cause of your suffering, nor are they the cause of your salvation.

They are equal passengers on the same journey. What you have felt, they have also felt. Like you, they are learning to see their own patterns of self betrayal. Like you, they are learning to say yes to self and no to giving their power away.

Be patient. This is a journey to full empowerment. When the self is empowered fully, abuse will be impossible.

## AWAKENING TOGETHER

*When you give the gift of unconditional love,*
*even the most subtle forms of abuse and inequality vanish.*

When you and your partner commit to a spiritual relationship, you agree to help each other become conscious of the patterns of self-betrayal. Your intention is not to stuff your fear, anger, shame or insecurity, but to create enough safety in your relationship that your pain can come up and be healed.

You agree to refrain from blaming or shaming each other. When you notice that your partner is projecting, you do not try to fix her, but you stay conscious of who she really is. And so you call her gently back to herself.

Most of all, you just listen. You don't agree or disagree with what she has to say. You know your opinion means nothing and, if anything, will take her away from her process. You just listen compassionately. You listen without judgment or, if you find yourself judging, you become aware of your judgments and bring yourself back to your heart.

You listen with an open heart and an open mind. And your listening becomes a grounding rod to truth. The more you listen to her without judgment, the more her self-blame slows down. Gradually, using the pathway of your love, she returns to herself.

This is the gift that you and your partner give to each other. This is the pearl of great price. When you give this gift of unconditional acceptance and love, even the most subtle forms of abuse and inequality vanish, and you become equal partners in the dance of life.

## NAMASTE

*Each Self is the unqualified presence,*
*yet each must approach God in its own unique way.*

Namaste. I accept your humanness and mine. And I also bow to the divinity in each of us. I accept our absolute spiritual equality as beings. And I also accept that we each forget who we are.

I celebrate the fact that we are waking up together, and I appreciate the fact that, as each of us pushes up against our fear, we nod off to sleep.

I acknowledge both the absolute and the relative, for both are present here. The gentle voice of God and the passionate cries of the wounded child commingle here, in this mind, in this world. Joy and sadness commingle. Strength and tears, beauty and betrayal, silence and cacophony interpenetrate.

It is a simple world, breathing in and breathing out, approaching the divine and moving away. And it is also complex in its near infinite variety of forms.

Each Self is the unqualified presence, yet each must approach God in its own unique way. Within oneness, paradox abounds.

Here we dwell together, my brother and sister. Here in the silence, each of us with our unique heartbeat, our own dance, our own call for love and truth.

Yet despite the division into bodies, despite the fragmentation of the mind, only one heart opens here. And that heart includes yours and mine and that of all beings who have ever lived in time and space. That heart belongs to God. His patient heart. Her infinite blessing on us all.

My wish for you is a simple one. May you find that heart in your heart. May you find your voice in that silence. May you awaken to the truth of who you are.

*Namaste!*

# BOOK 3

# Miracle of Love

*The power of love will make miracles in your life*
*as great as any attributed to me.*

# Prologue

*There was a time when I had twelve apostles.*
*Now I have thousands.*

A teaching lives only to the extent that people understand it and live it. It is like a musical composition. It doesn't come alive until someone performs it.

Performances can be wide-ranging in their accuracy and inspiration. Those who are deeply moved by a piece, understand all aspects of it, and have the skills to play it, will give the best performance. They in turn will inspire others to listen and to play.

When I lived, my words and my deeds were congruent. I spoke simply and clearly. My actions were consistent with my words. That is why people were moved by what I had to say.

When you understand my teaching and practice it in your daily life, you will be a beacon for others. Through you, my teaching will come alive. Through your life, I will live.

This is my second coming. I will not come again in a physical body. I will come through your words and actions as you attune to me, just as I have always done.

There was a time when I had twelve apostles. Now I have thousands. Every time a person turns to me in surrender, he becomes my instrument. Through his hands and heart I work to spread love in the world.

Every time a person releases her grievances and offers forgiveness to others and to herself, I stand at her side. I am the one who holds her in my arms and comforts her. I am the one who bows with her at the feet of the invisible God.

My disciples practice love and forgiveness every day. They are not perfect in their practice. But they are sincere. They make mistakes, come to recognize those mistakes, and endeavor to learn from them.

My disciples are wise, but they do not parade their wisdom. They do not seek to attract attention to themselves, but work to empower others in their thoughts, their speech and their actions.

No one else can bring you to me until you are ready. And when you are ready, you do not need another to intercede on your behalf with me. You have only to ask, and I will be there for you.

Unlike many whom you know, I am not fickle. I do not come and go away from you. Even when you reject me I do not stop loving you or cease to see your greatness. For I have learned from my Father and Mother how to love without ceasing, and how to give without expecting anything in return.

When you are ready, you too will learn. If you are turning these pages, that time may be now. As you open to the truth herein, that truth will open in you.

CHAPTER SEVENTEEN

# My Teaching

*Words and concepts cannot open your heart.*
*Only love can open your heart.*

It is nearly 2,000 years since my birth and my teaching, which was once like a raging stream, has shrunk to barely a trickle of water. You have rationalized me and put me in my place, an exalted place perhaps —but a distant one. You have placed me above you where I will not challenge you. By making me a deity, an only son of God, you excuse yourself from having to live up to my example. Yet my example is the heart of my teaching. If you do not try to emulate me, what is the meaning of your belief in me?

Mine is not an intellectual teaching. It is a practical one. "Love your neighbor" is not an abstract concept. It is a simple, compelling idea that invites you to practice. I did not invite you to an evening of discourse and argument. I did not ask you to profess or debate the scriptures. I asked you to do what you find so difficult to do: to go beyond your limited concept of self. Any of the practices I gave to you will keep you busy for a lifetime. Although they are simple to understand, their challenge lies in the practice.

If I died for your sins, then there is nothing left for you to do. Why then not ascend to heaven on the strength of your belief in me?

I will tell you why. Because, in spite of your belief, you are not happy. You are not at peace. You have placed me above you where I cannot touch you.

Take me down from the pedestal, my brother or sister, and place me at your side where I belong. I am your absolute, unconditional equal. What I have done, you too will do, and more. You will not be saved by my thoughts and actions, but by your own. Unless you become the Christ, peace will not come to the world. If you would see me as king, then king must you yourself be.

Do not put this distance between us, for I am no different from you. Whatever you are—a beggar or thief, a holy man or a king—that I am too. There is no pedestal I have not been lifted upon, nor any gutter I have not lain in. It is only because I have touched the heart of both joy and pain that I can walk through the doors of compassion.

I was born to a simple woman in a barn. She was no more a virgin than your mother was. You make her special for the same reason that you make me special—to put distance between us, to claim that what I did you cannot do.

If my life has any meaning to you at all, you must know that I do not claim a special place. Neither Mary nor I is more spiritual than you. We are like you in every way. Your pain is our pain. Your joy is our joy. If this were not true, we could not come to teach.

Do not hold us at arm's length. Embrace us as your equal. Mary could have been your mother. I could have been your son.

## LOVE IS YOUR TEACHER

*All darkness is a journey toward light.*
*All pain is a journey toward love without conditions.*

The light of truth lives even in the darkest of places. There is no such thing as total absence of light. Darkness cannot exist except in reference to the light. No matter how great your pain, it is measured in the degree to which you feel the love's absence or loss. All darkness is a journey toward light. All pain is a journey toward love without conditions.

That is why you are here—to enter the darkness you perceive in yourself and others and to find the light which lives there. Once you find the light, no matter how tiny or insignificant it seems, your life will never be the same. A light bearer never questions the light s/he carries. As a result, s/he can offer it to others patiently and without fear.

You who seek converts in my name, know that your actions betray your own fear. For love is gentle and kind. It gives without thought of return. It does not ask people to change, but accepts them as they are. No one can minister in my name and withhold love and acceptance. S/he who offers love with conditions, no matter what those conditions are, takes my name in vain.

You must recognize your own fallibility, as I was forced to recognize mine. When you make up the rules, love is constricted or denied. No one is as great as Love, not you nor I. It is to Love that you must bow. Love is, and will always be, your teacher. Will you be its student and learn what it has to teach you? Or will you insist on writing the syllabus and interpreting the text?

## THE JEWISH PERSPECTIVE

*When it comes to God and Jesus, only one of us is dispensable, and I assure you it is not God.*

When you are a Jew, you do not stop being a Jew and become a Christian. You remain always a Jew. And if you are a true Jew, then you are always asking questions of God.

You are always pushing God to the limits. Every day when a Jew prays, s/he asks God "why?" knowing that God alone has the answers. It is blasphemous when a Jew thinks that s/he knows, for only God knows. At best, s/he can have a glimpse of the mystery.

If you wish to follow my teaching, you must first fulfill the Jewish part of your Judeo-Christian legacy. You must know that God has the answers, not you nor I. You must submit to life as it unfolds, knowing that there is a purpose, even if you cannot see it.

Your attitude must never be full of pride or the pretension of knowing. You must always say "No matter what I seem to know, God knows more than I. God is mysterious. No matter how hard I try, I cannot fathom the Divine way. At best I can have experiences of grace and glimpses of the divine plan. I am the student. God is the teacher."

Many Christians think that they can have me and dispense with God. But it is not true. Without God, I am nothing. It is precisely because I dwell in respect and rapture at the feet of God that I am able to extend the divine blessing to you.

My friends, understand that when it comes to God and Jesus, only one of us is dispensable, and I assure you it is not God. You do not need me to come to God. You need only come to the Divine with boundless love and respect. You need only come with a sincere desire to learn. That is how I approached God and that is how you too must approach the Divine, whether or not you believe in me.

You Christians place far too much emphasis on your belief in me. I say, forget me, and remember your Creator. Then, you will be remembering me by your example, not just by your words. If you know me in your hearts, you know that I am not much for words. Show me what you believe not just through your words, but through your actions.

## DEEDS NOT WORDS

*The language of love is not a language of words.*

Anyone who practices being loving returns to the divine home. It does not matter what path s/he takes or what s/he calls it.

No one way is better than another. You will not get home faster if you believe in me than you will if you believe in Krishna or Buddha. The man or woman who loves the most makes the most progress. That is the simple truth.

Religions, sects, dogmas are nothing but obstacles on the journey home. Anyone who thinks he has the one and only truth builds his house on quicksand. It will not take long before he discovers that his pride, narrow-mindedness, and lack of tolerance toward others were the cause of his undoing.

If you are a loving person, does it matter if you are Jewish, or Muslim, or Taoist? That love expresses itself regardless of what you believe. The language of love is not a language of words. A few simple words and a heartfelt gesture are enough to convey your love and acceptance of another person.

Words and concepts will not open your heart. Only love can open your heart. When you open to the love that is available to you and extend it freely to others, the words that you need will be given to you. You will not have to struggle to know what to say or to do.

When love is in your heart, the path opens before you. Actions flow spontaneously from you. There is no self-consciousness, ambivalence, or deliberation. For these are not the qualities of love. Love is unconditional and direct. It always finds the beloved, even when she is hiding.

## THE SHEPHERD RETURNS

*Today you will drink deeply from the fountain of my love.*
*Tomorrow you will be the fountain.*

There is no one who will refuse love when it is offered without conditions. And who will offer it but you, my brother or sister?

Today you will drink deeply from the fountain of my love. Tomorrow you will be the fountain. Tomorrow you will carry the gift you have been given into the world. You are the hands of God bringing comfort and healing. And as you give, so you will receive.

In the past, you have given and received through the lens of your fear. But that time is over. Now you know that your fear can never keep you safe. It just holds you apart from the love you want. It keeps you in exile from those who love you and need your love.

You can remain apart from the community of the faithful as long as you want. But the love of that community will not leave you, nor will it cease expecting your return. For your gift is needed, my brother or sister. And until you learn to trust that gift and give it, you cannot be happy.

When you are ready to return home, your family will welcome you. The family of faith never rejects anyone, no matter how scared or confused that person may be. For this family is the embodiment of love. It is the living example, the word made flesh as the heart opens to love and mind opens to non-judgment.

Come, brother and sister. Lay your burdens down. Why hold onto your pain and suffering when love's promise can be fulfilled right here, right now? Why hold onto shame or blame when the breeze of forgiveness blows through the land, uplifting hearts burdened by grievances and thoughts of retribution? Lay your burden down, my friend. Can't you see that your worries and fears and all the attachments they uphold will not fit through the doorway of truth?

The time of ambivalence and deliberation is over now. When the door opens, you will walk through it. For that is why you came. And no attachment to the affairs of the world can prevent you from fulfilling your spiritual destiny. Like all children, you will return home. And returning, you will go forth as I did and guide others to the source of joy and peace.

When the flock is lost, the shepherd appears. And you, my friend, are no less a shepherd than I. In the times that come, many shepherds will be needed. Many witnesses to the power of love and forgiveness will be asked to stand up and serve. Through their example, my teaching will live and flower as it never has before. For when one person is certain of the kingdom and offers a loving hand, others follow easily.

## CHAPTER EIGHTEEN

# My Disciples

*Love is the only door to a spiritual life.*
*Without love, there are just dogmas and rigid, fearful beliefs.*

Practice my teaching of love and forgiveness. Practice giving and receiving love in all of your affairs—in your family, with your friends, in your community, even with strangers.

Do not let the differences in your beliefs, your culture, or the color of your skin keep you apart from each other. For these things are just the external mantle covering the truth of who you are. If you want to know the truth, you must learn to look beyond appearances. You must learn to look not just with your eyes, but with your heart. When you do that, you will not see an adversary, but a brother, a sister, a friend.

When you look with the heart, you feel your friend's pain and confusion. You feel compassion for the universal experience of suffering, which you both share. From that compassion, love is born —not the love that wants to fix or change others—but the love that accepts, affirms, reaches out, befriends and empowers others.

Love is the only door to a spiritual life. Without love, there are just dogmas and rigid, fearful beliefs. Without love, there is no compassion or charity. Those who judge others, preach to them, and seek to redeem them are just projecting their own fear and inadequacy. They use the words of religion as a substitute for the love they are unable to give or receive. Many of those who are most forlorn and cut off from love live in the shadow of the pulpit and mount the steps of judgment every Sunday to spread the message of their own fear. Do not judge them, for they are in their own painful way crying out for love. But do not accept the guilt they would lay at your feet. It is not yours.

Those who live a genuinely spiritual life—regardless of the tradition they follow—are centered in their love for God and their fellow beings. When they meet, they have only good wishes and praises for one another. For them, labels mean nothing. For those who practice their faith, God is the only King of Kings, and men and women, no matter what they believe, are absolute, unconditional equals. All are equally loved and valued by God. There are no outcasts, no heathens.

I have said it before and I will say it again: religious dogma, self-righteousness, and false pride create division, ostracism, and alienation. They are the tools of judgment, not of love.

My disciples learn to look upon all that happens with an open heart and an open mind. They grow increasingly willing to surrender their narrow beliefs and prejudices. They refrain from condemning themselves or others for the mistakes they make, but try to learn from these mistakes so that they will not repeat them.

My disciples grow more respectful and intimate in their relationship with God every day. They learn to let the indwelling God lead the way in their lives. Thinking of me and attending to my example helps them do this.

Being a Christian is not as easy as you think. It means that you open to the possibility of your own Christhood. You accept your potential to become one with God, to open your heart and your mind to God's love and guidance. It means that you stop finding fault with others and begin to look at your own fears as they arise, taking full responsibility for your thoughts and feelings, instead of projecting them onto others. You become honest with yourself, and gentle with others. Your life is your teaching, and it is lived with loving deeds, not with harsh, unforgiving words.

"How can you be a Christian and not practice giving and receiving love without conditions?" Better to throw away all your other beliefs and hold to this practice than to study scripture and practice judgment.

The path I have laid out for you is an open one. Anyone who wants to can follow it. No prerequisites are necessary—no baptisms, confessions or communions. Nothing external can prevent you from embracing my teaching.

But this does not mean that you will be ready to walk this path. If you are still holding onto dogma or creeds, you will not be able to take the first step. If you are convinced that you or anyone else is evil or guilty, you cannot step forth. If you think you already have the answers, you may begin to walk, but you will be on a different path.

My path is open to all, yet few will follow it. Few are willing to give up what they think they know to learn what they know not yet. This is how it was when I first walked the path, and it is how it is today. Many are called, but few answer the call.

That is how it is. Do not despair about it. For if you have chosen to walk the path, it matters not what choice others make. Your happiness is your responsibility.

As you walk with the light in your hands, people will approach you and ask how they too can find the light. And, if you are my disciples, you will say to them: "The light is already within you. You have but to recognize it." You will not ask them to jump through endless verbal hoops or participate in rituals that mean nothing to them. You will embrace them spontaneously. You will welcome them into your community and there they will feel at home. For there is no one who does not feel at home when s/he is loved and accepted unconditionally.

If you want to enter the path I have set out for you, you must learn to see innocence in yourself and others. You must learn to look with your heart rather than with your eyes and to offer forgiveness as necessary to everyone, including yourself.

You live in a world where everyone is made guilty. Everyone is made wrong. And most teachings come down on you like a sledge hammer, offering shame, punishment and condemnation.

My teaching is not like that. I tell you that you are not evil. You are not guilty, no matter what you have done, no matter how many mistakes you have made. I recall you to the truth about yourself. You are a daughter or son of God, no less loved than Mary or me.

Once you accept God's love for you, you will learn from your mistakes. You will no longer throw your life away. Forgiveness will lie in the place where evil once seemed to be. And compassion will be offered, where anger and envy once held sway.

Love brings everyone into line. It connects you to your true nature. Your challenge is always a simple one—to open to the love that is there for you.

You do this by refusing to condemn others, by not judging, not complaining, not finding fault. You do this by celebrating your relationships and feeling grateful for the love and nurturing that you have in your life. You focus on what is there, not on what is not there. By finding the good in your own life, you reinforce it and extend it to others.

As a son or daughter of a loving God, your purpose is to embrace the love that is offered to you and offer it back to others, using whatever skills and talents you have. It matters not what the form of your offering is. What matters is simply that it is given with love.

## WHO ARE MY DISCIPLES?

*By teaching love, they are filled with peace.*

My disciples do not put obstacles in the way of those who would enter the path to truth. They hold the door open to all who are ready to walk through it.

They live the love they talk about. They model the teaching.

My disciples know that I did not come to die for their sins, but to recall them to their innocence. Because they know their innocence, they can see it in others, even when others feel unworthy and guilty. My disciples see the light in each soul. They do not focus on the darkness. For they know that darkness is ultimately not real. They focus on the indwelling goodness of all beings, for evil is but the absence of something that can never be totally taken away.

By seeing the light in themselves and their brothers and sisters, my disciples are constantly baptizing and offering communion. Even as people are confessing their sins, my disciples are affirming the Christ within them. Their work is always healing. Like me, they recall people to the truth about themselves.

My disciples do not focus on what is missing or what needs to be corrected. They focus on what is always there and can never be taken away. They focus on what is right and what is good. They do not look for weaknesses and thus they instill strength. They do not look for wounds, and so they help people find their gratitude.

My disciples know that every unkindness that one person does to another is done because there is an apparent lack of love in that person's life. One who attacks others cannot know that s/he is loved.

My disciples teach love by being loving and accepting others as they are. In all their actions, they teach others that they are worthy of love. By teaching love, they are filled with peace. And the more peaceful they feel, the more loving they can be.

My disciples know that people often forget the truth about themselves. They become lost in their roles and responsibilities. They take each other for granted. People often feel threatened and build walls of self-protection. They forget to open their hearts. My disciples do not chastise people for forgetting. They simply remind them gently, over and over again, that they are capable of giving and receiving love.

My disciples reinforce the good and the true, and let illusion and falsehood fall away by themselves. They do not berate people for making mistakes, for that would just reinforce the guilt they feel. Instead, they praise people for having the willingness to learn and grow from the mistakes they make.

## A LIVING EXAMPLE

*Forgiveness cannot be offered to the world except through you.*

My teaching is about becoming conscious of the truth and living it. It is not enough just to know the words. Words are easily forgotten. Words must become practice.

You have focused so much on how great I am you have forgotten your own greatness. You have neglected the fact that forgiveness cannot be offered to the world except through you. And you cannot offer it, unless you have accepted it for yourself.

When you commune with me, it is not my body and my blood that you consume, but the spirit of forgiveness, which uplifts your hearts. When you raise the cup, remember your innocence and that of all other beings. That is the lifeblood, the legacy of truth that you must remember and extend to others.

You think I am special because I was crucified. Yet you are nailed to the cross every day. And when you are not being nailed, you are doing the nailing. There is nothing special about being crucified.

Some of you also believe that I alone was resurrected. Yet you are raised from death by the power of love every time you remember who you are or who your brother is. Every time love is given or received, death is vanquished, for everything dies, except love. Only the love you have given or received lives forever.

You may think that by believing in me you are guaranteed some special place in the afterlife. That is not true, unless your belief in me has inspired you to give love or receive it. If you have not opened to love in your life, your belief in me or in anyone else means very little.

When you remember me, remember what I have empowered you to do in your life, and do not dwell on the "miraculous" things I have done. The power of love will make miracles in your life as wonderful as any attributed to me. For love is the only miracle, not you or me.

You are here to embrace the miracle of love and pass it on to others. Yet do not take credit for what love has done or will do. The credit belongs to the one who loved us without conditions long before we knew what love was, or what its absence would mean to the world.

You have all strayed from the fold. You have all forgotten the Creator's love. I come to you as a reminder of that love. When you remember my birth into this world, remember my purpose for coming. It is your purpose too.

Your birth into this embodiment is no less holy than mine. Nor will the love you extend to others be any less important than the love that has been offered to you through me. Like me, you are a doorway to the infinite and eternal and each time your heart opens, spirit makes its appearance in the world.

You are the light of the world. You are the Lamb of God come to remind us that we are loved.

## THE BODY AND THE WORLD

*To worship the body is as unhelpful as it is to demean it.*

Being in the body is both a privilege and a hardship. Many lessons are learned thanks to the opportunity the body provides. Yet you must remember that everything the body can do for you will one day be undone. What will the pleasures of food, drink, sex, sleep, or entertainment mean when the body is no longer? To worship the body is as unhelpful as it is to demean it.

The body is a means. It has a purpose. I used my body to complete my mission here, just as you must use yours. I experienced physical joy and physical suffering, just as you no doubt have. No one comes into the body who does not explore both ecstasy and pain, love and death.

The body is a vehicle for learning. Please do not disrespect or demean it. Please do not make it into a god that you worship. Don't make it more or less important than it is.

When you enjoy and care for your body, it can serve you better. But no body is perfect. All bodies eventually break down. Bodies are not meant to last forever.

Those who speak of physical ascension or immortality have missed the point entirely. Everything in physical experience is by nature limited. It becomes physical by virtue of the limits that are placed around it.

The more limits you have, the greater the "density" or "gravity" of your experience and the less choices seem available to you. Ego-orientation, selfishness and greed are dense. Compulsive activity or addiction to substances is dense. "Dense" means that your behavior is repetitive, predictable.

Some people are born handicapped. Others handicap themselves. Those who are met with judgment and criticism shut down their hearts and live narrow, circumscribed lives. Those who are met with love and acceptance open their hearts and become beacons of joy and creativity.

There is no original sin. There is no original density. Fear and contraction lead to dense, impenetrable states of mind and matter.

Physical reality seems to be terribly restrictive, but it does not have to be so. I once asked you to be in the world but not of it. I suggested that you be in the body, honor it, and use it as a vehicle for spreading love and acceptance, without being attached to it.

I also asked you not to build your house on sand, where every storm takes its devastating toll. Some things are temporary and temporal, and some are eternal. The body is not eternal. The best it can be is a willing servant.

## PEACE ON EARTH

*When love is present, the body and the world are lifted up.*

Peace is the lightest and most emancipated state you can experience while in a physical body. It has no goal except itself. It has no agenda.

One who is at peace has great flexibility, great patience, and great compassion. S/he has no need to try to fix anyone, no need to improve the world. One who is at peace naturally improves the world just by being. S/he breathes peace, talks peace, and walks peace. There is no effort, no attempt to fix.

Nothing in the world is broken. The perception of pain is healed just by seeing it differently. When you look through the eyes of love, there is no situation which cannot be accepted as it is. There is no injustice anywhere apart from the eyes of the beholder. And it is the beholder, in the end, who must let his pain go and see the world differently.

The laws of the world are the laws of the ego. They are based on suspicion and distrust. They seek to control people's behavior. Control is dense. The more you need to control others, the more your own destiny is predictable and controlled. The laws of Spirit are based on trust and compassion. They see the best in each person and so bring it forth.

Just as I challenged the laws of the world in the name of a higher law, so will you. It is not enough to live your life in a state of fear. It is not enough for you to cower in a corner and let other men and women dictate to you.

You must stand up and be counted. But please do so lovingly, compassionately, and respectfully. Do it knowing that there is no enemy out there. Each brother or sister, no matter how angry, fearful or distraught, deserves your support and your respect. And how you act means as much, if not more, than what you do or what you say. Angry words or actions do not serve you or anyone else.

When you act in a loving way the Spirit is awakened in others. The body and the world are lifted up and infused with light, possibility and celebration of goodness. The world you see when Spirit is present in your heart and your life is not the same world that you see when you are preoccupied with your ego needs. The world that you see when you are giving love is not the same world that you see when you are demanding it.

If you want to go beyond the body, learn to use it in a loving way. Think and speak well of yourself and others. Be positive, and constructive. Don't look for problems. Don't dwell on what seems missing. Give love at every opportunity. Bring it to yourself when you are sad. Bring it to others when they are doubting or negative.

Be the presence of love in the world. That is what you are. Everything else is an illusion.

## CHAPTER NINETEEN

# A Relationship Path

*Love comes only from your own consciousness.*
*It has nothing to do with anyone else.*

Each person must learn to see how s/he creates personal suffering by holding a negative attitude toward the events and circumstances of life. If you don't see how you do this, you will do it unconsciously. And then you won't understand why your life is difficult. You will blame others for your problems: your parents, your spouse, your children, your boss, maybe even God.

I ask you to take responsibility not just for what you do, but for what you think. I ask you to understand the power of your thoughts to create negative emotional states, from which ill-considered actions arise. See how the thought "Nobody loves me" leads to the state of feeling disconnected and envious of others who seem to have love in their lives. See how the thought and the feeling of being unloved push others away. It becomes a self-fulfilling prophecy. By thinking this thought, you separate yourself from the very love that you want.

Next time the thought "Nobody loves me" comes into your mind please be aware of it. If you speak or act in a way that separates you from others, please notice it. Don't judge yourself or try to change anything. Just bring your awareness to the whole dramatic cycle from thought to action. Become aware of how your negative mental and emotional states create suffering in your life. Every time you succeed in separating from others, you substantiate your belief that

"Nobody loves me." But this is your personal creation. It is not true that nobody loves you.

As you watch your drama unfold, it will be easier for you to take responsibility for it. Then you will begin to tell the truth to yourself. When the thought "Nobody loves me" comes into your mind, you will recognize it and reword it in a more truthful and responsible way: "I see that I am not feeling loved right now."

Instead of trying to make others responsible for your not feeling loved, you will be taking responsibility for it. This simple shifting of responsibility for your negative feeling states from "others" to self is the beginning of healing and correction.

When you know that you are not feeling loved, you naturally ask "How can I feel loved right now?" What you realize is that the only way you can "feel" loved is to "think" a loving thought. Loving thoughts lead to the emotional state of feeling loved. And out of this positive emotional state actions arise which connect you to others.

Now, it doesn't matter if this loving thought is about you or about someone else. Any loving thought will do. When you offer love to another person, you are also offering it to yourself.

When fear and doubt arise in your psyche, you either entertain them or you don't. If you entertain them, you will end up believing that someone else is responsible for your unhappiness and you will feel powerless to change it. If you don't entertain negative thoughts when they arise, you will remind yourself again and again that you are responsible for everything you think, feel, and experience. If you want a different experience, you must choose a different thought.

The reason that you are always looking for love from other people is that you do not realize that love comes only from your own consciousness. It has nothing to do with anyone else. Love comes from your willingness to think loving thoughts, experience loving feelings, and act in trusting, love-inspired ways. If you are willing to do this, your cup will run over. You will always have the love that you need, and you will take delight in offering it to others.

The fountainhead of love is within your own heart. Don't look to others to provide the love you need. Don't blame others for withholding their love from you. You don't need their love. You need your love. Love is the only gift you can give yourself. Give it to yourself and the universe resounds with a big "Yes!" Withhold it and the game of hide and seek continues. You keep "looking for love in all the wrong places."

There is only one place you can look for love and find it. No one who has ever looked there has been disappointed.

## THE DRAMA OF RELATIONSHIP

*Don't allow your happiness to be dependent*
*on your partner's happiness.*

Other people do not make you happy or sad. You are the one who is responsible for your happiness or sadness. Learn to take other people off the hook and bring love to yourself.

When people judge you, find fault with you or withhold their love from you, realize that they do not feel loved and understand clearly that you are not responsible for how they feel. Don't accept blame or react to the other person's negativity. Go into another room. Take a walk by yourself. And work on bringing love and acceptance to yourself.

When your love for yourself fills you up direct that love toward the other person. Be willing to overlook his negative behavior. Understand that his negativity and self-protectiveness come from his own fear. Feel compassion for his suffering, even if it is self-created. Extend to that person the love you have found inside yourself.

Love does not complain, argue or blame. Love simply embraces the other exactly as s/he is. Love overlooks fear, because fear is not ultimately real. It is a temporary wrinkle in the fabric of life. Wrinkles do not last forever. In the next moment the fabric can be pulled tight and the wrinkle will disappear. Love honors the fabric and knows that it is flexible enough to adjust to new conditions.

Practice this in your intimate relationships. No partner is happy all of the time. Don't allow your happiness to be dependent on your partner's happiness. That will just drag both of you down. Tend to your own garden, and offer your partner a rose to smell. Refusing to tend your garden and complaining that your partner never gives you roses will not make either one of you feel better.

When one person is cranky or sad, the other must dig deep inside to find the source of love. When she finds the light within, she must carry it for both people for a while. That way the other person does not forget that the light is there, even if he can't see it in himself.

This does not mean that one person should do all the supporting. Relationships require a give and take. But it does mean that there will be times when each partner will have to rise to the occasion and maintain the connection to Source in the face of the other person's fear and mistrust. That is never an easy thing to do. But it is often necessary in the course of a committed relationship.

## COMMITMENT TO SELF

*In a healthy partnership, the commitment to self
and the commitment to the relationship
are equal in depth and intensity.*

When you are committed to yourself, you can make commitments to others. But try to make commitments to others before you have committed to yourself, and you will leave in your wake a trail of heartache and broken relationships.

If you do not do what is necessary to create and maintain your happiness, who will do it? Do you expect your partner to make your decisions and live your life for you? Of course not! You must make your own choices. You are responsible for your own happiness.

So go for it! Give yourself permission to move toward your joy and express your gifts. Your willingness to do this is essential to your creative fulfillment. Nobody else can do this for you.

When you have a partner, this responsibility to yourself continues. You cannot give this responsibility to anyone else. It is yours and yours alone. No matter how close you are to your partner, s/he can never be responsible for your successes or failures in this regard.

In a healthy relationship, both people support each other in taking responsibility for their own happiness and creative fulfillment. They offer each other encouragement and positive feedback. And then they let go. They trust the other person to find her own way. They don't judge her goals or interfere in her attempts to realize them.

In a healthy relationship, people are not enmeshed in each other's creative process. Even when they work together, they find a way to support each other's autonomy.

Unless each person has this autonomy and the time and space to grow, he won't command his partner's respect. But autonomy is only one ingredient. Equally important is a shared vision.

Both people must have dreams, values, and aspirations that they hold in common. They must have a vision of a shared life in which they move together as a couple.

When either the autonomy or the shared vision of the partners is weak, the relationship will not prosper. In some relationships, the shared vision is strong, but the autonomy is not sufficient. The couple does not thrive because the individuals are not being challenged to grow. In other relationships, autonomy is strong, but the shared vision and experience is weak. The partners express themselves well as individuals, but do not spend sufficient time together. Their emotional connection is attenuated, and they begin to lose sight of their reason for being together.

Neither of these extremes is helpful. Couples need to work on expressing themselves as individuals, as well as on strengthening their sense of common purpose. In a healthy partnership, the commitment to self and the commitment to the relationship are equal in depth and intensity.

## CREATING THE LOVE YOU WANT

*Your partner is the midwife to your birth into your full potential.*

You cannot force another person to love you the way you want to be loved. Demanding specific expressions of love will only make it more difficult for others to respond to you in good faith.

To be sure, you can ask for what you want. Clear communication is important. But once you have communicated what you want, you must back off and give the other person the time and the space to honor your request to the best of his or her ability.

Any effort your partner makes to respond to your request should be positively reinforced. Finding fault with her efforts to please you because they aren't perfect or don't match your pictures of the way things should be will jeopardize her responsiveness in the future. When you notice your partner's efforts and praise them, you help her feel joy and satisfaction in giving to you. That makes her want to give more.

Criticizing your partner for not measuring up to your expectations is the fastest way to destroy your relationship. Criticism is not constructive. Gratitude and praise are the building blocks of mutual bliss.

When you don't receive what you asked for, acknowledge what you did receive, and ask again for what you did not receive. Do not ask with anger or resentment. Ask in a kind and respectful way.

When you ask respectfully and your partner is still unable to respond to you, you must face the fact that she is either unwilling or unable to meet your needs. Usually, when you are honest with her, you find that she shares your disappointment and frustration.

When this happens, you have a choice. You can part ways or you can try to move your commitment to higher ground. You can stop focusing on what you are not receiving from each other, and instead focus on what you are giving to one another. Often, it is helpful to take a short break from the relationship so that you can learn to see it in perspective.

In the event you decide to separate, do so in a loving way, without holding onto resentments or grievances. It is not easy when a relationship ends or changes form, and gentleness on both sides is extremely important if healing is to happen for both people.

When you complete a relationship, consider what you have learned from the other person and be grateful for your experience together. Be cognizant of the issues that separated you and take responsibility for your part in them. When you begin another relationship, be aware of how similar issues arise and see if you can deal with these issues in a more generous and responsible way.

If you are learning from your relationships, you will feel that you are making progress being a better partner. You will bring increasing honesty and integrity to your relationship and you will be better able to create intimacy with your partner as a result.

When the same lessons come up with different partners, bringing familiar discomfort and frustration, you need to consider the probability that something needs to shift inside of you before you can be in a successful relationship with another person. A good therapist may be able to help you look at your relationship patterns and understand how they can be transformed. When you have gained insight about the ways that you resist intimacy and push love away, you can work consciously to stay open to people who are trying their best to love and accept you. And you can learn to share aspects of yourself that you have heretofore kept hidden.

Every relationship carries with it great potential for learning. When you are willing to learn and to grow, your relationship will bring a blessing, whatever its outcome. No relationship lasts forever. Each has its natural beginning and end. People come together because they have important things to learn together. When those lessons are learned, they move on to other challenges with other teachers. That is how it is.

The key is not to worry about how long a relationship lasts, but to give it your best energy and attention. Neither you nor your partner will ever be perfect in your ability to give or receive love. Don't try to be. Just try to be a little more open to give and a little more open to receive than you were before. Remember, you are learning. You are going to make mistakes. You are going to come up short and so is your partner. But accept your mistakes and bless them. Accept your partner's mistakes and send him blessings for his willingness to keep opening to love. That is all either one of you can do.

There is nothing more healing than the practice of forgiveness in your primary relationships. No other area of your life offers you as many opportunities to understand your wounds and heal them. Your partner is the midwife to your birth into your full potential. Thanks to him or her, you learn to surrender the dysfunctional patterns that compromise your happiness. Through the mirror your partner holds up to you, you discover your wholeness and learn to give your gift to the world.

CHAPTER TWENTY

# Creativity & Abundance

*The energy inside you is never the same energy.*
*You are never limited to the past.*

All energy is potentially creative. That potential for creation becomes limited as energy expresses itself in form. It is the nature of form to limit and constrict. By limiting its creative potential, form channels and directs energy in specific ways.

Form emphasizes some aspects and de-emphasizes others. It prioritizes. It constructs a picture. Without form, there would be no works of art. Manifestation is a commitment of energy to a certain direction or goal. It is the movement from unlimited to limited, from abstract to concrete, from unseen to seen.

All creativity is a dialogue between energy and form. It is therefore meaningless to talk about energy without also talking about form.

You are an animated form, an energy body. Your body/mind consciousness is a temporary container for the universal energy of creation. This energy expresses through you in a unique way, through your genes and chromosomes, as well as through your personality structure.

As your mind/body consciousness expands with love, you become more open to giving and receiving the universal energy of creation. Conversely, when you contract in fear, you become less able to give or receive this dynamic creative energy.

The energy of creation wants to expand and open you up and the structure of your mind and body resists that expansion. Structure belongs to the past, while energy only exists in the moment. It is like water that flows by you as you watch from the bank of a river. It is never the same water you are looking at. In the same manner, the energy inside you is never the same energy that it was five minutes ago. It is always new energy.

That is fortunate indeed, because it means that you are never limited to the past. Every adjustment you make in consciousness in the present has an immediate effect on the energy that is able to move through you. As your physical body becomes more healthy and your personality structure becomes more flexible and integrated, you become increasingly able to give and receive energy, physically, emotionally, mentally and spiritually.

You are an ongoing dialogue between energy and form. When you are fearful, you contract on all levels of being. Energy gets trapped in your body/mind and you experience physical tension or pain, emotional upheaval, and mental anxiety. These symptoms, when not addressed, may lead to bigger ones: physical illness, the break up of a relationship, work or money problems.

On the other hand, when you are feeling love, energy flows effortlessly through you. You are physically comfortable, emotionally open, and mentally present and alert. You experience gratitude for your life and openness to new possibilities.

A fearful attitude toward life leads to defensive, controlling behavior that pushes love and abundance away from you. A loving attitude leads to trusting behavior that honors other people and inspires them to support you.

Love opens the mind/body vehicle to its maximum energetic potential, enabling others to "feel" the energy of acceptance, gratitude, and kindness flowing directly to them. This opens their hearts and minds to their own potential and empowers them to share their creative gifts with others. This is how abundance is generated in the world.

## EGO BLOCKS TO ABUNDANCE

*Selfish actions are not supported by the universe.*

The energy of creation moves through you to others and through others to you. While this energy supports you in essential ways, there can be no personal ownership of it. No one has a special connection to the energy. As soon as someone claims ownership of it, his or her connection to the energy is disturbed.

When your relationship to each other is one of mutual trust and mutual respect, you create an energetic connection which is supported by the love energy of the universe.

Your alignment with the energy of creation requires the relinquishment of your ego agenda. Your ego agenda operates from the belief that you can manipulate people and events to obtain the outcome you want. Your ego agenda is selfish and short-sighted. It does not consider the good of others, and therefore it does not consider your good, although you may believe that it does.

When you cheat someone out of something s/he deserves, you lose not only what you thought you would gain, but what you would have gained if you had acted in a less selfish way. Every attempt to gain in a selfish manner eventually leads to loss and defeat, because selfish actions are not supported by the universe.

Those who take advantage of others may have great determination and skill, but they cannot compensate for the loss of their connection to the energy of creation. Others equally determined will join together and, supported by invisible forces, defeat them in the end, for David always defeats Goliath. Not because he is bigger or stronger, but because his intention is clear and he has love in his heart.

While fear might sometimes seem to marshal more forces on its side than love, it can never hold those forces together. Fearful forces are always pulling apart. When the selfish expectations of one group are no longer met, it defects or goes over to the other side.

Love has greater sustaining power than fear because it is peaceful and patient. When it does not attract help right away, it does not despair, but finds comfort and faith in the strength and clarity it already has.

I have said that "those who live by the sword will die by the sword." Those who try to take advantage of others will fall victim to their own erroneous actions. That is the nature of the karmic journey. Every time you attempt to injure another, you really only injure yourself. For everything that you think and do toward others returns in the end to you. Only one who truly forgives and eschews vengeance breaks through the vicious egoic cycle of violence.

If you want to open to abundance in your life, you must give up the idea that you can gain through someone else's loss. That is the fearful thinking of the ego mind and it must be recognized and refused if new patterns are to be set into motion in your life.

Fortunately, there is another way, a way that begins when you recognize that your good and that of your brother or sister is one and the same. When you accept your equality with others, then you reconnect to the energy of creation, and that energy supports you.

Because you are supported, you do not toil in vain. Results come spontaneously and on their own timetable. But you are always being asked to relinquish your expectations so that the work can move through you and with you.

While you may have ownership of your area of the work, you never have exclusive ownership of the work as a whole. For the work of creation is essentially collaborative. It cannot be done without the contribution of many people. Your piece needs to fit with other pieces, or the integrity of the whole will be compromised.

The demands of this path are as great as those made by the ego's path of manipulation and struggle. But the rewards of the path of Spirit are far greater, for those who follow this path find true happiness. Because they serve others, love serves them. Because they give without thought of return, the universe brings to them unexpected gifts. Because they live joyfully in the present, the future unfolds gracefully before them. When challenges come, they rise to meet them. When disappointment arises, they look within and surrender the emotional barriers that prevent them from feeling love's presence in their lives.

## FOUR STEPS TO FREEDOM FROM FEAR

*No matter how hard it tries, fear cannot bring love.*

You believe that your ego knows what is good for you and can bring you what you want. This is not true and has never been true.

You listen to the ego's voice because you are fearful. If you were not fearful, you would listen to a different voice.

The ego seems to offer you a way out of fear, but how can that which arises out of fear lead you out of fear? It cannot be done. Only that which arises from a place of non-fear can show you a way out of fear.

The key to everything is your recognition of your fear. Once you know that you are fearful, you know that any decision you make while in this state will be counterproductive.

When you are in fear, your only constructive course of action is to recognize your fear, realize that you are incapable of making good decisions, and begin to work on accepting your fear and moving through it.

Here are four simple steps that can help you do this.

1.  First, recognize your fear. Notice the signs that fear is coming up for you: rapid, shallow breathing, pounding heart, nervousness, anxiety, attack thoughts, anger. Be aware of your physical, emotional, and mental state without judging it or trying to change it. Acknowledge it to yourself and, if another person is involved, to the other person.

2.  Second, recognize that the solution the ego offers you is motivated by fear. Understand that your ego will always have a solution to every perceived problem. But, when you listen to that solution, you don't feel any more peaceful. Indeed, you often feel more charged with anger, more victimized, more suspicious of other people and defensive toward them. The ego's solution cannot bring you peace.

3.  Third, accept your fear. Get your arms around all of it. Say to yourself, "It is okay that I am afraid. Let me be with my fear and tune into why fear is coming up for me right now." Don't

be analytical about this. Don't go up into your head. Stay in your emotional body and listen to what's there. You will know when you have listened enough because you will begin to feel more peaceful, even though you don't have a solution to your dilemma.

4. Fourth, tell yourself, "I don't have to decide anything now. I can wait until my fear subsides and insight comes to make any decisions that need to be made."

By doing these four steps, you will bring love and acceptance to yourself. Out of this compassionate place, a non-fearful solution to your dilemma can be found.

But do not put pressure on yourself. Pressure is just more fear coming up. Keep loving yourself and accepting your fear. Be patient and let the answer come from a non-fearful place in your psyche.

Know that the ego does not have a solution for any of your problems. In spite of its perpetual promises to you, it does not know what you need. No matter how hard it tries, fear cannot bring love. Indeed, the harder it tries, the more it fails. And the more it fails, the harder it tries.

There is no end to this downward spiral of laborious and useless effort until fear is accepted as it is and no longer expected to bring a solution. When it's okay to be afraid, fear is off the hook, and so are you.

## HEARING GOD'S ANSWER

*As long as you need to be in charge, God can't step in.*

Fear is never the enemy, nor is the ego. Everyone has fear. Everyone has an ego. You are not being asked to get rid of your fear, but to be aware of it and accept it. You are not being asked to get rid of your ego, but to acknowledge it compassionately, while seeing clearly that it cannot bring you understanding or peace.

If you want to hear God's answer, you must first hear the ego's answer with compassion. You must say to the scared, hurt, angry one within you, "I see that you are afraid and that is okay. I understand what you want to do. I will consider it. But for now I would like to be open to the possibility that there is another way to look at this." This simple act of speaking to the fearful aspect of self with loving kindness accomplishes a shift in the psyche away from fear.

You cannot be aware of God's presence until you have addressed your fear in a loving way. Through your compassionate acceptance of all aspects of yourself, you prepare a place in the temple of your heart for God to come.

Do this simple practice and you will see. You will experience the presence of love within. Your grievances will fall away. And you will be vibrating with acceptance of your life and everyone in it.

When problems arise and fear comes up for you, remember "It's okay to be afraid. It's okay not to know the answer." God cannot take charge until you realize that you don't know and ask for help. As long as you need to be in charge, God can't step in.

And who is God but the one who loves and accepts you without conditions, under all circumstances, now and for all time? That being is not outside of you, but in your heart of hearts. When you ask sincerely, this is the One who answers. When you knock, this is the One who opens the door.

You cannot come to God when you are in fear and you think you know the answers. First, you must acknowledge your fear and your ignorance. And then you must bless yourself so deeply that even your fear and your ignorance are acceptable. That is the way to the God within who loves you without conditions.

And who else would you call upon in your struggle? Would you settle for the conniving voice of the fearful child in you who feels unloved and victimized and would attack or betray others to save his/her own skin? I don't think so!

When you know the choice is between the whining child and the loving Mother, you won't have any difficulty knowing who will comfort you. And when you listen to the voice of the Mother, the fearful child is comforted too.

## THE MYTH OF EVIL

*Every block to love lies in your own heart*
*and it is there that it must be dissolved.*

The devil does not exist except in relationship to God. He is the one who abandons love. He is the one who thinks he can create apart from God. That is his delusion and it gets him into serious trouble.

The devil does not exist apart from you either. If you can be tempted by him, then there is part of your mind that has already abandoned God. Otherwise you could not be tempted.

Consider this: if God is all-powerful, then the devil can stand apart from God only with God's permission. If there is a devil—if there is evil in the world—it can only exist because God allows it to exist.

Why would God allow evil to exist in the world? Why would God allow one of his angels to fall? The answer is a simple one. God gave you free will. The devil is simply the personification of free will gone wrong. Those who fall from grace have simply made a wrong choice. Fortunately, they are not condemned forever. They can atone. They can learn to make a different choice.

People are not essentially bad. Their actions may be unloving or cruel, but that is because they do not feel loved. Often, they have been abused by others. When you bring love and offer them a different choice, they can transform their lives. Redemption is not just a possibility; it is the inevitable result of all trespass. Those who stray from the fold can, and will eventually, return to it.

This is the pathway God has created for all those who choose to stand on their own. They will lose their way. They will suffer. And they will find a way to shift their perceptions and open their hearts, so that they can find their way back home.

If you can change the consciousness of a person so that his actions become loving instead of unloving, would this person still be bad? Of course not! As long as redemption is possible, absolute evil cannot exist.

You cannot facilitate change by shaming and punishing people who hurt others or themselves. You do not empower a guilty man by reinforcing his guilt.

Instead, you tell him that he is worthy of love. You tell him that he is not "bad," that others are mistaken about who he is. Those who abused, neglected, or humiliated him did not know who he was. But you know. You can see the goodness within him and you are willing to accept him and be his friend.

If you want someone to act in a loving way, you must be willing to love him. Only your love for him will teach him the meaning of love. Empty words and promises will not do.

You learn to bring love to the enemy outside and the enemy within. You learn to love your ego and the wounded child within. You learn to see with compassion your own capacity for unloving thoughts and actions. You learn to bring love so that this fallen angel, this wounded child hidden in the manger of your heart, may be redeemed and recognized for who s/he is. Until you do this, you cannot experience your wholeness.

Inner and outer healing are inextricably related. As long as you find an enemy within or without, you are fighting the truth about yourself and others. As long as you see evil as something that has reality apart from your own fearful thoughts, you are crucifying yourself and condemning the world.

Such thoughts and beliefs are not helpful. I have told you before and I will tell you again: Be careful whom you condemn. It might be you.

In each devil you perceive, there is an angel you must discover, an angel who has fallen and needs your love to ascend. When you offer that love, you will find that you too have risen.

Each one of you must rise above your fears and prejudices or risk remaining apart from love. For every block to love lies in your own heart and it is there that it must be dissolved.

Don't wait for heaven to come to spread your love around. Do it now. For heaven is here right now. It is in your heart when you open to love. It is in your eyes when you see with acceptance and compassion. It is in your hands when you reach out to help. It is in your mind when you see "good" instead of evil.

How you see the world determines what the world will be for you. As long as you are here, this will be true. So do not seek to change other people or the world around you. But look within your own heart and mind. Hear the criticism, the judgments, the cries for vengeance and you will know where love needs to be brought.

You cannot save your neighbor when your own heart is full of fear. Attend then to your own fear and be not concerned with the fear of others. Be the bringer of love to your own experience and others will take note. Only when you have accepted healing for yourself can you become an instrument for love and healing in the world.

## UNDERSTANDING AND COMPASSION

*God is not able to stop loving anyone.*
*For God is love, always love, in every moment.*

Everything is God, including that which tries to live without God. For what tries to live without God is simply a part of God that doesn't accept itself. It is God pretending not to be God.

People who are called "evil" are not separate from God except by their own actions. They feel unloved and act in unloving ways. But God has not stopped loving them. God is not able to stop loving anyone. For God is love, always love, in every moment.

Every sin is but a temporary moment of separation. It cannot be final. Every child who strays from God's love will return, because it is too painful to be separate from the Source of life. When the pain becomes too great, every being turns back. There are no exceptions.

The world is a classroom for redemption. Everyone who comes here tries in one way or another to live apart from God's will. Each person experiences fear and listens to the ego's voice. Some simply realize more quickly than others that they can't find love in separation.

And everyone wants love. Even the ego craves love. It just does not know how to create it. And so the child who divorces the parent still dreams of the parent's love, but does not know how to accept it when it is offered.

You must learn that God's will for you is not separate from your good, even if your ego feels threatened by it. When you are willing to give up your ego's interpretation of the events and circumstances of your life, their true meaning can be revealed to you.

As you learn to open your heart, you move through your fear and leave it behind you. For you know that fear cannot lead you home. And love cannot mislead you.

## THE ECONOMY OF LOVE

*The economy of love is based on surrender.*
*The economy of fear is based on control.*

Peace and happiness will not come to the world until it comes into the hearts and minds of the people who live in the world. As each person feels the presence of love within, it is easier for him to offer it to others.

People whose minds and hearts are open experience and extend love, gratitude and abundance as a matter of course. They don't have to do anything special. Being open, what they need comes to them. Being caring and compassionate, they give away what they don't need to others who need it. This is the law of love. It is based on trust and faith.

People who align with the law of love do not have to try to hold onto or protect what they have. For they know that everything they have is merely given to them temporarily. It will stay with them as long as it is needed. And when it is no longer needed, it will go.

People who align with the law of love learn to release their attachments so that they can open to the next stage in their growth. They learn to surrender the ego's terms and conditions to make room for God's will to take root in their lives.

The economy of love is based on surrender. The economy of fear is based on control. The economy of love is rooted in the understanding that there is enough for everyone. The economy of fear is rooted in the belief that there isn't enough to go around.

If you look around, you will see both economies at work. The economy of fear seems to be more prevalent than the economy of love, but if you look carefully you will see that the former is losing strength to the latter. That is because the more fearful people become, the more they must learn to rely on love to survive. While conditions seem to be getting worse, in fact they are getting better.

That is the good news. The bad news is that very few of you believe this. Most of you believe the doomsday prophets who say the world is condemned to unimaginable suffering and distress. This belief induces more fear and has the potential to become a self-fulfilling prophecy.

The real struggle before you today is not a struggle between good and evil, but a struggle between your belief in goodness and your belief in evil. Each of you must fight this battle in your own consciousness. And that is where your suffering either deepens or dissolves.

Believing in evil, you contract emotionally, become more defensive, and cut yourself off from the energy of creation. That leads to a consciousness of scarcity.

Believing in good, you expand emotionally, open up to others, and engage with the creative energy of the universe. That leads to a consciousness of abundance.

Contrary to popular opinion, abundance does not mean that you have a lot of money or material possessions. Abundance means that you have what you need, use it wisely, and give what you don't need to others. Your life has poise, balance, and integrity. You don't have too little. You don't have too much.

On the other hand, scarcity does not mean that you don't have enough money or material possessions. It means that you don't value what you have, don't use it wisely, or don't share it with others. Scarcity may mean that you have too little. It may also mean that you have too much. Your life is out of balance. You want what you don't have, or you have what you don't want or need.

I assure you that you will not increase your happiness by increasing your material possessions. You increase your happiness only by increasing your energy, your self-expression and your love. If that also increases your pocketbook, then so be it. You have more to enjoy and share with others.

The goal in life should not be to accumulate resources that you don't need and cannot possibly use. It should be to earn what you need, enjoy and share joyfully with others.

The abundant person has no more or less than she can use responsibly and productively. She does not obsess on protecting what she has or in obtaining what she does not need. She is content with what she has and is open to giving and receiving all the resources that God brings into her life.

CHAPTER TWENTY-ONE

# Love and Freedom

*What is empowering for the individual
and what strengthens the group culture
are by their very nature often at odds.*

As dogmatic, hierarchical religious teachings are appropriately rejected, a socio-spiritual gap is created. No longer willing to let outside authorities dictate to them what to believe, people try to find their own way of connecting with God, purpose and meaning in their lives. While this search may be liberating and fruitful for some, it is confusing and emotionally draining for others who may need more social participation and structure in their lives. It is not surprising, perhaps, to see some "recovering new-agers" gravitating toward conservative or even fundamentalist churches which offer a stable community where regular fellowship thrives and parents can raise their children in a safe, supportive environment.

The great gift of the new age movement is the freedom it gives individuals to explore many different approaches to spirituality so that they can make their own eclectic and creative synthesis of ideas. It empowers people to ask their own questions and find their own answers. However, those religious structures that emphasize self-exploration and foster diversity often lack the kind of social and emotional cohesiveness found in more homogeneous religious communities which require individuals to conform to the group norms.

For many people, there is a clear choice between freedom and belonging. The more freedom one needs, the less chance one will find a community into which one can fit comfortably. What is empowering for the individual and what strengthens the group culture are by their very nature often at odds.

The weakness of the new age movement is its lack of spiritual depth and emotional congruence. The plethora of self-help books, workshops and seminars synonymous with the phrase "new age" comes in response to a tremendous groundswell of interest in non-dogmatic, non-authoritarian approaches to spirituality. Unfortunately, the fervor of interest in new approaches leads to the development of heavily marketed, superficial tools that promise life changing experiences without delivering them.

The downside of new age consciousness is its "quick fix" mentality, its inference that the answer to all of your problems lies in something outside yourself. If one tool doesn't work, you can always find another one that does. When there are a thousand approaches to truth, all of them touted by one persuasive person or another, it is hard for people to choose one of them and stick to it. Superficiality and dilettantism tend to be the rule.

Not everyone who embarks on a journey of self-empowerment is capable of navigating the spiritual marketplace, sifting and shredding, and finally making an eclectic synthesis of tools and techniques that leads to the experience of inner awakening. While some have used this freedom to explore well, there are more casualties in the age of drive-in spirituality than there are success stories.

Confusion, contradictory beliefs, addiction to books, workshops and new promises of fulfillment lead to a spiritual vacuum or cul-de-sac. Many new age advocates do not know what they believe or where to turn. Many have not found connection to a loving community. Some have lived selfish, me-centered lives that do not lead to deepening insight or compassion.

The wings that have been given to this generation grow tired now. As many move into the second half of life, there is a need to settle down and grow roots. There is a need for friendship, eternal values, and beliefs that encompass and speak meaningfully to the pain and suffering of the past.

## A FREE AND LOVING COMMUNITY

*Real love does not seek to bind, to control, or to enslave,*
*but to liberate, to empower,*
*to set others free to find their own truth.*

The great challenge before you today is to learn how to come together to create community based not on dogma or external authority, but on mutual equality and a deep respect for each person's experience. The question is "How do you accept and appreciate the differences between you while maintaining emotional connection and continuity? How do you experience freedom and love at the same time?"

Since most forms of love tend to be conditional, love is offered only when there is perceived agreement. To love someone who disagrees with you is rare. To feel emotionally connected to someone who has a very different set of experiences is unusual.

Real love is unconditional. It requires you to see beyond appearances, to see others from an inner conviction that all people carry the divine spark within them.

Real love does not seek to bind, to control, or to enslave, but to liberate, to empower, to set others free to find their own truth. What church or temple has this for an agenda? What religious structure gives its members the freedom to self-actualize in the name of love?

What church extends love and inclusion to all? What society reaches out to those who live on the fringes and keeps inviting them back in? What community of human beings is dedicated to seeing beyond its fears and learning to love its enemies?

When I asked for a church, was this not what I asked for? Did I not ask for a community which would recognize the Christ presence in all human beings, a community where no one would be ostracized or cast out? What is salvation, I ask you, if you do not offer it to everyone, regardless of his appearance or beliefs?

Love asks you to give and receive freedom. It asks you to encourage and empower others.

There are never any guarantees in the act of loving. If you look for agreement or favorable response, you cannot love freely. And if love is not free, it is not love. It is bargaining, negotiation, commerce.

Perhaps you begin to see what a church like the one I called for would do for the world you live in. It would make no one wrong, but encourage each person to find out what is right for him or her. It would trust and support the love and the light that dwells in each human being. It would not foster a world divided into rich and poor, haves and have-nots, but it would create a world in which each person has enough and is not afraid to share what s/he has.

A church and a society founded in my name would live by the principles I taught and teach. It would extend love and support freely to all. It would make no one wrong, condemn no woman or man, nor ostracize any human being from the community of faith. It would not be defensive, greedy or proud, but open-minded, generous and humble.

These qualities lie within each one of you. You have only to cultivate them. There is not a single one of you who cannot love unconditionally. But you must be encouraged to do so. My church is a church of encouragement. It calls you to realize the highest truth about yourself and about your brother and sister.

## HONORING FATHER AND MOTHER

*I challenge you to accept each person*
*who comes before you as a Child of God.*

If you follow my teachings, you must know that I call upon you to become the embodiment of unconditional love, non-judgment and compassion. I challenge you to accept each person who comes before you as a Child of God, no less perfect than you or I am. I challenge you to give to each the love and freedom that God has given to you. I call you to love and let go, to nurture and empower, to comfort and inspire.

Love is peaceful, but not static. It is dynamic, but not overwhelming or controlling. It gives the gift you need to receive and receives the gift you need to give. It is both feminine/receptive and masculine/active.

If you want to be a vehicle for love, you must practice both giving and receiving, leading and following, speaking and listening, acting and refraining from action. Love flows to and from you naturally as you accept the polarities of your experience, integrate them, and realize your wholeness.

You are a child of the Father and the Mother, as am I. As a man, you must emulate the father and embrace the qualities of the mother. As a woman, you must emulate the mother and embrace the qualities of the father. Just as God is neither male nor female, but both together, so are you a synthesis of male and female qualities within a particular body/mind vehicle.

Women have an equal place in my teaching. They have always had that place and they always will have it. Those who have denied women their rightful place in my church have twisted and distorted my teaching.

Gays and lesbians, blacks, Asians, Hispanics, born-agains, fundamentalists, Buddhists, Jews, even lawyers and politicians all have a place in the community of faith. Anyone is welcome. No one should be excluded. And all who participate in the community should have the opportunity to serve in leadership positions.

My teaching has never been exclusive or hierarchical. You have imposed your prejudices and your judgments on the pure truth I have taught. You have taken the house of worship and made it into a prison of fear and guilt. My friends, you are mistaken in your beliefs.

But it is not too late for you to learn from your mistakes. Repent from your unkind actions and words. Make amends to those whom you have injured or judged unfairly. Your mistakes do not condemn you unless you insist on holding onto them. Let them go. You can grow. You can change. You can be wiser than you once were. You can stop being a mouthpiece for fear and become a spokesperson for forgiveness and love.

No ship has ever been refused refuge in the harbor of forgiveness. No matter what you have said or done, I will welcome you home with open arms. All you need do is confess your mistakes and be willing to let them go. The past cannot condemn you if you are willing to open your heart and mind right here and now.

## LIVING A SPIRITUAL LIFE

*A spiritually awakened person knows*
*that love is the answer to every perceived problem.*

Spirituality and religion are not necessarily the same thing. Religion is the outer form; spirituality is the inner content. Religion is the husk; spirituality is the seed. Religion is a set of beliefs; spirituality is a continuum of experience.

You can be spiritual and not attend church or temple. You can find your spirituality in intimate sharing with others, in communion with nature, in being of service. Spiritual experience is simply that which relaxes the mind and uplifts the heart. Meditating, walking in the woods or by the ocean, holding an infant, or looking into a lover's eyes—these are all spiritual experiences. When there is love and acceptance in your heart, your spiritual nature is manifest and you can see the spiritual nature of other people.

To be spiritual is to see yourself and others without judgment, to see not just with the eyes, but with the heart. To be spiritual is to accept and appreciate "what is," instead of finding fault with it and seeking something else.

A spiritual person sees beauty everywhere, even in suffering. Wherever hearts are touched by the poignancy of life, there is beauty. Whenever people learn their life lessons and let the past fall away, beauty is present. There is beauty in the rain and clouds, and beauty in the sun. There is beauty in aloneness and in intimacy, in laughter and in tears. Wherever you turn, beauty awaits you.

A spiritual person does not focus on what appears to be ugly, cruel, or manipulative. S/he sees all these behaviors as coming from a lack of love. S/he gives love whenever it is asked for, even if it is requested in a fearful or aggressive way. A spiritual person looks upon her own suffering and that of others as a temporary disconnection from the experience of love.

A spiritually awakened person knows that love is the answer to every perceived problem. If life does not unfold the way you want it, you have disconnected from love and acceptance. To reconnect, you need only surrender your expectations and accept what comes into your life with gratitude.

Spirituality is the consciousness that life is okay the way it is. It doesn't need to be changed or fixed. It just needs to be accepted. A spiritual person is peaceful, upbeat, helpful, encouraging. S/he doesn't complain about the past or look for happiness in the future. S/he doesn't try to fix other people or ask to be fixed. S/he lives in the present moment, filled with gratitude and acceptance.

Everyone is spiritual, but not everyone takes the time to explore their spirituality. Many people become lost in the drama of their lives. They spend most of their time dealing with survival issues. They do not take the time to watch the sunset or smell the roses. They are missing out on a great deal of joy and beauty. If they would just stop, take a deep breath and look for a moment, they would realize what they are missing.

There is a discipline involved in living a spiritual life. You need to take care of yourself and say no to people who would draw you into their dramas of suffering and victimhood. You learn to bless them and give them the space to have the experience they wish to have. You see the futility of trying to rescue others from their dramas and you know that your ability to help anyone depends on your maintaining your own health and balance.

When you rest in your Self, you see that there are no problems to be fixed. Life just needs to be accepted in a heartfelt way. In that acceptance, peace and happiness are established and all that seemed to be obstructing love is finally washed away.

## WHO NEEDS RELIGION?

*A barren tree will make no fruit. A religion that does not help*
*its followers connect to love will not prosper.*

The truth is that no one needs religion. You don't need to hold onto the husk. But you do need to break it open and plant the seed.

Whatever your religion, it has dogmas and interpretations that disguise the truth. All religions are heavily burdened by the prejudices and narrow ideas of followers who never opened to truth and beauty in their lives. What you have is a record of their fear, not an invitation to love.

But if you dig deeply enough in the garden of your faith, you will find the voices of truth and beauty that help you to open your heart to love's presence. And that is where you must focus. That is where you will plant the seed of faith that will take root in your life.

There are many beautiful trees that flower in the springtime. Each tree has its special beauty. Seen together, they make an extraordinary garden. So it is with approaches to the divine. Each approach has its own beauty and integrity. It speaks to certain people and not to others. That is the way it should be. One tree is not better than another. One religion is not better than another.

Each religion has attached to it a climate of fear and rigidity that can destroy the tree before its seeds can be carried forth on the wind. This is true in every tradition.

If you belong to a tradition, you must find the seed, separate it from the husk, and see that it is planted in your lifetime. You must find the core teaching that connects you to love and pass that teaching on to your children. That is the only way that a tradition stays healthy. The form should change to better speak to the time and place, but the essence of the teaching must be continually discovered and resurrected.

A barren tree will make no fruit. A religion that does not help its followers connect to love will not prosper.

You do not have to belong to a religion to awaken your spirituality. But it is easier to awaken to the truth and beauty of your life if you belong to a loving community of people. Such a community need not be religious. Many secular communities such as twelve step groups provide their members with the same emotional support and empowerment that some people find in religious organizations.

You don't have to belong to a community to open your heart to love, but it sure makes it easier if you do. Even if you meet with just two or three other people who are loving and supportive, you will find that it helps you transcend your personal drama and stay open to the purpose and meaning that are unfolding in your life.

The Affinity Group Process provides you with a very simple way of staying connected to love in your life. It is particularly helpful if you aren't comfortable with religion and don't have a secular support group in your life.

The Affinity Process can also help large congregations stay connected to love. As organizations grow outwardly, they often forget their purpose and they cease to be nurturing places for their members. Bringing the Affinity Process into such an environment can reawaken the original inspiration and loving interactions which made the organization popular to begin with.

In the long run though, no organization is going to provide you with ready-made spiritual sustenance. The best a church or temple can do is help you connect to love. Once that connection is made, it is up to you to nurture that love at home with your family, at work, and in all of your interactions with others.

Leading a spiritual life is essential for your fulfillment. But no one can or should tell you what that spiritual life should look like. Your journey is a unique one and you are guided most appropriately by the Spirit within you. As you listen to your inner voice and learn to rely on it, you won't need to depend on your parents, your minister, or other authority figures for guidance. You will establish in your Self. You will become authentic.

When the truth has been nurtured within you, it asserts itself clearly in your life. As you become more fully empowered, you may leave your support group, your church or your temple to follow your calling. Then, wherever you go, you give and receive support without hesitation. For when love is awakened within you, it is given freely to all who need it.

In truth, each one of you is a minister in training. And you will be called to serve your brothers and sisters when your connection to love is firmly established. When that call comes you will have no choice but to answer it. For it is the reason for which you came, the purpose for which you are ideally suited in temperament and ability.

God knows your purpose, even if you do not know it yet. But God lives within you, not outside. And if you would know your purpose, you must ask the divine being within. That is the only one who can guide you home.

## AFFIRMATION AND NEGATION

*To find real truth, real love, real essence,*
*you must stop accepting their imitations.*

If you want to connect deeply with your spiritual nature, you must understand clearly what needs to be affirmed and what needs to be denied. On the simplest level, truth is affirmed, and falsehood is denied. Love is affirmed and fear is denied. Essence is affirmed and appearance is denied.

The problem with affirming truth, love and essence is that we often don't know what they are. How can you affirm the truth if you don't know what it is? How can you affirm love if you are fearful or ambivalent about it? How can you affirm essence if you are always looking for the approval of others?

Often, to approach affirmation genuinely, we must practice negation. If I am confused, I must acknowledge "This confusion is not the truth." If I am ambivalent in my feelings, I must admit "This ambivalence is not love." If I am looking for external reinforcement for how I feel, I must see that "This search for approval is not essence."

By being clear about what truth, love and essence are not, I create the space within me to realize what they are. And so the process continues. "Truth is not prejudice or narrow opinion; love is not expectation or the desire to rescue or fix another; essence is not the search for agreement, approval, or belonging."

In Zen Buddhism, there is a practice of negation that says "Neither this nor that." There is no preference or taking sides. This helps one resist the temptation to find truth in intellectual concepts. Truth is deeper than concepts.

Lao Tzu told you, "The way that can be spoken is not the true way." Truth lies in the heart along with essence and love. They cannot be found with the mind or spoken with the lips. They can be embodied and expressed only by one who does not need to be right, loved back or approved of. Real truth, real love, real essence have no opposite, for they do not come from the realm of duality.

To find real truth, real love, real essence, you must stop accepting their imitations. If you accept conditional love, you will not experience love without conditions. If you accept any form of dogma, judgment or prejudice as truth, you will not know the pure truth of the heart. If you seek the approval of other men and women and are attached to the way they receive you, you will not tell the truth to others even when it is called for.

You must negate all imitations. As long as love is offered with conditions, as long as truth is offered with judgment of others, as long as essence is puffed up and attached to self-image, it will be an imitation.

If you mistake the false for the true, you cannot affirm what is true or deny what is false. That, my friends, is the difficulty of words and concepts. To penetrate to the core, you must go beyond words and concepts.

When you speak of love, please ask yourself, "Is my love free of conditions?" When you speak of truth, please ask yourself, "Is my truth free of judgment or opinion?" When you speak of essence, ask yourself, "Am I attached to the way people perceive or receive me?"

Freedom to be yourself requires more detachment than you think. As long as you want something from anyone, you cannot be yourself. Only when you want nothing in particular from anyone, can you be free to interact honestly and authentically with others.

I do not say this to discourage you, but to prepare you for the depth and breadth of the journey you are on. To be a self-realized person requires that you disconnect from all expectations and conditions whether they come from you or from another.

Your goal is to accept every person you meet just the way s/he is and to be yourself regardless of how other people receive you or react to you. When you meet someone who repulses you or pushes your buttons, you are not seeing truth or essence in that person. If you feel expansive when people love you and depressed when people dislike you, you are not established in the truth of your own essence.

Love is the most difficult thing in the world and the easiest. It is the most difficult thing because you have so many attachments and expectations that block its flow toward you and from you. It is the easiest thing because, when you drop those attachments and expectations even for a moment, love comes to you and emanates from you spontaneously and without effort.

CHAPTER TWENTY-TWO

# Abuse and Forgiveness

*Do not accept less than you want and deserve
and you will not bring inappropriate relationships into your life.*

People who are afraid of love ask for it nonetheless. Yet when it comes to them, they are unable to receive it. They want love to come in a perfect shape and size and it never comes that way.

Real love comes from essence, not appearance. It is practical and immediate, not ideal or abstract. People who can't look past appearances won't recognize the beloved even when s/he stands before them.

People who are afraid of love are ambivalent about giving and receiving. When you are aloof, they feel safe and desire your presence. But when you come close, they get scared and ask you to back off or go away. This emotionally teasing behavior enables them to be in relationship while avoiding intimacy.

If you are drawn into such a relationship, you must face the fact that you too may be afraid to receive love. Why else would you choose a partner who cannot give it? More specifically, you may believe that the only way you can receive the love you want is to put up with someone's constant criticism and rejection of you.

On some level, you are what you attract, so blaming the other person for showing up in your life is a futile attempt to shift the responsibility away from yourself. If you want to understand and learn from what happened, you must ask yourself "How does this person reflect my own fear, insecurity and emotional ambivalence?"

Only when you do that can you break the magic spell.

Freedom comes when you take the other person off the hook and realize that the real issue is your own self-worth. Your partner's criticism and lack of acceptance of you is just a mirror for your own lack of acceptance and criticism of yourself. Low self-esteem is frequently mirrored in critical or abusive relationships.

Your job is not to judge other people, analyze them or try to fix them. Accept them as they are. Send them love. But don't live with them or be their partner. Stop compromising yourself. You deserve love without having to put up with criticism or abuse. Only if you are afraid that no one will love you the way you are would you settle for love with such unfortunate conditions attached to it.

If you are willing to be a victim, you will be sure to attract an abuser. Your lack of faith in yourself attracts another who is similarly insecure. What the other person does to you is just an external version of what you are doing yourself.

Don't blame the other person. Take responsibility for the fact that you allowed the criticism to continue and be clear that you are making a different choice. Own the problem and the solution.

Loving and taking care of yourself are essential steps in attracting a relationship that will honor you. Do not accept less than you want and deserve and you will not bring inappropriate relationships into your life.

Look with care when a potential partner comes into your life. Is s/he gentle and forgiving with you, or is s/he critical and controlling? Say yes to the former and no absolutely to the latter. Unless you can say no to potential partners who are incapable of honoring you, how can you attract a partner who will love and accept you as you are?

## YOU BRING IN WHAT YOU ALLOW

*When there is a strong desire in the heart and clarity in the mind, the creative process flows easily.*

None of you are victims of someone else's actions toward you. You bring into your life what you allow to come in. If you say "no" to what you don't want, you bring in what you do want. It is that simple.

The only factor that makes all this complicated is that you don't always know what you want or, if you do, you don't trust it and remain committed to it. When your unconscious desires are different from your conscious goals, what you bring into your life reflects a mixture of both.

Your creative capacity functions both consciously and unconsciously. Mind is creative, whether or not it is aware of itself.

If you want to create consciously, you must bring your unconscious desires and fears up for acceptance and inspection. Then, you will understand why your experiences often differ remarkably from what you consciously intend.

When you understand your desires and fears, you can make choices that do not violate the more childish, vulnerable parts of your psyche. This may mean that your goals become more immediate, short-term and realistic. But this is a positive step, insuring that your long-term goals will not be undermined by the scared and wounded aspects of your psyche.

Expecting too much from yourself or from others is as dysfunctional as expecting too little. Wanting a job or relationship you don't have the skills or maturity to handle is counterproductive and creates severe anxiety. It is far better to seek out a less challenging job or relationship and do well at it than it is to shoot too high too soon. Small, progressive victories build confidence on all levels of the psyche, integrating child and adult perspectives and strengthening trust that will be needed for more difficult challenges that lie ahead.

To create what you want means to get clear about what you really want on all levels of your being. When the spiritual adult and wounded child want different things, manifestation is always mixed. That is why the time you take to integrate and unify the different needs and wants of your psyche is time well spent. When there is a strong desire in the heart and clarity in the mind, the creative process flows easily.

If you want to succeed in your relationships with others, take the time to get to know yourself. Then it will be clear when and to whom you must say no and when and to whom you must say yes. Remember, what comes to you is not always what it seems. The knight in shining armor may be an insecure abuser in disguise, and the one offering comfort and support may be a wolf in sheep's clothing.

Always look beyond appearances, for nothing is as it seems to be. When you know what you want and what you need, be patient and wait for it. Many will come to you claiming to be the one you asked for, but only one will be authentic. Usually, it won't be the one who comes with lots of smoke and mirrors. More often than not, it will be the simple unassuming one, the one who doesn't use big words or promise great gifts, but who takes your hand and looks into your eyes without fear.

## EQUALITY AND MUTUAL RESPECT

*Giving your power away to others is not spiritual.*

In order to experience equality with others, you must be willing to treat others with dignity and respect. Moreover, you must be clear that you expect to be treated in a respectful manner by all of the people in your life—spouse, parents, children, friends, people at work, even strangers.

If someone acts in a judgmental, critical or attacking way toward you, please tell that person immediately how you are feeling. Do so without blaming or attacking back, but ask clearly to be treated respectfully. That is your right. And that is the other person's responsibility.

Don't allow someone to treat you in an unkind or an unfair way without standing up for yourself. Mind you, I am not telling you to attack back or retaliate. I am simply telling you to stand up for yourself and insist that you be treated with respect. When you turn the other cheek, you are telling your abuser to think again and make a different choice.

The important thing is to oppose what is disrespectful when it happens. Otherwise you will feel resentful and entitled to make judgments of the person who criticized or attacked you. That is passive-aggressive. Retaliating slowly over time is no better than retaliating in the heat of the moment. The key is not to retaliate at all, but to stand up for yourself clearly and forcefully without impugning the dignity of the other person.

Unless you know in the core of your being that you deserve to be treated kindly, you will put up with unnecessary abuse and allow yourself to become a victim. Being a victim who gives power away to others is not spiritual. It is irresponsible to yourself and to the other person.

You do not empower another by giving your power to him. Instead, you give him a false sense of responsibility and control, which prevents him from taking appropriate responsibility for his own life. This arrangement is codependent and mutually invalidating. When one person does not carry her own weight, the other person has to carry her weight as well as his own. The result is that both people become weak, tired, discouraged and resentful.

For a relationship between two people to work, each person must take responsibility for treating the other with dignity and respect. This creates a foundation of trust and mutual regard on which genuine equality can be built.

## FORGIVENESS

*Through the practice of forgiveness,*
*imperfect people become whole,*
*and broken relationships are healed and strengthened.*

No matter how good your relationship is, you and your partner will forget to honor each other. You will get stressed out and project your pain onto each other. You will attack and defend, give and receive guilt, and generally make a mess of things. These are the times when your relationship is asking you to grow in wisdom and emotional strength.

Your intimate partnership is a microcosm of your entire journey. Since there are no perfect partners out there, your challenge is to accept and honor the imperfect one who stands before you and, yes, to honor yourself, even though your life also is riddled with mistakes.

If you and your partner can forgive each other's transgressions and reestablish your trust in one another, then you can deepen in your love and your capacity for intimacy. This is the challenging part of relationship.

Anyone can enter into relationship. Falling in love is easy, especially when hormones are at work. And leaving isn't much harder, especially when people are blindly projecting their fears onto each other. But what most people don't seem to be willing to do is to practice forgiveness together. And that is why so many partnerships fail.

Forgiveness is the key to success in every relationship. Indeed, if you and another person are committed to practicing forgiveness you can live together successfully, even if you don't have a lot in common.

On the other hand, if the two of you are not willing to practice forgiveness, then nothing you try will work. No, not religion, or psychotherapy, or relationship workshops. If one of you is willing and the other is not, then the odds are a little better, but still not so good, unless the willing one sets such a strong example that the unwilling one becomes willing. While one person can practice forgiveness, and this is always helpful, it takes two to heal the wounds of mutual trespass.

If you decide to leave one relationship because you are unwilling to forgive, what makes you think that you can succeed in another? It's true, people are different and some people push your buttons more than others, but everyone is imperfect and everyone is going to push your buttons at one time or other. Your ability to create a successful relationship depends not so much on your choice of partner, but on your willingness to forgive yourself and the partner you choose.

By all means, hold out for the partner you want. Insist on common goals, shared interests and mutual attraction. Abandon any relationship that appears to be abusive, even though you might eventually learn something there. Don't play the game of love with half a deck.

But realize, my friends, that no matter how well or how poorly you choose a mate, the practice of forgiveness will be necessary. It is the one constant. It is the key to your ultimate happiness and that of your partner.

Through the practice of forgiveness, imperfect people become whole, and broken relationships are healed and strengthened. Through the practice of forgiveness, you learn what real love and real essence are all about. Through your forgiveness, your mate is transformed into the Beloved, the perfect teacher come to set you free of judgments and illusions.

That synergy of lover and beloved is the great promise of relationship. When two people surrender fully to their union, they become one in heart and mind. They become the nurturing Mother and empowering Father, redeeming all wounded children from the suffering of the past. They become living witness to the redemptive power of love.

## VALIDATION

*When the emotional body is triggered,*
*many traumatic memories and experiences can surface.*

Almost all fear, anger, and hurt stem from your feeling unloved and unappreciated. When you respond to another person in a hurt or angry way, s/he feels invalidated by you. The downward spiral of mutual attack and invalidation continues until you are both thoroughly alienated from each other.

When you recognize that you and your partner are moving into the game of, "I'll hurt you because you hurt me," you must stop immediately. Tell your partner: "I don't want to do this. Let's take some time to tune into what's going on inside before this situation escalates and we turn off our love completely."

Just stop and say, "I'm going to take a walk. I'll be back when I understand better what's happening inside. I want to talk with you when I'm feeling okay, not when I'm feeling hurt or angry."

When you walk, realize that what you are feeling—unloved and unappreciated—goes very deep. It is not just a response to this particular incident with your partner. It is a response to every experience you've ever had in which you felt attacked, judged, rejected, abandoned, or betrayed. When the emotional body is triggered, even though the trigger seems insignificant, many traumatic memories and experiences can surface. The sadness that comes from feeling the loss of love can be intense.

Your partner is not responsible for the depth of sadness you feel. S/he is just the trigger. So take him or her off the hook, and see that the job of bringing love to the sad and wounded parts of you belongs primarily to you. Be gentle and loving with yourself. Understand that all you want from your partner is reassurance that s/he loves you and wants to be with you. When you return to your partner, ask for that reassurance.

But be clear that you cannot depend on your partner for validation. Self-validation is necessary. Even in the healthiest relationships, there are times when one partner is unable to give what the other person needs.

People who have not learned to validate themselves have a very difficult time in relationships. They expect more attention and approval than most people are capable of giving. That means they are rejected a lot, and that only adds to their insecurity.

When you learn to love and validate yourself, you are not needy and easily threatened when your partner gives attention to someone or something else. You learn to give her space to be herself and express aspects of self that she cannot express with you, and you feel free to do the same.

When the relationship permits each individual to self-actualize, it is easier for the partners to find a shared space that is authentic and nurturing to both people. Finding that shared reality is both the challenge and the reward of every committed relationship. In the process, both people grow beyond narrow self-interest and learn to serve the higher purpose of their union.

CHAPTER TWENTY-THREE

# Staying Connected to Love

*You are here to find out that the Source of love lies within.*
*You do not have to seek love outside of yourself.*

Love is omnipresent in the universe, yet you have a hard time staying connected to it. Why is this?

The reason is that you believe that there is something wrong with you. You are afraid of being judged or rejected by others. For most of your life, you have accepted other people's ideas and opinions as the truth about you. You have established the authority for your life outside yourself. You have accepted as truth what mother, father, teacher, minister or other authority figure said about you. Yet what they said was just their opinion, not the truth, about you.

All human beings betray themselves in the search for love and acceptance. They internalize the feedback they receive from others and develop their self-image based on it.

In other words, the "you" that you know is a creation of other people's beliefs and judgments which you accept as true about yourself. Even your so-called "personality" is a set of behavior patterns you adopted to accommodate the needs and expectations of the significant others in your life.

Where then is the "real you" in the equation of self and other? The real you is the unknown factor, the essence that has been heavily clothed in the judgments and interpretations which you have accepted about yourself.

This is true for everyone, not just for you. People relate to each another not as authentic, self-realized beings, but as personae, masks, roles, identities. Often, people have more than one mask that they wear, depending on whom they are with and what is expected of them.

The True Self gets lost and forgotten among all these disguises. And its great gift of authenticity is not seen or acknowledged.

The True Self is not bound by the limitations, judgments and interpretations that the persona lives with. Indeed, it can be said that Self and persona live in different worlds. The world of Self is bright and self-fulfilling. The world of persona is dark and needy, seeking light and fulfillment outside itself.

The Self says, "I am." The persona says, "I am this" or "I am that." The Self lives and expresses unconditionally. The persona lives and expresses conditionally. Self is motivated by love and says "I can." Persona lives in fear and says "I can't." Persona complains, apologizes and makes excuses. Self accepts, integrates and gives its gift.

You are Self, but believe yourself to be your persona. As long as you operate as persona, you have experiences that confirm your beliefs about yourself and others. When you realize that all personae are just masks you and others have agreed to wear, you learn to see behind the masks.

When that happens, you glimpse the radiance of the Self within you and within others. You see a bright being, eminently worthy and capable of love, dynamically creative, generous and self-fulfilling. That is your inmost nature. And that is the inmost nature of all beings.

When you accept your True Self, your arguments with others cease. For you no longer do battle with their personae. You see the light behind the mask. Your light and their light are all that matter.

When you contact the truth about you, you recognize that a great deal that you have come to accept about you is false. You are not better or worse than others. You are not stupid or brilliant, handsome or ugly. Those are just judgments someone made that you accepted. None of them is true.

When you know the truth about you, you understand that you are not just a body, although you need to accept your body and take care of it. You are not just your thoughts and feelings, although you need to be aware of them and see how they are creating the drama of your life. You are not the roles that you are playing—husband or wife, mother or father, son or daughter, employee or boss, secretary or plumber—although you need to make peace with whatever role you choose to play. You are not anything external. You are not anything that can be defined by something or someone else.

The purpose of your journey here is to discover your True Self and leave the persona behind. You are here to find out that the Source of love lies within your own consciousness. You do not have to seek love outside of yourself. Indeed, the very act of seeking love in the world will prevent you from recognizing it within yourself.

You can't see the light in others until you see it in yourself. Once you see it in yourself, there is no one in whom you do not see the light. It does not matter if they see it or not. You know it's there. And it is the light you address when you speak to them.

The world of personae is a chaotic and reactive world. It is fueled by fear and judgment. It is real only because you and others believe in it and define yourselves by the conditions you find there. But those conditions are not ultimate reality. They are simply a collective drama of your making. Yes, the drama has its own rules, its costumes, its inter-relationships and its plan of action. But none of this matters when you take your costume off and step off the stage. Mind you, the play will go on. It does not depend on you alone. But when you know it's just a play, you can choose to participate in it or not. If you participate, you will do so remembering who you are, understanding the part that you play without being attached to it.

Suffering ends when your attachment to all conditions dissolves. Then, you rest in the Self, the embodiment of love, the Source of creation itself.

## WHO IS THE CHRIST?

*Christ is the True Self fully acknowledged and empowered.*

The Self is all-powerful. The persona is not. The only reason the persona seems to be powerful is because you are invested in it. The persona is a temporary container for Self, which is deeper than any experience or set of conditions.

When you remember Self, you go beyond your attachment to the idiosyncrasies of your persona. You experience a peace and a freedom that lies beyond the conditions that appear to bind you.

As Self, you are never a prisoner of conditions. How could you be? If you see yourself as a prisoner or a hapless victim, you are in your persona. When you dwell in your Self, you know yourself to be totally innocent and free, regardless of what others may believe about you.

Christ can be crucified, but he cannot be forced to hate those who attack him. He stands committed in his love, regardless of the hatred that dwells in other people's hearts. Christ is gentle with himself and all others, yet he will defend the truth fearlessly. No one can intimidate him, nor would he intimidate any brother or sister. His only call to his siblings is a call to awaken and accept the mantle of love.

Christ is simply the True Self fully acknowledged and empowered. He is the revelation of truth, the Spirit awakened in the flesh. Do not think that I alone am Christ or you will miss the entire point of my teaching. Every one of you is challenged to awaken to your True Self. When you do, you too will be the anointed one.

Waking up to the truth about who you are does not make you special or give you special privileges. You will still inhabit a human body. You will still live in a world dominated by masks and roles, but you will live in that world without buying into it. You will live in the world of persona, but you will not be of that world. You will be of the world of Self, where all are equal and all are worthy of unconditional love.

## CONFESSION AND ATONEMENT

*Your only purpose here on Earth is to accept your innocence
and to help others accept theirs.*

Why do you suppose I asked you to confess your sins? Do you honestly think it is because I wanted to give some priest artificial power over you so that you would have to beg forgiveness from him and from the authority of the Church?

What nonsense!

I asked you to confess your sins so that you might lighten your load, so that you might release the judgments you make about yourself and others. You cannot walk next to me so long as you carry those judgments with you. They are too heavy a load. You cannot take them where you and I must go.

I ask you to confess your sins and your pain in a private place where no other man or woman enters. Forgive your mistakes. Vow to learn and to do better by yourself and others. Connect to love in your heart and take that love with you when you leave. Find this inner temple when you become burdened by the affairs of the world and your attachment to them.

Take sanctuary there. Go there to release your worries, your fears, your guilt about what you have said and done. Go there to allow your heart to heal and strengthen so that you make amends with anyone you have slighted and treated unkindly. Go to find peace, so that you can make peace with your brothers and sisters.

I ask you to confess your sins, not to hold onto them. I ask you to forgive yourself, not to let some priestly hierarchy hold you in perpetual bondage.

If you have been holding yourself prisoner, know now that it is time to set yourself free. No matter what you have said or done, you do not deserve to suffer. Your suffering will not feed the hungry or heal the sick.

Take the forgiveness I offer you so that you can come back into your life with a clear vision and a strong heart. I offer you freedom, not for yourself alone, but for the sake of all those who need your love and your service. Take the branch of peace and carry it forth into the neighborhoods where people need empowerment and hope. Your love can heal all the wounds of the past, if you will only believe in yourself and in the power of love.

Accept my forgiveness that you may offer it to others and be a force for healing and reconciliation. Nothing else can bring you joy or redemption.

Do not let the world tell you who you are. For you are not what others tell you, even if you appear to be fulfilling their expectations. Consider it well, my friend, do you want to continue to live in fear and sorrow, just because others expect you to be hard and tough? Will you squander your life just to protect an image that someone else gave you long ago?

I say it is time to cast that image away. It is not who you are. It will not bring you peace or happiness. Let it go. And let me help you learn of yourself anew.

When I went forth to serve my brothers and sisters, I took the name Emmanuel so that I would always remember that God was with me. By remembering God, I was able to see my innocence, as well as the innocence and purity of all of the beings I beheld on my journey.

You must do the same. You must carry God with you in your heart and remember that your only purpose here on Earth is to accept your innocence and to help others accept theirs. That is why you have come to me.

I will use everything that you bring to me as a tool for healing and redemption. It does not matter if you have been a criminal, a drug dealer, an alcoholic, a prostitute, a corrupt preacher or politician. I will send you back amongst the people whose fears and habits you know and together we will bring them home. No, not by condemning their actions or trying to fix them, but by loving them, seeing them whole, and reminding them of the truth about themselves, which they have forgotten.

## MINISTRY OF LOVE

*Do not impose your beliefs and opinions on others.*
*Respect their right to decide what works for them.*

When you are secure in your experience of the divine, you do not need to convince anyone else to believe as you do. Yet, because your experience is significant for you, you are happy to share it with others.

Nevertheless, you must understand that you are helpful to others only to the extent that you encourage them to use whatever portions of your testimony are uplifting and empowering to them. They must decide what is helpful and what is not, not you.

When you seek to impose your beliefs and opinions onto others, you are not respecting their right to decide what works for them. This is manipulation, not ministry.

You place so much value on words and concepts, yet I tell you this is not where the experience of conversion happens. Conversion happens primarily in the heart, and not so much in the mind.

People are not converted to some concept of God, but to an experience of love. One who does not believe in something beyond his small ego suddenly opens to a loving presence. That is the experience that changes lives.

People are not converted by adopting a set of beliefs and parroting them to others. Conversion does not happen through proselytizing. It does not happen when you preach narrow, intolerant ideas that make you right and others wrong.

People are converted by the power of love when you love and accept them unconditionally. You don't need to change their beliefs or customs, or fix their lives. You just need to demonstrate the power of love in the way that you speak and act toward them. That is what gets their attention.

No one can resist a person who radiates love. Everyone comes to sit at his or her feet. Can you imagine that? These people are not even invited, never mind proselytized, yet they come anyway. They come because love calls to them and they respond.

You do not have to go out aggressively to spread my message. You do not have to hit people over the head with it and drag them back to your churches or synagogues. Just love each other, and people will come. They will come and fill themselves to the brim, and they will return home with their cup running over. That is the way my teaching spreads.

You do not have to be perfect to be a mouthpiece for my teaching, but you do need to be humble. You have to meet people where they are. And you need to be honest about where you are. Pretense will not work. If you lie to yourself, you will lie to others, and if you lie to others, you will eventually be found out. So save yourself some valuable time and tell the truth from the beginning.

No one is perfect. I am no more perfect than you, and you are no more perfect than the least of your brothers or sisters. Every one of you makes mistakes. Every one of you has much to learn about giving and receiving love.

You don't get to heaven by pretending to be there when you aren't, nor do you get there by pretending that you have some impossible handicap. Heaven is available to all who are willing to learn about love.

Are you willing to keep learning? If so, the doors of heaven will keep opening to you. Every time you walk through one door, another one will open. For there are many rooms in the house of love. And each room must be explored fully.

When you let love into your heart, the process of exploration ceases to be work and drudgery. On the contrary, it becomes energetic and fun. You discover that you have many gifts that you can share with others along the way. And you learn to receive with gratitude the gifts that others need to share with you.

Do not look down on or despise another's gift. Even if it doesn't seem to measure up, please accept it anyway. Look into your brother's eyes and see how much he wishes to give the gift, and you cannot refuse to accept it.

## LIVING THE MIRACLE

*When the door needs to be celebrated, it ceases to be a door.*

Sometimes you think you need a miracle, but all you need is a little common sense. Sometimes, you think you need God and his angels to do it for you, but all you need is to walk through your fear.

There are many miracles that happen all around you, but you do not notice them because you are expecting fireworks. Miracle-making is a process. When you are doing the best that you can in your life, when you are moving through your fear, seeing your projections, and reaching out lovingly to people who are dispirited or afraid, you are living that process.

Some of you think that God does all the work. I hate to disappoint you, but you do 90% of the work in every miracle that transpires. God does just 10%. God inspires you and guides you, but you do the work.

Yet you cannot take credit for the work you do in God's name. All credit goes to God, because without God healing would not happen. All the work that you do would be for naught.

You and I are just messengers. Any one of us could be the door. The door does not need to be celebrated. Just being the door brings its own ecstatic rewards.

When the door needs to be celebrated, it ceases to be a door. When people grasp the finger pointing to the moon, they can no longer tell where it is pointing.

Don't make yourself important. Let the glory go to others and you will be glorified truly. When you do not call attention to yourself, you become capable of working deeply in every moment. No one interferes with your work. Indeed, only the most discerning notice what you do.

It is a rare person who can go about her work without calling attention to herself, without seeking publicity, without building an organization around her. It is a rare person who inspires without taking credit, who heals without charging a fee and gives without asking anything in return. You may seek her, but you will find her only if you are prepared to walk in her footsteps.

The greatest teachers are the most humble, the most loving, the most empowering to others. If you wish to find such a teacher, you must look beyond appearances. Find the man or woman who promises you nothing, but loves you without hesitation. Find the teacher who makes no pretension to fix or to teach, yet who opens your heart when s/he looks into your eyes.

When you think of great teachers, you think of glitter, flowing robes and great crowds of people gathered together. But none of these trappings are required. Indeed, they often get in the way.

CHAPTER TWENTY-FOUR

# Releasing the Ties That Bind

*Fear in one person tends to invoke fear in another.*
*That is the equation of mutual trespass.*

When you see another as less than yourself, you are seeing through your fear. And fear, as you know, is blind.

No one is less worthy than you, even if that person's behavior toward you is unwarranted and objectionable. His fear makes him act toward you in a belligerent way. Your fear makes you think of him and act toward him in an equally belligerent way. Fear in one person tends to invoke fear in another. That is the equation of mutual trespass.

The only way out of the cycle of mutual attack and defense is to see your attacker as he really is. When you see him as a human being who is responding to you out of fear, you can speak and act in a way that will lessen his fear. That means you don't attack back. It does not mean that you allow him to intimidate you.

Each of you must find a way to stand up lovingly for yourself without putting other people down. Your regard for yourself is essential. It is precisely that self-regard that must extend to include the other person.

Extending your love in the face of someone else's fear is the most difficult thing you will ever have to do. Yet it is essential that you learn how to do this.

There are many people who are anxious or afraid and are acting out in angry ways. I'm not just talking about murderers, thieves, and rapists. I'm talking about people who cut you off in traffic, call you names, threaten you or spread untrue rumors about you.

Many people are time bombs of anger waiting to explode. If you engage with them in an un-centered way, you can trigger their rage.

To handle these situations skillfully, do your best to refrain from making judgments about others and try to keep your heart open to them, even when they treat you unfairly. By all means let them know that you want to be treated with respect, but offer them the same respect when you confront them.

Don't confront people out of anger. When you react in an angry or defensive way to someone's attack, you will only make the situation worse.

You do not have to respond to the fearful words and actions of other people. You can respond to what lies behind their words and actions. You can give them the love and respect they are seeking from you and then their hostility toward you will cease.

I never said that this path would be easy. There are real challenges here which you must learn to meet. You too become fearful and act in hostile ways toward others who don't deserve your anger or your blame. You must learn to apologize to others for these attacking behaviors. You must see the times when you are callous and unloving and take responsibility for treating people with greater gentleness and respect.

This is a two-way street. Everyone who has been mistreated by another has mistreated others at one time or another. All of you have the same lessons to learn in this regard.

## LEAVING HOME/COMING HOME

*I have asked you to stand alone, not because I wish to isolate you, but so you can know the truth and anchor in it.*

If you think that I or anyone else has something you don't have, you are already giving your power away. You need to learn nothing is missing in you whatsoever. You need to learn to trust yourself and see the unlimited resources that are available to you as a spiritual being.

Do not limit the possibilities that lie before you. Do not shut the doors of opportunity with negative thinking. Be open. Be willing.

Let go of your specific expectations, but hold onto the belief that your needs will be met in ways that you cannot even begin to understand. Be surrendered. Rest in your faith that God has only good things for you. Know that even the tests and the lessons are there to make you stronger and more flexible in your ability to love.

Let God be your teacher. Let the Tao flower in you. You don't need to control things anymore. When you are willing to be helpful, life flows through you. You become the channel, the means by which love without conditions can reach into the world.

Do not give your power away to others. Nobody else knows what is good for you. Nobody else knows what your mission here is all about. Stay away from psychics, teachers, therapists and gurus who would direct your life through their own limited beliefs about themselves or you.

You have everything you need to be guided wisely in your life. Trust in this. Trust in your connection to the Source of all things. You are no further away from God than I am. You don't need me to bring you to the feet of the Divine. You don't need your partner or your teacher to bring you there. You are already there.

God is incapable of moving away from you. God is ever-present in your life. When you do not feel the divine presence, it is because you have moved away. You have given your power to some earthly authority. You have left the place of the indwelling God in search of something special in the world. That search always comes up empty, but that doesn't mean that you won't keep trying to find the answer somewhere outside of yourself.

Many of you think that I want your exclusive allegiance. Nothing could be further from the truth. When I ask you to believe in me, it is to empower you to know that you can do as I have done. But you can do this with me or without me. It does not matter. Your salvation does not depend on me. You are the Lamb of God. You are the one who has come to forgive yourself and release the world from her chains of envy and regret.

If you have a teacher who empowers you, I am happy. It does not matter to me if that teacher is a Buddhist or a Jew, a Christian or a Moslem, a shaman or a businessman. If you are learning to trust yourself, if you are becoming more open in your mind and your heart, then I am happy for you. It does not matter what specific path you are on, what symbols you believe in, or what scrolls you consider sacred. I look to the fruit of all those beliefs and endeavors to see if you are stepping into your divinity or giving that power away to someone or something outside yourself.

No, I do not want your exclusive allegiance. I simply ask you to choose a teacher and a teaching which empowers you to discover truth within your own heart, for there alone will you find it. When you give your power away, to me or to anyone else, I know that you have not heard me.

How many times have I told you I am not the only son or daughter of God? All of you share that lineage with me. You are God's children. You carry divine love and wisdom within you. All the answers to your problems lie within you.

I stand before you as a model of one who realized his divinity while living in a body in this world. I demonstrate to you the power that manifests when one listens to one's inner voice and follows it, even when other people judge or object. I stand for the inner authority of the universal heart-mind which holds everyone in equal reverence. I know that when you trust the divine within, you cannot help but become authentic.

I have tried to show you a way of cutting yourself loose from parental authority, cultural authority, and religious authority. I have tried to tell you that who you are is far greater than all that. I have told you that the laws and customs of men and women are limited by the conditions of their experience. They cannot see beyond them.

But there is a Reality that is beyond that narrow subjective reality. And you can find it, from the inside out, for it is the very ground of your being. It is who you are when you strip away all the false beliefs you have accepted from parents, family, culture and church or synagogue.

I have asked you to have the courage to stand alone so you could step into your life and shed the narrow identifications which prevent you from knowing who you are. I have asked you to leave your home and your work, so that you could stand back and look at your life from a distance, seeing the self-limiting, fear-based patterns of behavior. I have asked you to stand back so that you would realize that you do not have to sell yourself short. You do not have to give your power away to customs and traditions that don't honor your spiritual roots and branches.

A young person must leave the home of her parents and open to new experiences if she is to create a home of her own. For the same reason, you may have to leave your school, your career, your religion, and your relationship so that you can discover who you are apart from the roles that you play and the social structures that define your life.

You are not just a son or a daughter, a husband or a wife, a carpenter or a plumber, a black person or a white person, a Christian or a Jew. You are much more than any of that. Yet if you identify with these roles, you will not discover the essence within you that goes beyond them. Nor will you find a way to transcend the inevitable division these external definitions will create in your life.

I have asked you to leave home so that you could one day return knowing what "home" really is. I have asked you to go on a pilgrimage in which you shed your external identity so that you can discover what your true identity is. I have asked you to listen to others with respect, but never to accept their ideas and opinions as an authority in your life. I have asked you to find that authority within, even though no one else in your life agrees with it, and I have asked you to follow that inner authority even in the face of outright criticism from your friends, your family, your church, your race, your political party, and your country.

I have asked you to stand alone, not because I wish to isolate you, but so you can know the truth and anchor in it. For there will be times when you will have to stand in that truth in the midst of a crowd of people who would ignore it, condemning their brothers and sisters, as they once condemned me. There will be times, my friend, when you will be the voice in the wilderness that helps people find their way back home. And you could not become that voice if you did not learn to stand naked and alone with the truth.

When you know how to stand alone, it is easy to stand with others who uphold their own truth. You aren't threatened by what they believe or what their experience is. You honor all that. You honor every authentic path to divine wisdom and love. And you take great delight in being with people who are comfortable being themselves.

# LETTING GO

*When ties bind, you have no choice but to give them up.*

Most external changes follow on internal shifts of allegiance and attention. When one ceases to be committed to a relationship or a course of action, a shift takes place. Energy is withdrawn from one direction and placed in a new direction.

You can argue until you are blue in the face about whether it is right or wrong that someone's commitment changes, but it won't do you any good. You cannot prevent other people from going forward in their growth, even if you don't agree with their decisions.

Don't play the role of martyr. If you look deeply enough, you will see that every apparent "loss" you experience brings an unexpected gain. When one person leaves a relationship that is not growing into deeper intimacy, the other person is set free too. But s/he must be willing to let go to appreciate the gift of freedom which has been offered.

Wanting someone who doesn't want you is a way of punishing yourself. After a while, you will get tired of your masochism and realize that you have other choices about where to put your energy.

When you cease to be committed to your career, it falls apart. When you stop being committed to your relationship, it begins to crumble. It is no longer as nurturing, as supportive, as fun as it used to be. You can blame this change on your partner or your boss, but you will be missing the whole point. The relationship or the career no longer works because you are no longer giving it your love, your support, your commitment.

Neither holding onto the other person nor blaming him or her will help you get on with your life. If you don't want to live your life in the shadow of a ruptured union, where negative emotions are constantly recycled, you must learn to let go.

Perhaps the greatest gift that you can ever give to yourself is to set someone or something you love free. Staying in a relationship which does not have the full commitment of both people is not constructive for either person. Either mutual commitment must be re-established or the process of letting go must begin in earnest.

When something in your life is not working, you often try first to fix it. Then, if that doesn't work, you may pretend for a while that it's fixed even though you know it isn't. Finally, you realize that your playacting isn't fooling anyone and that your heart just isn't in it. That's when you are ready to let go.

As long as you hold onto a role or relationship that has served its purpose in your life, you will be holding yourself hostage to the past. Letting go is an act of courage. There is always some degree of pain in the release of someone or something that once brought you joy and happiness. You will have to be patient and mourn the loss. But when your mourning is over, you will arise as a new person. You will open to opportunities you never could have dreamed of. As you explore these new opportunities, you will step back into your life with confidence and faith. Your life will be renewed and you will be reborn as the phoenix is from the ashes of the past.

The fire of change is never easy to weather. But if you surrender, the conflagration is quickly over. In the enriched soil, the seeds of tomorrow can be sown.

I have told you that unless you die and be reborn you cannot enter the kingdom of heaven. No one comes here to Earth without suffering the pain of loss. Every identity you assume will be taken from you when it is time. Every person you love will die. It is just a matter of time. And it is just a matter of time before you too leave your body and the world behind.

All sacred teachings exhort you not to be attached to the things of this world, because they are not permanent. Yet you get attached nonetheless. That is part of the process of your awakening. Getting attached and letting go. Embracing and releasing. Personally, I don't think it is necessary to avoid attachments. But it is essential to realize when they become dysfunctional. When certain ties bind, you have no choice but to give them up. Learning to let go is one of the great lessons of this embodiment.

With letting go comes a new freedom for you. That is what it means to be born again.

You will experience many small deaths in the course of your life, many times when you must let go of the arms that once comforted you and walk alone into the uncertain future. Every time you do so your fears will rise up and you will have to walk through them. Often, you will believe that if you let go you will die, but you will find out otherwise. When you let go of what no longer works, you are guided to what does.

Don't be impatient. No one is reborn instantaneously. It takes time. It is a process. Just know that the more that you surrender, the easier it will be for you.

The tide goes out and comes back in. People let go of one attachment only to form another one which challenges them more. Life is rhythmic, but progressive. As earth and water breathe together, the shape of the beach changes. Storms come and go.

In the end, a profound peace comes and pervades the heart and mind. Finally, the ground of being is reached. Here the changing waters come and go, and the earth delights in them as a lover delights in the playful touch of his beloved.

A deep acceptance is felt and, with it, a quiet recognition that all things are perfect as they are. This is grace, the presence of God come to dwell in your heart and in your life.

## CHANGE AND THE CHANGELESS

*Human nature may be different, but divine nature is the same.*

Although some things change, other things never do. Thoughts change, emotions change, houses and jobs change, bodies change, the world changes. But the core of you does not change.

On the surface, each one of you looks different. Differences in physical appearance, personality, temperament, culture, religion, national heritage, all contribute to your uniqueness. As long as individuals respect one another, the diversity created by individual uniqueness is a positive phenomenon.

Growth too is a unique proposition. People grow in different ways. Experience teaches some people to be more assertive and others to be less. Some people grow to become more gregarious; others learn how to be happy alone.

But everyone who is here needs to breathe air, to eat, to drink water. Every person needs acceptance and love to flower. When people are nurtured physically, emotionally, intellectually and spiritually, they are happy and joyful. For this is their natural condition.

When you learn to accept yourself and others just as you are in the present moment, you live in your natural state. You move with life as it unfolds, accepting and working with what is.

Tao flowers in you. You dwell in the universal heart-mind. When you look at two people who live in this place, you know them to be the same, even though they look different. The same light shines in their eyes, even though one has brown eyes and the other green. Both have an easy and relaxed smile, and you feel equally safe being in their presence.

Human nature may be different, but divine nature is the same. When divine nature and human nature blend together in a person's heart/mind, you have all of the strengths of the individual's authentic gifts and temperament without the insecurity, anxiety, and divisiveness of ego consciousness. Each person can be unique without threatening or undermining the uniqueness of anyone else.

This blending of the personal and universal reflects psychological integration and interpersonal harmony. It demonstrates congruence within and without.

All human beings have the potential to dwell in this state of peace and happiness. To do so they simply have to shed the ego-identifications which reinforce their judgments and create discord and struggle with other people.

In this state of consciousness, that which changes and that which does not change come together. Individual differences survive without being divisive. Yet when one is asked to surrender the personal wants and needs, it is not difficult.

That which changes arises out of the changeless and returns to it. You cannot imagine the point of origin or the point of return, but you have known moments in your life free of self-consciousness or fear, moments when you felt connected to everyone and everything without trying.

The closer you get to this state when you are in the body, the less you fear the moment of death. For you have brought the universal into the personal, the divine into the human, the unconditional into the conditional. When the body/mind container is filled by Spirit, it expands and breaks apart so that the energy can go where it is most needed.

When your personal journey comes to fruition, your impersonal journey begins. The Divine Presence in which you have your being decides what you will do and where you will go. You are here to love and to serve. You do not need to ask who, where, why or how. Those questions cease to be relevant when you no longer live for yourself alone.

## CHAPTER TWENTY-FIVE

# Re-Union

*Christ Consciousness has one thought, one agenda,*
*one will, one love for all beings.*

Imagine living with another person without trying to change him or her in any way. Imagine that your only calling is to accept where that person is, at any time, and to accept where you are in that same moment. Imagine not having to put pressure on others to meet your needs or expectations and knowing that others will not put pressure on you.

Imagine that your relationship with your partner is a continual dance in which moving in a complementary way is the only goal. Each one of you is constantly making little adjustments so that you can stay together in a comfortable way. None of these adjustments takes much thought. It is just what you do when you are dancing.

Imagine a dance in which each person takes turns leading. Sometimes one person feels the music more deeply than the other and takes the lead. Another time the other person is more tuned in and leads the way. This happens by itself, out of the mutual regard and attunement of the partners, not because of some prearranged agreement about "equal time."

Imagine having a "we" awareness, where you once had an "I" awareness, being as devoted to your partner's comfort, pleasure, and well-being as you are to your own. Imagine understanding that any disconnection with your partner is a disconnection with self.

Your unconditional love and acceptance of your partner is your best and easiest pathway to God-communion. With your partner, you learn to be both lover and beloved. You learn to give and receive unconditional love and acceptance.

When you have learned to do this with one person, you become capable of doing it with others. One becomes many and many become one. Christ consciousness is established in your heart and mind and no one can be excluded from your love. What you give to one, you give to all. What you receive from one, you receive from all.

The Christ Mind is the end of separate thoughts, separate agendas, separate wills. The Christ Heart is the end of disparate feelings and special love. The Christ Consciousness has one thought, one agenda, one will, one love for all beings.

But none of this will mean anything to you until you learn to love one person as you love yourself. For most of you, this is the doorway you will open to the divine.

So choose your partner well. If you choose one who dances too slowly, you may be held back. If you choose one who dances too fast, you may break your ankle trying to keep up.

Find a partner who dances at the same speed that you do, one you can empower and assist, one who will complement you and help you realize your potential. That is the purpose of a spiritual relationship.

## LETTING YOUR PARTNER BE

*Relationships are a two-edged sword.*

By now it should be clear to you that it is in your relationships that you learn and grow the most. Yet relationships are a two-edged sword. They promise bliss, yet bring up the most primitive emotions. They promise companionship, yet challenge you to deal with seemingly irreconcilable differences. They promise an end to loneliness, yet open the door to a deeper aloneness.

You may think of a relationship as a pill you take to bring you relief from boredom or loneliness. But all pills have side effects. For every high you experience, there is a corresponding low.

If you want to avoid the low moments, you should avoid having intimate relationships. Unfortunately, if you do this, you will avoid your own psychological and spiritual growth. That growth comes from experiencing the highs and the lows of relationship and every-thing in between. It comes from experiencing all aspects of the other person, just as you must experience all aspects of yourself.

For a while, it may seem that you lose yourself in the other person. But this happens only in the early phases of a relationship. When you live with a person, it doesn't take long for everything that is there to come out on the table.

When that happens, you need every skill you have to prevent the relationship from self-destructing. When your partner's fears and insecurities come to the surface in the relationship, you can either react with your own fears and insecurities, or you can find a way to bring understanding and compassion.

That sounds easy enough, but it is very difficult to do. To let your partner be when s/he is experiencing fear, doubt, ambivalence, victimhood, or anxiety about the future is a tremendous challenge. You must detach from what is being said so that you don't react to it or take it personally. Yet, at the same time, you must keep your heart open, and stay emotionally present. Instead of engaging with your partner's fear and negativity, you must look beyond the specific words that are being said and realize that s/he is just asking for your love and reassurance. If you give that, and ignore the rest, you can help bring him/her back on track.

Giving your partner space when s/he is determined to stay in a space of victimhood, blame and self-pity is as important as giving praise, encouragement and affection when s/he can receive it. What you don't say or do is as important to the health of your relationship as what you do say or do.

The two most important rules of thumb are:

1.  Don't try to fix your partner, even if you think s/he wants you to.

2.  Don't feel responsible for your partner's sadness, fear, or anger. When your partner is unhappy, lovingly detach and let her be.

Don't engage. Don't try to fix. Don't feel responsible. Just let her be and know that s/he will find a way to reconnect with herself and ultimately with you.

## MIRROR OF INNOCENCE

*You must be willing to be occupied and cleansed
by something greater than yourself.*

When the snow falls, it covers ground, plants, trees, houses and roads with a white mantle. Everything looks fresh, new, innocent. Forgiveness comes in the same way, undoing the grievances of the past, replacing judgments with acceptance. In the light of forgiveness, you see your problems and challenges differently. You feel capable of meeting your life just the way it is.

Forgiveness is as far-reaching as a snow. It reaches out and touches everything in your life. For forgiveness to bless you, you must be willing to receive it, as the ground receives the snowfall. You must be willing to be occupied and cleansed by something greater than yourself.

In every successful relationship, forgiveness is an ongoing practice. It is a daily, weekly, monthly cleansing. Without forgiveness, there can be no communion between you and your partner. Instead, old wounds will be aggravated by hidden resentments.

This will not do. Negative thoughts and feeling states must be cleared on no less than a daily basis. Do not go to sleep angry at each other. Do not let the sun rise or set without making peace with each other. The sacredness of your union must be nurtured and celebrated. Give it the time it deserves. Be ready to let go of thoughts and feelings that can only injure and separate.

In your dance together, find a way to soften and come together when you feel angry and apart. Find a way to let your armor dissolve as you look in silence into each other's eyes.

Your partner is not your enemy, although s/he sometimes seems to be. The separation you feel from one another is a function of your mutual fear. Come to each other as equals and admit your fear.

Surrender your need to be right or to make your partner wrong. You are both right in your desire to be loved and respected by your partner. You are both wrong in your attempt to blame the other person for your unhappiness.

Relationship is a dance in a theater of wounds. As hard as you try to avoid hurting others, someone is always crying out in pain. Sometimes, an apology is necessary. But most of the time it is clear that one person's pain is triggered by someone else's. It's no one's fault. That's just the way it is.

After you have danced enough, you no longer take the drama so personally. You just get better at dancing out of your pain toward your joy. When you do that, the whole atmosphere on stage changes.

To some, the earthly journey seems to be an arduous trek through a veil of tears. But even to these travelers, there are moments when the sun comes out and rainbows arch across the sky, moments when the pain slips away and the heart is filled with unexpected joy.

Even when the dance is difficult, you feel grateful for the opportunity to participate and to learn. Life is essentially dignified.

It is true that you sometimes resist learning your lessons. But learn them you do. You move onward and upward and, as you do, matter and mind become imbued with Spirit. Once identified with a specific mindset and a specific body, you are eventually set free to love without conditions and to receive the love that is offered you without resisting or defending.

That is the nature of your journey here. It is a good journey. May you take the time to appreciate and enjoy it. May you open your eyes and see the sun peeking through the clouds. May you see the light reflected by the snow-covered ground and the white boughs of the pine trees. Light sparkling in all directions, embracing all of you, right here, right now.

*Namaste.*

# BOOK 4

# Return to the Garden

*God knew you would find the light in the darkness
and that it would guide you back home.*

CHAPTER TWENTY-SIX

# The Life of the Witness

*There is no way, no truth, no life, except through you.*

You have heard me say that "I am the way, the truth and the life." That statement is equally true for you. The truth, the path to the divine, the life of the witness runs through your heart. There is no way, no truth, no life, except through you.

Please understand this. It is the core of my realization and my teaching. God does not exist apart from you. God is the essence of your being. S/he is the essence of all beings. God dwells within your heart and within the hearts of all beings.

It is not necessary to seek God, because God is already the essence of who you are. To connect with God, simply remove all that separates you from your own essence. Remove all judgments and thoughts that do not bless you and others. These are not your essence. They are false ideas that you carry around. They are the veil, the illusion that appears to separate you from your own heart and the heart of God. Remove the illusions, lift the veil, and you will rest in the heart. Rest in the heart, and God will abide with you.

## OPEN HEART AND MIND

*Becoming aware of your fear is essential*
*if you wish to reconnect to love.*

When you are judging another or yourself, neither your mind nor your heart is open. When you are complaining, blaming, holding grievances, pushing love away or finding fault with your experience, you are contracted in heart and mind. Behind this contraction is a simple fear that you are unworthy.

Becoming aware of your fear is essential if you wish to reconnect to love. You cannot open your heart or your mind as long as your fear remains unconscious. You must bring your fear into conscious awareness.

When you see the fear that underlies your judgments and your attack thoughts, just let it be. Don't beat yourself up for having these thoughts or push the fear away. Just be with the fear and know that it is okay that you are afraid. Tell yourself "I know I'm scared and feeling unworthy. That's why I'm blaming others or finding fault with my life."

Gently take the responsibility away from others: "It's not anyone else's fault that I don't feel good enough. I don't have to project my fear and unworthiness onto someone else. I can look at my fear directly and see that I need to bring some love and acceptance to myself. I can be with my fear in a compassionate way."

When you are able to hold your fear in a compassionate way, you reconnect to your heart. You open your mind. You feel energy as you release others from blame and open to your own love. Your consciousness expands. You stop seeing your situation in a limited way.

Love is the essence of who you are. Everything else that you think or feel about yourself or anyone else is just an illusion. Illusions are born when you stop loving yourself or another. The only way to dissolve illusions is to start loving right now in this moment.

If you want to reconnect with God, love yourself. Love the person who is in front of you. Be compassionate with yourself and with others.

## THE FRIEND

*God and the Friend are always one.*

The friend is always there. You have merely to call on him or her.

The friend is the Christ within you. It doesn't matter what you call him or her. The friend is the one who has your greatest good at heart. The friend is the one who also has the greatest good of others at heart.

The friend is the one who is free of judgment, the one who accepts you and everyone else unconditionally. This friend is within every mind and heart. S/he embodies essence. S/he is the voice of God in your experience.

Some people call the friend Christ. Some call the friend Buddha, Krishna, or Ram. Names do not matter. The friend is the embodiment of love. S/he has many names and faces.

God and the friend are always one. When you approach the friend within, God hears your footsteps.

## IN THE BEGINNING

*In every form born of love, the spark of love inheres.*

In the beginning was God, Original Presence, Indivisible and Boundless Love. In the act of Creation, God expressed Its essence in many different ways. Thus, Love became embodied. Out of oneness came diversity.

In every form born of love, the spark of love inheres. In each of the ten thousand things, the original essence remains. Thus, within your heart and mind right now is the original spark of Creation. It belongs to you and can never leave you. No matter where your life takes you, no matter how far you stray from the path, you cannot extinguish the spark of divinity within your own consciousness. It was and is God's gift to you.

You can forget about the gift but you cannot give it back. You can ignore or deny it, but you cannot un-create it. The deeper the darkness through which you walk, the brighter the tiny spark becomes.

It calls to you like a beacon reminding you of your essence and your place of origin.

When you acknowledge the spark and nurture it, the light within you grows. The more attention you give to it, the more the light within you expands. Soon it seems that your whole being is surrounded by light. Even total strangers feel the rays of your love touching them.

You enter the spiritual path when you acknowledge the spark within and begin to attend to it. That is the moment when you stop being a victim and begin to take full responsibility for your life. The spiritual path culminates when you fully realize your God nature and that of all the other beings around you. Then you too become the Friend, the Christ, the Buddha, the compassionate one.

## ATTENDING TO THE SPARK

*To see the truth, you must lift the veil.*

The spark can be detected only when you are looking for it. It requires a conscious effort. If you live your life reactively, you never notice the spark. You see only the darkness.

To see the spark, you must come to understand that you are not defined by what happens outside of you. Although you have to deal with what happens, you are always free to respond to it creatively. To respond creatively means to choose from a position of strength, from an awareness that you have a number of options.

You cannot respond creatively if you feel attacked by life. When you feel attacked, you respond reactively and defensively. Victims see very few options, nor do they act from a position of strength.

When you are in touch with the light within, everything that you do is done out of the consciousness of that light. Your actions are empowered by the understanding that the love and the wisdom of God abide within you. You know that you cannot be forsaken by God, regardless of how external reality appears to you.

To be sure, your fear can be triggered. You can forget the light within and see only the darkness before you. You can feel attacked or rejected by others. You can even feel attacked or rejected by God.

But all this happens because you look away from the light, instead of toward it.

When you look outside for proof that God loves you, you find a mixed bag. Sometimes God seems to favor you and sometimes God seems to have forgotten you exist. But remember, when you look outside, you don't find God, because God isn't out there. God is within. God isn't in how life appears. That's just the veil. To see the truth, you must lift the veil.

God is in the truth of who you are. God isn't the temporal, the changing, the inconstant. God is the eternal, the unchanging, the constant, because God is love and never stops being love.

But if you aren't looking within, you can live your whole life and never know that God exists. You can think that life gave you a raw deal. You can be bitter, resentful, and angry. There's nothing to be done about this if you insist on looking outside of yourself for validation or approval.

An about-face is necessary. You must turn to the place where God abides. You must look into your own heart. You must find the place in you which is unconditionally aligned with love.

You can't do this while you are blaming others or holding onto grievances. That is still looking without. Nor can you do it when you are feeling guilty and beating yourself up for making mistakes. That is just taking the veil and putting it on the other side. You must take the veil down completely. All judgment of self and other must go. All apparent "knowledge" must be surrendered. You must come to God empty, with open arms. To rest in the heart, you cannot bring your judgments, your interpretations, or your fixed ideas. They must be left at the threshold. When you enter the heart you must enter with openness and trust.

You can enter the heart only if you are willing to walk in forgiveness with yourself and others, even if that willingness seems only to be in the moment. That is all God needs anyway . . . just a moment of your time and attention . . . just a moment when you drop your defenses and open to the presence of love. It does not matter that you have judged in the past or may judge in the future. All that matters is that right now you are willing to lay your judgments down.

## BURNING BUSH/BOTTOMLESS WELL

*Your heart is the place where love is born.*

When you know that the Source of Love lies within you, you can leave your worries behind and enter the sanctuary for rest and renewal. Your heart is the place where love is born. It is the bottomless well from which you can draw as often as you need to. Every time you come to the well, you drink the waters of life. Your spiritual thirst is quenched. Your sins are forgiven. You are baptized, healed and renewed.

Whenever life shows up differently from the way you expect it to, whenever the problems of life seem to overwhelm you, there is only one place that offers you sanctuary. You must learn to make your pilgrimage there on a regular basis.

Don't look outside of yourself for answers. Don't seek refuge in the ideas, opinions and advice of other people. Don't go into your head and try to figure things out. Surrender all of that, and seek the place where love begins, in your own heart. It is your responsibility to reconnect with the Source of love when you need to. No one else can do it for you.

It doesn't matter what spiritual practice you do as long as it takes you into your heart and helps you connect with the Source of Love. If it does that, then stay with it throughout all the twists and turns of your life. Hold to your practice. It is your lifeline. When storms come up unexpectedly, it keeps you afloat. Ever so gradually, it brings you home.

When the spark in your heart is attended to, it grows into a steady flame. When the flame is fed by acts of loving kindness to self and others, it becomes a blazing fire, a source of warmth and light for all who encounter it. When Moses saw the Burning Bush, he knew that it was God revealing Himself. What he did not know was that Bush was not in the world, but in the heart.

## I AM THE WAY

*To follow me means more than preaching my words.*
*It means following my example.*

I am the way not because I am special but because I have aligned with Love, the essence of my being. You too can align with Love. I ask you to look to my example, not because I want you to worship me or put me on a pedestal, but because I want you to understand what is possible for you. I am the mentor, the model. I not only speak the truth; I also embody It.

When I said "I am the Way," I wanted you to see how the word became flesh, how what I taught was demonstrated in my life. I wanted you to realize that I offered you a living teaching, not just a set of abstract beliefs. I wanted you to know that to follow me means more than preaching my words. It means following my example.

There is nothing special about who I am or what I have done. If you insist on calling me "Lord," do not do so out of envy or littleness, but out of the awareness that this same "Lord" you see in me is within you. If you call me Rabbi, do so because you see the light which is in you made manifest in my presence. Power is not separately vested in me or in you, but it abides in what we experience together when our hearts are open.

## LOVE YOUR NEIGHBOR AS YOURSELF

*You cannot advance your life by hurting another,*
*nor can you help another by hurting yourself.*

I have asked you to see me as a brother, because I am your absolute equal. I have asked you to see one another as brothers and sisters for the same reason.

As soon as there is the slightest perception of inequality between any of you, you have left your hearts. You have abandoned the truth.

Do not justify your thoughts or actions of separation, but acknowledge that you are not in your right mind, and return to the consciousness of equality, acceptance and inclusion. I have told you many times that your good and that of your brother or sister are one and the same. You cannot advance your life by hurting another, nor can you help another by hurting yourself. All attempts to break this simple equation lead to suffering and despair.

If you wish to prosper, love your neighbor. Care for her happiness in the same way that you would care for your own. For in honoring her, you honor the divine in yourself and so strengthen your love and your faith.

## LOVE EVEN YOUR ENEMY

*You cannot love me and hate them.*

Even those who oppose you deserve your love and your blessings. They are your absolute equals too. You cannot love me and hate them. If you hate them, then you offer me the same hatred.

There is no brother or sister who is unworthy of my love. If there were one such, then my awakening would not be complete. That is why I have told you that there are no exceptions to the law of equality. If you would condemn any one of my brothers or sisters or withhold your love from them, then you are not following my teaching or my example.

## TURN THE OTHER CHEEK

*Every attack is a call for love.*

I have advised you that if someone injures you, you should not attack back, but instead turn the other cheek. Turning the other cheek does not mean that you condone the attack or that you are inviting the other person to attack you again. Quite the contrary, by turning the other cheek, you are inviting your brother or sister to make a different choice.

When you understand that every attack is a call for love, you begin to realize that your response to attack can totally transform it. Someone attacks you out of fear and unworthiness, and you respond with the love you know that person needs. That offers the person a choice s/he did not know s/he had before.

The reality is that people will attack you and you will attack them. And it will be for the same reason. Neither one of you feels worthy of love and you mistakenly think that the other person is blocking your access to the love you want.

Ironically, the other person is the doorway to the love that you want. Your enemy is your ally in disguise. If you offer your enemy love, you will make peace with yourself.

When someone responds to your attack with acceptance, compassion and love, how can you attack them again? When they refuse to take offense, and just ask you to see who they really are, how can you refuse to see?

All attack happens because you dehumanize the object of your attack. You make that person "less than" you. In this way, you justify your attack. But the justification is always false because it violates the law of equality. You are never justified in attacking anyone.

While you may refuse to condone a person's actions toward you, do not cast that person out of your heart. Offer him the love and the respect that will inspire him to engage in caring, responsible actions in the future. Give him an opportunity to make a different choice.

To turn the other cheek does not mean that you refuse to stand up against injustice. Quite the contrary. I encourage you to oppose injustice wherever you encounter it. Take issue with actions that are uncaring, hurtful, disrespectful to yourself or others, but do so in a loving way. Do so in a way that respects the people whose actions you oppose. For they are your brothers and sisters too.

Your proper attitude toward all people should be one of mutual respect. However much you might take issue with others, they remain your equals. Their opinions, beliefs, values, likes or dislikes are as important as your own. Offer respect and ask for it in return. It is your birthright.

## INNOCENCE AND GUILT

*It is always easier to see your enemy outside
than to confront the enemy within.*

The part of you that condemns another person is the part of you that feels unworthy. If you felt worthy, you would not judge or attack others. You would see the pain that underlies their hostility and feel compassion for them.

When you are established in your own innocence, you know that no one, no matter how terribly they act toward you, can take your worthiness away. You know in the depths of your being that you are lovable. Nothing happening outside of you can challenge that internal conviction. That is why I could look on my crucifiers with compassion. When I said "Forgive them, Father, for they know not what they do," it was the absolute truth. They did not know.

The executioner sees the unworthiness of his victim, but he cannot see his own unworthiness, for to see it would undermine his ego structure, his false strength, his fearful compact with the crowd. To see his own unworthiness would take him into the depths of despair. Is it any wonder that most people turn away from the confrontation with the shadow within and instead project it onto others?

It is always easier to blame or attack others than it is to acknowledge your own fears and mistakes. It is always easier to see your enemy outside than to confront the enemy within. To acknowledge the disowned aspects of self and bring them into conscious awareness, to accept and love the parts of yourself that you judge, hate or feel guilty about is a far more challenging task.

Yet the truth is that you don't begin to walk the spiritual path until you are willing to take responsibility for bringing healing and wholeness to your own psyche. Spirituality happens from the inside out. It happens as you learn to love and accept yourself at deeper and deeper levels of being.

As long as you are trying to change or fix something outside of yourself, you continue to hide your pain and guilt. Your professed spiritual beliefs are like a band-aid covering a festering wound. It is only a matter of time before the wound must be addressed.

## BORN AGAIN IN GRACE

*Grace happens when you accept.*
*Struggle happens when you reject or try to fix.*

You begin the path of ascension when you hit bottom and come face to face with the depth of your self-judgment and fear. You take your first few steps on the way to wholeness when you stop acting like a victim and blaming others for your pain, when you know that your healing has very little to do with anyone else; it's mainly about your relationship with yourself.

You begin to surrender to love when you become willing to feel your pain and move through it. You become vulnerable, accessible, willing to be present and feel whatever you are feeling. Your heart begins to open.

To be reborn in spirit means that you finally know without any doubt that your responsibility is to love and honor yourself and others. You commit to love and forgiveness not just as ideas, but as a way of life. You agree to treat others as equals, to hold their good equally with your own.

To be born again means that you understand that God has never abandoned you. You simply turned away from God in your pain, your fear, your guilt and your feelings of unworthiness. In a real sense, you abandoned yourself.

In your fall from Grace, you forsake the light within. You create yourself in your own image, instead of understanding how you are a reflection of the Divine. You rely on your ego structure to meet your perceived needs and, without the inner light guiding you, you experience life as hardship and struggle. Even easy tasks become difficult.

Grace does not come from without but from within. It comes through your inner alignment with Spirit. When you are in constant dialogue with all parts of yourself, you learn to honor yourself more completely. You do not commit to activities about which you are ambivalent or have misgivings. You learn to listen to yourself more deeply, so that you can act with integrity.

Because you wait for integration and clarity within, your outer actions create harmony, instead of conflict. Your life slows down and becomes more spacious. You are less anxious and pressured. You do less, but what you do is far more effective than what you did before when you were under pressure to decide before you were ready.

By honoring yourself, you also honor others. You don't give mixed messages. You don't make promises you are unable to keep.

None of this would be possible if you had been unwilling to face your fears. Grace cannot come from the denial of the shadow side. It can't come from resisting life or pushing away parts of yourself that you don't want to face. Grace comes from the integration of dark and light, from the inner marriage of male and female, heart and mind, wounded child and spiritual adult.

Grace is the movement from inner wholeness to outer wholeness. Sin is the movement from inner conflict to outer conflict. When the spiritual adult aligns with the wounded child, sins are forgiven and karmic conditions are dissolved.

All healing happens thus: As illusions are surrendered, truth appears. As separation is relinquished, the original unity emerges unchanged. When you stop pretending to be who you are not, who you are can be clearly seen.

The second birth is the letting go of all that is false (persona) so that your true spiritual identity can be experienced. It is the letting go of your prejudice and conditioning so that which is unbiased and unconditional can be welcomed into your life.

Grace happens when you abide with what is. Struggle happens when you push what is away or try to bring something else in. Grace happens when you accept. Struggle happens when you reject or try to fix. Grace is natural. Struggle is unnatural. Grace is effortless. Struggle is arduous.

Grace means acting "with" God. Struggle means acting "without" God. You have tried it both ways and you have seen the results of each way demonstrated. There is no question which way feels the best. Yet you keep mistaking one way for the other. You keep mistaking the voice of ego for the voice of Spirit. You keep getting in the way.

When you get in the way, you suffer. You know that you are not in your right place. That is when you must acknowledge your mistake and move out of the way. Doing so removes the ego blockage within consciousness and restores the flow of grace in your life. Then, you become an instrument for the Divine Will.

## CHAPTER TWENTY-SEVEN

# Learning to Bless

*When your intention is to bless, you cannot hold onto the past.*

It is the intention that you hold that really matters. Do you intend to bless or to curse, to accept or to find fault?

Every moment is new. It doesn't matter what happened yesterday or last year. Right now you have a new choice to make. Is your intention to bless or to curse? Are you holding onto your grievances? Have you released the past?

When your intention is to bless, you cannot hold onto the past. You must let it go. If you have closed your heart or your mind, you cannot bless. You can only judge, blame, complain or condemn.

And if you want to judge, just be aware of it. Just be aware: "I am still carrying a past hurt, a past wound. I am not ready to bless." Realize that whatever you say or do in this moment will be a judgment or attack. In this moment, all you can do is be with your fear, your hurt, your anger, your judgment.

That's the truth of what's happening and there's no harm done. There's no harm when you refrain from speaking or acting when you are upset. There is just the experience of being present for yourself in your pain and feelings of separation.

When you can be with yourself in this way, you bring love in. The more love you bring in, the more you begin to accept and to bless yourself and your experience.

Whose job is it to weather these moments of separation when you feel cut off from others or from God? Is it not your job? How can you make it anyone else's responsibility?

So you ask: "Do I intend to bless or to curse?" and you become aware of your intention. And if your intention is to bless, then you know that your words and actions will be helpful. And if your intention is not to bless, then you know that nothing you say or do can be helpful now.

Your spiritual goal is to know that everything you think, feel or do is coming from love. If it is coming from love, you will be an instrument of love and understanding in the world. If it is not coming from love, then you will be sowing seeds of strife.

When you are at peace, you do not create conflict. You extend peace. When you are clear, you do not create confusion. You extend clarity.

Whatever is within you will be expressed outside of you. This is the law of manifestation. If you want different outer results, you must take care of what you harvest within.

Negative conditions do not arise when you dwell in silent awareness of your own inner states. You take responsibility for the contents of your own consciousness. You do not project your discomfort onto others.

When someone else projects onto you, blaming you for their pain or discomfort, you must take care not to react to their accusations. They are not in their right mind. If you react, you too will not be in your right mind.

Listen with compassion to another person's cry for attention and for love. When you listen with compassion, you won't feel attacked, even though you know the other person is trying to blame you. You will just tune into how much pain the person feels and how difficult it is for him or her to face that pain.

Don't accept the blame another person places at your feet, but don't try to defend yourself either. The person is simply mistaken about you. You know that. And so you can stand lovingly in the truth of who you are.

When you are aligned with love, you can listen without judgment to other people. You can empathize with their pain and encourage them to value themselves. Because you don't take offense when people inappropriately blame you, you refuse to be a target for their projections. You don't engage their pain with your pain, their anger with your anger, or their unworthiness with your own. You mirror back to them their innocence by refusing to make anyone guilty.

By speaking and acting only when you are able to bless, you stand free of the painful drama of mutual trespass and betrayal. Waves of illusion wash over you, but you stand simply and firmly in the truth of who you are.

## HOLDING ON TO THE LOVE

*The challenge is to let the form go, but hold onto the love.*

You come into relationship to one another in different ways: as children, parents, siblings, friends, workmates, teachers, students. What is important is not the form of the relationship, but the love that abides within the form.

Relationships constantly change form. Children grow up and become parents, parents surrender their bodies to the next adventure, friends move apart, lovers break up, and so it goes. No form remains the same.

Growth must continue. Forms must come and go. That is the bittersweet quality of life. If you become attached to the form or throw away the love just because the form is changing, you will suffer unnecessarily. The challenge is to let the form go, but hold onto the love.

To love another is a spiritual act. It is an unconditional gesture. When you love someone now, there is no limit placed on that love. It is timeless and eternal. Real love continues to be itself. If it is here now, it will be here always. It does not change. The form that love takes will change, but love itself will not change. It will simply find a new form for expression.

Too often you deny the love you have for one another when the form changes. That is just another kind of attachment to form. It says: "I must have love in this particular way or I do not want it at all." That is childish. When you grow up, you realize that you can't always have things exactly the way you want them, especially when other people are involved.

When one person no longer wants to keep an agreement, the agreement is off. You can't hold another person against his or her will. If you try to do so, you will push love away. Love survives the ending of agreements, if you will allow it to.

Love and freedom go hand in hand. Love cannot be contained in a specific form. It must break free of all forms, all conditions, if it is to become itself fully. Resisting this organic process just creates separation.

Grant to the other person the freedom to be who s/he is and the form will take care of itself. Try to take away that freedom and the form will become a prison for both of you.

True relationship happens only among people who regard each other as equals. It happens only among those who honor and respect one another. It happens only when people are present for each other right now.

If love is present now, then you need take no thought for the future. You need to think about the future only when you aren't fully present right now.

When love is lacking, then you want guarantees about love. When love is here, guarantees are not necessary.

Everything comes into being right now. The alpha and omega of existence are present in this moment. There will never be more love than is possible here and now.

The greatest love that you can attain is attainable right now. It cannot be experienced in the past and future.

The attachment to form is about the past or the future. It is never about now. When love is present now, form is irrelevant. If you love someone now, it does not matter what s/he looks like, what s/he is saying, or how s/he acts. It just matters that you love her and accept her. And if s/he feels your love and acceptance, then s/he has the freedom to be herself in that moment.

When you hold onto the love, you become its embodiment. Forms may change, but you continue to love each another through all those changes.

Love and freedom are inseparable. If there is love, there must be the freedom to choose a form that works for both people. And to do that you must hold onto your love for one another and let the form go when it no longer serves your highest good.

This takes courage. It takes heart. It takes patience. But that is the nature of love. And those who love each other through all the conditions, all the ups and downs of life, are patient and courageous beyond measure.

## FACING YOUR FEARS

*You too have your time in the desert*
*when you must face your fears and doubts.*

When events and circumstances trigger the wounds of the past, it is easy to feel overwhelmed. But if you are going to grow, your past must come up for healing.

Share what is coming up for you with others, but don't try to make them responsible for it. Your anxiety and pain is not caused by other people. It is a condition of your own consciousness. Take responsibility for what belongs to you. Own it, look at it, and let it go. Let the fears of the past be resolved in the present.

Once you face your fear, it diminishes. It may even go away. If it comes up again, listen to it as a parent listens to a scared child. Be compassionate with that child but clear that her fears are without substance. This comforts the child and she feels safe.

When I was in the desert for forty days, I experienced every voice of fear you can imagine. These were not devils outside of me that had come to tempt me. They were voices in my own mind that caused me to doubt myself or others.

You too have your time in the desert when you must face your fears and doubts. This time of inner testing always precedes the revelation and acceptance of your life purpose. For if you cannot move through your own fears, how can you begin to deal with the fears of others when they project them onto you?

If you are not whole and strong in yourself, how can you be

a beacon of love and light for others? The kind of strength and integration I am talking about here is not to be taken lightly. Can you meet your devils and learn to love them? Can you listen to the scared voices within your mind and reassure them? Can you affirm that you are worthy in the midst of a steady stream of doubts about your worthiness? Can you love when fear comes up?

These are the critical questions. Before you begin your life work, these questions must be answered. You must enter the darkness of your own psyche carrying the light of awareness. Every fear which undermines your self-esteem must be faced. Unless you are strong enough to face your fears and hold them compassionately, you cannot take your appointed place in the scheme of things.

Don't be surprised if your commitment to self is tested when your life purpose is revealed to you. Do not take this as a sign that something is wrong. Nothing is wrong. It is simply time to demonstrate that you are ready. While it may seem that you are trying to convince someone outside yourself, this is not true. You are proving everything to yourself. You are the only one who needs to be convinced.

When you know without a doubt that you are worthy, when you are willing to trust yourself completely, then your purpose on this planet can unfold. Then you can emerge from the desert, having discovered the oasis, the bottomless well of love and compassion which rests beneath the shifting sands of your fear.

## THE DANCE OF ACCEPTANCE

*The more you accept your life as it is,*
*the easier the dance becomes.*

So much of your life you spend judging yourself and others. Imagine what it would be like to affirm and bless all that you now judge or find wanting.

It is a radical act to accept what happens in your life exactly as it is. When you do that, you stop questioning the validity of your experience.

Your challenge lies in being with your experience or, when you can't be with it, being aware of your resistance, your judgments, your negative interpretations of it. Being aware of the thoughts that separate you from life creates a bridge back to simple acceptance of the moment as it unfolds.

When you see your resistance, you don't judge it. You don't beat yourself up. You just notice your fear without judgment. When you identify fear, it no longer has the ability to run your life.

Acceptance is a lifelong dance. You get better at it the more you do it. But you never dance perfectly. Fear and resistance continue to come up and you do the best you can. Sometimes they slow you down, but slowing down might be exactly what is needed. In the dance of acceptance, unconscious becomes conscious. Your fear becomes your partner.

You dance with the inside and outside situation. You dance with what happens and with what you think and feel about it. The inner and outer dance are going on all the time. There is never a time when you can get off the dance floor and go and take a nap.

The Tao never ceases. Even in stillness there is movement. The stream never stops flowing. If it is not visible on the surface, then it continues underground.

You live in a dynamic universe: always moving and changing. Sometimes you get tired and you want to get off the merry-go-round. "I shall dance no more," you self-righteously proclaim. But then, unexpectedly, you fall in love, or someone makes you a business offer you can't refuse. As soon as you begin to understand that the Emperor has no clothes, his designer shows up with the latest fashions.

No matter how hard you try, you cannot get out of the drama. You can't stop the dance. It goes on with you or without you. That's why your only hope of having a harmonious experience is to learn to move with the flow instead of against it.

When you accept the eternal nature of the dance, it is easier to accept its specific content in the moment. That content may be that you are having a panic attack, yelling at your spouse or kids, drinking too much, or contemplating suicide, but as long as you know that it's part of the dance you can find a way to embrace it.

Even if you trip over someone's toes, you can regain your balance. That's one of the laws of the dance. So you learn to take a deep breath and keep moving. When you lose the rhythm, you listen for a moment to the music and pick it up again.

Mistakes are part of the dance. But some of you don't know this. Your business fails or your partner leaves and you put a bullet in your head. You play for very high stakes. You think the dance is about success or failure, black or white.

In fact, it's about both, constantly. The dance is a dance of the opposites, a play of contradictions. It is paradoxical. It has always been paradoxical.

One of the greatest paradoxes is this one: You can't be in the dance if you are trying to figure it out! If you are always thinking about how to move your feet, you are going to have a very hard time dancing. But if you just move your feet, you will be dancing. You may not be doing the dance someone else is doing, but you will be dancing your dance. And your dance is as good as anyone's.

The greatest act of acceptance is to know that what happens is perfect for you. You are not given more than can you handle, nor is anything lacking in your life. To be sure, you can look at your neighbor's yard and think the grass is greener. Maybe he has a bigger house and a nicer car. But you can't see what that means to him. You can't see if he's happy about his house or his car. You can see only if you are happy about it.

And, if you are not happy about it, then you can be sure you are feeling unworthy and unappreciated. And so that is what you must dance with. When you are not accepting your life as it is, you must dance with your lack of acceptance. You must learn to be with your resistance, your envy, your jealousy in a loving way. And that's quite an extraordinary dance.

The more unhappy you are, the harder the dance becomes, because you must dance with your unhappiness. That's why acceptance is so important as a spiritual practice. The more you accept your life as it is, the easier the dance becomes.

## RULES VS. GUIDANCE

*Those who have the greatest need to tell others what to do have the least faith in themselves.*

Everyone wants rules to live by. But rules are not always helpful. They can too easily be used to persecute others.

The truth is that you do not know what is good for others. Indeed, you often do not know what is good for you. The humility that results from this understanding is essential to living a spiritual life.

Since what you say and do can potentially be hurtful to others, it is better to remain neutral than to speak or act without insight and understanding. Don't wave your holy books in front of people. Don't insist that they live the way you think they should live. If you are concerned about them, love them. Don't try to convert them.

If you have chosen a path, live that path. Demonstrate that you are capable of speaking and acting in a loving, compassionate way. This will get people's attention much more than preaching will.

Your job is not to preach to others, but to find the way to the truth of your heart. You alone know what course of action is best for the fulfillment of your purpose here. But that knowledge is often buried deeply in the heart. Sometimes, it takes a lot of listening to connect with your own wisdom. In some cases, connecting to yourself is not possible until you stop listening to what other people think you should do.

But your responsibility doesn't end here. Once you have heard the voice of your heart, you still have to listen to it. You still have to act in a manner consistent with it. And that might mean taking some risks. It might mean shifting your priorities.

Your inner wisdom will not keep you in a rut. It will bring out the tow truck so you can stop spinning your wheels and get back on the road of your life. But first you have to sign the permission slip.

There is always some kind of payoff in staying stuck. Do you know what yours is? Do you prefer the certainty of prison to the wide open spaces of the world? At least you know where you will sleep and what times your meals will be ready.

When you are used to living by other people's rules, it can seem overwhelming to set your own priorities and make your own decisions. You don't know whether you can handle the responsibility. But if you don't learn to take responsibility for your life, who will? If you don't find your purpose and follow it, how will you find fulfillment?

You can spend your life working for other people and living by their rules, but it won't help you find your path. You must "leave your nets" before you get caught in them.

Working for others should at best be a temporary proposition. Work for others while you learn the skills that you need to work for yourself. Live by other people's rules until the opportunity presents itself for you to act on your own priorities.

Your life must be progressive. You must keep taking the next step. Be faithful to your ideals. Follow your beliefs. Prove them out. Show yourself and others that they work. Be a beacon of love and compassion. Empower others to find their own truth.

This is how the work extends. . . . Not by preaching. Not by telling people what you think is good for them or allowing them to prescribe for you.

If you look carefully, you will notice that those who have the greatest need to tell others what to do have the least faith in themselves. They haven't even begun to hear the voice in their own hearts; yet they are up on a soapbox telling others what to do.

Such is the absurdity of false witness. When you are in a rut and you are too afraid to step out of it, the first thing you do is try to attract some company. It is not uncommon to build a temple over a ditch and call it God's sanctuary.

I have told you many times to be careful. Things are not always as they seem. Wolves are disguised in sheep's clothing. Prisons of fear and judgment masquerade as temples of love and forgiveness.

It helps to keep your eyes open. Don't join the crusade until you see the fruits of people's actions. Words are cheap and often misleading.

If each of you would nurture the truth within your hearts, you would collectively give birth to a very different world. It would be a world of realization, not sacrifice, a world of equality, not prejudice, a world of insight and respect, not collusion and despair.

Nobody else can take responsibility for living your life. Not your parents, or your partner, or your children. Not your church, your friends, or your support network. You alone must do it. Does this seem to be a lonely proposition? Well, perhaps in some way it is. But no more exciting task will ever come into your life.

So don't make rules for other people. That will just take the focus away from your life. Let others find their own way. Support them. Encourage them. Cheer them on. But don't think you know what's good for them. You don't know. Nor will you ever know. A co-dependent preoccupation with the lives of others keeps you from taking responsibility for your own life.

Stay in your life. Stay in your heart. Everything that you need to fulfill your destiny will be found within. Listen to your guidance, honor it, act on it, be committed to it, and it will unfold. When you are joined with your own divine nature, the doors you need to walk through will open to you.

## THE OPEN DOOR

*When the door in your heart is open,*
*all the important doors open in the world.*

Life has its own rhythm. If you are surrendered, you will find it. But surrendering is not so easy.

Surrendering means meeting each moment as new. And to do that, you cannot be attached to what just happened. You can appreciate it. You can savor it. But you must let it go where it will.

You can't control what happens. You can only be open to it or resist it. If you have expectations, you will be resisting. Don't resist. Don't have attachments to the past or expectations of the future.

Just be where you are. Bring everything into the now. Bring the attachment, the expectations into the present. Be aware of your resistance. See the drama of your disappointment. See that you did not get what you wanted. See how it makes you feel. Watch it. Experience it. But don't lose yourself in the drama.

When you can see the drama without reacting to it, you can stay anchored in the here and now. You can remain present. You can see which doors are closed and which ones are open.

If you try to walk through closed doors, you will hurt yourself unnecessarily. So, even if you don't know why a door is closed, at least respect the fact that it is. And don't struggle with the doorknob. If the door was open, you would know it. Wanting it to be open does not make it open.

Much of the pain in life is as a result of people attempting to walk through closed doors or trying to put square pegs into round holes. You try to hold onto someone who is ready to go, or you try to get somebody to do something before s/he is ready. Instead of accepting what is and working with it, you interfere with it or try to manipulate it to meet your perceived needs.

Obviously, this doesn't work. When you interfere with what is, you create strife for yourself and others. You trespass. You get in the way.

That is why awareness is necessary. When you know that things are not flowing, you need to step back and realize that your actions are not helpful. You need to stop, pause, and consider. You need to cease what you are doing because it is not working and you don't want to make the situation worse than it is.

Stopping the offensive action is the first step in the process of At-One-Ment for your trespasses. Unless you stop, violation continues. The door stays shut. After stopping, acknowledge your mistake, to yourself and to others. Vow not to repeat your mistake again.

When you interfere in the natural order of things, there is suffering. As soon as you stop interfering, suffering stops. It is a simple movement from dis-ease to ease, from disharmony to harmony. You don't need to make the forgiveness process difficult or esoteric. It is a natural, organic process.

When the door is closed, you cannot enter. You must wait patiently or move along and see if another door will open. As long as you are forgiving yourself and others for your mistakes, there is a good chance that the right door will open. Only when you refuse to learn from your mistakes or hold onto your grievances does it seem that the doors are repeatedly closed to you.

Fortunately, God does not hold grievances. God does not punish you for your mistakes. God keeps saying to you: "That didn't work too well, did it? Next time, perhaps, you can make a different choice."

It isn't helpful to obsess about your mistakes and feel bad about them. Guilt doesn't help you act more responsibly toward others.

Guilt does not contribute to atonement. If anything, it impedes it. When something does not work, a correction must be made. Adjustments are a natural part of living in a harmonious way.

Grace comes when correction is constant. Fulfillment happens when you don't just talk about forgiveness, but live it moment to moment. Then, it does not matter how many times you stray from the path or put your foot in your mouth. You can laugh at your errors and put them behind you.

You cannot fit through the door if you are carrying the past around. Don't feel guilty. Instead, take responsibility for correcting your mistakes. That way you don't carry around a lot of excess baggage. The more responsibility you take for your thoughts, feelings, and experiences, the lighter you travel and the easier it is to correct for your mistakes.

Guilt is not constructive. If there is nothing you can do to make the situation better, then just accept it as it is. Sometimes, there's nothing to be done. It's no one's fault. Life is just as it is. And that's okay. In knowing that life is okay, no matter how ragged and unfinished it seems, there is room for movement. A shift can happen. A door can open.

The most important door is the one to your heart. Is it open or closed? If it is open, then the whole universe abides in you. If it is closed, you stand alone, holding the world off. Trust and the river flows through your heart. Distrust and a dam holds the river back.

A heart in resistance gets tired quickly. Life wears heavily upon it. But a heart that is open is filled with energy. It dances and sings.

When the door in your heart is open, all the important doors open in the world. You go where you need to go. Nothing interferes with your purpose or your destiny. Everything that you are unfolds naturally in its own time, without resistance or struggle. The unexpected happens without difficulty. Miracles are everyday occurrences.

## WALKING THE TIGHTROPE

*Every step is an act of balance.*

Even if you know a little bit, you rarely see the whole picture. Indeed, the more attached you are to any part of the whole, the less likely you are to see the big picture.

Some things belong to the past, not to the present. What happened in the past can prejudice you toward what is happening now. It can constrict you so that you don't open fully to the present.

Some things belong to the future, not to the present. The more invested you are in a particular outcome, the harder it is for you to accept "what is" and work with it.

The truth is that you don't know specifically what happened in the past or what will happen in the future. To live in the present, you need to stay centered in what you know now and put the past and the future aside.

If you keep bringing the past in or trying to plan for the future, you will move out of what you do know. You will get behind or ahead of yourself. You will sow the seeds of conflict within and without.

So this is a balancing act. You need to walk the tightrope between the past and the future. And you can't expect to walk without tipping to one side or the other. But when you do, you must lean the other way, so that you can come back to center.

Be honest with yourself. You don't know that the past is going to repeat itself. You don't know that your present experience is going to be the same in the future. Things may change or they may stay the same. Old patterns may dissolve or they may reappear. You don't know these things. All you know is how you feel about what's happening right now.

If you can stay with this, then you can be present and be honest about your experience. You can say what you are able to commit to and what you cannot commit to.

Things may change in the future, but you can't live now hoping they are going to change. You must be where you are, not where you want to be.

This is difficult work. Most mental activity is fear-based. It is about resisting "what is" or trying to change it. If you don't move through this resistance to a deeper level of self-attunement, you won't be able to claim the present moment. You will get lost in a reactive buzz saw of conflicting thoughts and emotions.

The past will be telling you "Don't open. It's too scary. Don't you remember what happened last month or last year?" and the future will be saying "This is taking too long; why don't we just jump in and do it?" You need to listen to both voices and then rebalance and come back to center.

That is what the tightrope walker must do. She can't worry about losing her balance in the past. She can't dream about a perfect performance in the future. She needs to focus on what's happening right now. She needs to put one foot in front of the other. Every step is an act of balance. Every step is a spiritual act.

## ATTACHMENT TO PAST OR FUTURE

*The time has come to anchor in the heart.*

Many people want to know what is going to happen to them in the future. They go to psychics, astrologers, tarot card readers and so forth, hoping to hear something that will make them feel better.

The absurdity of this can only be appreciated when you know that the future cannot be predicted. True, there are lines of force emanating from a person's consciousness. There are patterns that are set in motion. But every moment offers you a new choice and that choice may alter your destiny.

Unfortunately, the more preoccupied you are in finding out what will happen to you in the future, the less attention you can give to the choices you need to make now. That is why a fascination with fortunetelling is discouraged in many spiritual traditions.

The obsession some people have with the past can be just as dysfunctional as this preoccupation with the future. Many people go to therapists or psychics looking for knowledge of the past which could explain problems in the present. They engage in a variety of forms of psychoanalysis, dream therapy, inner child work, hypnotherapy, past life regression and so forth. While this work may help some people move on in their lives, it becomes a quagmire for others. A tool meant to help becomes a dogma. A technique meant to assist people in discovering the source of their pain becomes an invitation to wallow in it and become its perpetual victim.

When you emerge from such therapies with stories about childhood trauma or abuse, or memories of previous lifetimes, you would do well to ask if these stories help you to stay focused and empowered in the present moment. If they help you heal issues that are present in your life now, then they are therapeutic. But if they simply encourage you to become a victim, establishing an identity in your wound, then they are counterproductive. Generally speaking, the projected dramas of past or future are distractions that take you away from the real challenge of being present here and now.

It is important to watch how your mind continues to grasp for external answers to your problems and how fascinated you get in the imagery of change. What does not change is far less interesting to you. You don't like being told "There's nothing out there to get!" When the teacher tells you to go home and follow your breath, you are disappointed. You had hoped that s/he would send you on another retreat, another mission of mercy, another crusade to save the world.

There are enough windy, circuitous roads out there to keep you traveling for a long time. There are enough detours on the spiritual path to keep you spinning your wheels ad infinitum. After taking enough of them, you realize that none of them are going anywhere in particular. All paths eventually bring you back to the place where you started.

You have taken enough of these useless journeys. The time has come to anchor in the heart. You don't have to be concerned about what happened in the past or what will happen in the future. You don't need any more stories to put you to sleep.

## DROPPING YOUR STORIES

*When you try to fix yourself, you reinforce your belief
that something in you is broken.*

Your stories of the past reinforce your fears and justify your rituals of self-protection. Whenever you connect with what you want, you also connect with all the reasons why you can't have it. "I want to leave my job, but I can't . . . . I want to commit to this relationship, but I can't." On and on it goes . . . . the perpetual "Catch 22."

You want to bring new energy into your life and hold onto your old habits at the same time. You want change, but you are afraid of it. In some ways, you prefer your pain just the way it is because it is a known quantity. You think that if you make a change in your life things could get worse. You prefer a known pain to an unknown pain, a familiar suffering to an unfamiliar one.

Your ego is deeply committed to the status quo of your life. That's why the spiritual adult's heroic plans for the transformation of your life are inevitably undermined by the fears of the wounded child, who doesn't think s/he is lovable, and therefore cannot have a vision of a life without pain. To the wounded kid within, any promise of release from pain is a trick that entices you to let your defenses down and become vulnerable to attack.

So your fears keep you closed to the possibility of meaningful change in your life. What you say you want is not what you really want. The spiritual adult and the wounded child are at odds, and when that happens the wounded child usually wins. Unfortunately, that does not lead to happiness for either adult or child. It leads only to the prolongation of your familiar, internalized suffering.

Into this duplicitous environment of the psyche at war with itself then come a variety of professional fixers: psychiatrists, counselors, preachers, self-help gurus. Each claims to have the answer, but each solution offered just compounds the problem. When you think there is something wrong with you, your shame and unworthiness are reinforced. When you try to fix yourself, you reinforce your belief that something in you is broken.

Professional fixers believe your stories of brokenness and try to heal you. If your story isn't juicy enough, they help you make it more juicy. It's all about high drama, about sin and salvation. It never occurs to them or to you that maybe nothing is broken, that maybe there is nothing in you that needs to be fixed. It never occurs to either of you that the only dysfunctional aspect of your situation is your belief that something is broken, your belief that you will never get what you want.

The external problems you perceive are projections of the internal conflict: "I want but I cannot have." If you would allow yourself to have what you want, or if you would stop wanting it because you know you can't have it, this conflict would cease. Having what you want or accepting that you can't have it ends your conflict. It also ends your story.

If you have what you want or if you have made your peace with not having it, you have no story. There's no drama of seeking. To keep the drama of seeking going, you cannot find what you are seeking. Finding love, happiness, joy, and so forth ends the story. "And they lived happily ever after . . . ." Story over. Drama complete.

The truth is you are not ready to give up your drama. Your story has become part of your identity. Your pain is part of your personality. You do not know who you are without it. Letting your drama go means letting the past dissolve right here, right now.

If you can do that, it doesn't matter what happened in the past. It has no power. It doesn't exist anymore. You are writing on a clean slate. That means that you are totally responsible for what you choose. There are no more excuses.

When you no longer interpret your life based on what happened yesterday or last year, what happens is neutral. It is what it is. There is no charge on it.

The freedom to be fully present and responsible right now is awesome. Very few people want it. Most people wear their past like a noose around their necks. They insist on carrying their cross and wearing their crown of thorns.

You stay in the drama because you love it. You keep dragging your past with you because you are attached to it. And so you have to heal all the wounds you think that you have. It doesn't matter that those wounds are not ultimately real. They are real enough to you.

And so the drama continues. You can't tell a person who is in prison getting three meals a day that freedom is its own security. S/he wants those three meals a day no matter what. Then s/he will talk about freedom.

When you are attached to what you already have, how can you bring in anything new? To bring in something new, something fresh, something unpredictable, you must surrender something old, stale and habitual.

If you want the creative to manifest within you, you must surrender all that is not creative. Then in the space made by that surrender, creativity rushes in. If the cup is full of old, cold tea, you cannot pour new, hot tea into it. First you have to empty the cup. Then you can fill it.

If you want to give up your drama, first find out what your investment is in it. What is your pay-off for not finding, not healing, not living happily ever after?

And then be honest. If you don't want to move through your pain, tell the truth. Say "I'm not ready to move through my pain yet." Don't say "I wish I could be done with my pain, but I can't be." That is a lie. You could be done with it, but you don't choose to be. Perhaps you enjoy the attention you get being a victim.

Most people who claim to be on the spiritual path are just spinning their wheels. They are always making excuses.

When you have learned to accept responsibility, there are no excuses. You don't procrastinate or make empty promises. You wait until you are ready and you act clearly and decisively. When you are ready, there is no need to hesitate, for actions flow from readiness, and actions speak louder than words.

## FREEDOM AND COMMITMENT

*People are ineffective for two reasons.*
*Either they don't know what they want,*
*or they don't believe they deserve to have it.*

All of you have the freedom to do what you want. If you are not doing it, then you must not want it enough. Maybe you are trying to live someone else's dream, instead of your own.

You can be sure that your dream doesn't look like anyone else's. It is unique to you. When you compare yourself to others, you can't act in an authentic way.

When you are not committed to your dream, you aren't going to manifest it. Desire and commitment go hand in hand. Usually when there is a lack of commitment, there is a lack of desire too. If you don't really want it, you aren't going to put out the energy to create it.

People are ineffective for two reasons. Either they don't know what they want or, if they do, they don't believe they deserve to have it.

When you know what you want and believe that you deserve it, nothing can stop you from creating that in your life. Of course, when you manifest it, it might look a little different than you expected it to. Your ego might object to it. But that's a different problem.

Your job is not to know how manifestation is going to happen or what it is going to look like. Your job is to get clear on what you want and be totally committed to it. Then, however it happens and whatever it looks like, you better accept it. Because if you do not accept and celebrate the fruit of your labors, you will not reinforce your success.

Everybody wants a formula for manifestation, but few want to practice the formula. The formula's easy. The practice is what challenges.

## A FORMULA FOR CREATION

*Your job is to be clear about the goal, committed to it,
and grateful for its accomplishment in your life.*

1.  First, get clear on what you want. Unless you want something, heart and soul, you will have difficulty creating it. Take as long as you need to get clear. It might take a day, a month, a year, a lifetime. If you try to create without knowing what you want, you will waste time and energy. You will also be training yourself to be a failure. Don't ask for something you're not sure that you want.

2.  Believe in what you want and know that you deserve it. Move toward your goal steadily, no matter how implausible it seems or how many obstacles seem to be in your way. Without your total commitment, your goal cannot be realized. Do not waver in your commitment until what you want has manifested in your life.

3.  When you create what you want, celebrate it. Be grateful for it. Give up your pictures of the way you thought it would be. Drop your expectations. Embrace it just the way it is. Work with it. Use it. Love it and keep on loving it.

Your job is to be clear about the goal, committed to it, and grateful for its accomplishment in your life. You don't have to know "how" the goal is going to be realized in your life. Just do the best you can. Follow any strategy that feels right to you.

Remember, it is not the strategy that brings you toward your goal, but your desire to reach it and your commitment to accomplish it. When these factors are in place, the strategy you need will make itself known to you. When you know "what" you want and "why" you want it, "when, where and how" will be revealed to you.

All creation is really co-creation. You determine what you want, commit to it, and move toward it, and the opportunities you need to realize your goal come your way. To be sure, you must keep your eyes open and keep surrendering your expectations. But you do not have to make the opportunities happen. They happen all by themselves.

This is what effortlessness and non-striving teach you. You don't have to struggle. You don't have to sacrifice, beg, borrow or steal. You just have to be clear and committed.

Of course, there is one more important thing. You must believe that you are worthy of having what you want. If you don't believe that you are worthy, it doesn't matter how good your process is. You will find a way to undermine it.

As long as you feel unworthy, you will struggle. You will continually get in your own way. Only when you know that you deserve what you want can you realize your dreams and meet your goals.

CHAPTER TWENTY-EIGHT

# Acceptance and Trust

*Life always unfolds better when you get out of the way.*

It's a paradox. If you think it needs to be fixed, then fixing it will be impossible. If you realize that it can't be fixed, then it isn't broken. The key in this sentence is the word "you." What "you" think determines the drama, or lack of it.

The question always is: "Are you willing to accept this situation the way it is?" If you are, then you can learn from it and move on. If you're not, then you will prod it, poke it, prolong it, and generally make it much worse than it seemed to be.

By insisting on perfection, you experience imperfection. Only when you accept things just as they are do you experience the inherent perfection of all things.

When you accept your experience, you take the pressure off. You learn to be compassionate with yourself, with others, and with the situation at hand.

The problems you perceive when you are finding fault with your life often disappear when you can be okay with what is happening. Accepting life is like taking a deep breath and relaxing. The more you accept, the more peaceful you feel.

When you are peaceful, you don't need to fix anyone or anything. If something needs to change, the change will happen by itself. It doesn't need to be forced. It doesn't require great effort or manipulation.

When you are upset or agitated, you try to fix your problems and everyone else's problems. You contract, tense up, forget to breathe, and attack or run away. You act as though you are going into battle, except that the battle is taking place only in your own mind.

You are not going to stop this from happening. You are going to experience anxiety, frustration, fight or flight. The question is not "How can you avoid getting upset?" but "How will you handle things when you get upset?" Will agitation lead to panic? Will fear lead to paranoia? Will you turn purple because you forget to breathe? Or will you see that you are getting upset, remember to breathe, relax, and accept the situation as it is?

This is a spiritual practice. When you want to jump in and fix somebody, become aware of your own fear and anxiety. Remember that acting from that place of fear only exacerbates the situation. Slow down, pause, listen, breathe, and come back into your heart.

Acceptance doesn't happen overnight. It is a process. It doesn't ask you to make things better. It simply asks you not to make things worse. When you refuse to fix, you eliminate the impact of your judgments and interpretations on the circumstances of your life. And life always unfolds better when you get out of the way.

## LISTENING WITHOUT JUDGMENT

*You are not here to rescue others from their pain,*
*but merely to walk through your own.*

Sometimes you try to fix others in subtle ways. You listen to others with your own filters, agreeing or disagreeing with them, seeing what they are saying in the context of your own life and beliefs. You do not listen unconditionally, neutrally, without having an opinion. And so, in a certain way, you aren't really listening at all.

When your friends confide in you, you take this as an invitation to analyze their situation or give advice. Then you jump in with all your own issues and judgments. It is not surprising that others may feel attacked by you.

You need to learn to listen without judgment to what people are saying and to refrain from offering an interpretation or opinion about it. If people ask for feedback, tell them as accurately as possible what you heard them say. When you do this, people are pleasantly surprised. "Wow," they often say, "You really heard me!"

Being really heard is a rare event. How many times have you felt really heard? How many times have you listened to others unconditionally without trying to solve their problems?

When you give advice to others, you get involved in their problems. Why would you want to do this? Maybe because this is a way for you to try to work out your own problems! You project your dreams and fears onto other people's dramas. You watch soap operas for the same reason.

This is a waste of your time and theirs. You don't need to take on other people's problems and they don't need to take on yours.

Even if your intentions are honorable, it is unlikely that you will be able to help other people work out their issues. You can't really understand the context of another person's life. So the solutions that worked for you are not necessarily going to work for someone else.

When you try to fix or give advice to others, you are not being kind or generous. If you want to be kind to others, accept them the way they are and stop trying to judge, analyze, interpret, or change their lives.

If they want to share their problems with you, listen with compassion, but don't offer opinions or solutions. Just let them know that you have heard them. Encourage them to stay in their own process and find their own guidance. Know and feel confident that all the answers are within them, just as the answers you need are within you.

When you trust others to find their own answers, you treat them as spiritual equals. You don't pretend to know something they don't know. You grant people both respect and freedom. You trust the truth within them to light their way. That is love in action.

Not fixing others means that you don't take responsibility for their lives. That gives you the time and energy you need to take responsibility for our own life.

By taking good care of yourself on all levels—physically, emotionally, mentally, and spiritually—you are able to respond to others in the most compassionate, patient, and caring way. By contrast, if you neglect your responsibilities to yourself and try instead to take responsibility for others, you get depleted energetically. Then you aren't in a position to be helpful to anyone.

It should be a relief to know that you are not here to rescue others from their pain, but merely to walk through your own. This is your essential responsibility and will be throughout your embodiment. Even when you join your life with another person's life, this responsibility stays with you. Whenever you lose sight of this fact, you inevitably pay the price.

## THE AFFINITY PROCESS

*Affinity Group practice provides you with a hands-on practice of non-judgment, acceptance, and forgiveness.*

In order to help you develop skillfulness in listening, accepting, and not fixing, I suggest the Affinity Group Process. The Process invites you to hold a space of unconditional love and acceptance for all members in your group. A set of guidelines helps you to keep the group experience loving, safe, and compassionate.

Using the guidelines, you become aware of just how many judgments you are holding about others in the group and, ultimately, about yourself. You learn to hold these judgments compassionately and come back into your heart, where you can be emotionally present and listen without judgment.

You and other group members have the opportunity to talk about any matter which is heavy on your hearts and to be heard without judgment by the others. Often, by sharing your conflict or problem, something shifts inside them, enabling you to hold that problem in a lighter, less self-condemning way.

When problems are given into a state of consciousness which upholds the inherent perfection of life, there is nothing that supports the problem and, without support, the problem ceases to be. It remains a problem only if you hold onto it.

Using the guidelines of the Affinity Process, you learn to hold your fear and shame with love and compassion. You can then take this skill home with you and use it effectively in your relationships with spouses, children, parents, friends, bosses, and co-workers.

Affinity Group practice helps you surrender the blocks to unconditional love so that you can see and embrace your innocence and that of others. The process provides you with a hands-on practice of non-judgment, acceptance, and forgiveness.

## COMMUNITY SERVICE

*Wherever the process goes, healing happens,*
*often in unexpected ways.*

When you complete the Affinity Group Process, you are asked to share it with others in some area of your life: in a school, a nursing home, a prison, a church, a cancer treatment program, a homeless shelter, a business or government agency. It might be where you work, where you play, or where you volunteer.

This enables you to express your gratitude for a process that was given to you free of charge and it helps the process extend easily to others who want to experience it. In this manner, the Affinity Group Process moves energetically into homes and organizations throughout the community, helping people learn to listen to one another and communicate in a non-blaming way. Wherever the process goes, healing happens, often in unexpected ways.

While the process is not outcome-oriented, wonderful results happen when people feel listened to and accepted. Because the process teaches you to accept others unconditionally and respect differences, it enables people from all different races, religions, social and economic groups to bond spiritually and come to a deeper appreciation and understanding of one another.

This simple spiritual practice can bring the presence of love and compassion to your relationship with your husband, your wife, and your children. It can bring understanding to people at your work, in your neighborhoods, schools, hospitals, and prisons. It can bring together people from divergent groups in your city, your country, and ultimately the world that you live in.

There are no limits to what it can do. And all because you have taken up the mantle. All because of your commitment to learn how to hold the space of unconditional love and acceptance for yourself and others.

## RETURN TO THE GARDEN

*The Garden is not a physical place,*
*but a place within your heart and mind.*

When you learn how to hold what happens in your life gently and compassionately, when you learn to see the innocence of others and consider their happiness equally with your own, when you learn to practice acceptance, listening without judgment, and not-fixing with each person you meet, then you will find yourself standing at the gates of the Garden.

To return to the Garden, you must give up selfishness, greed, struggle, sacrifice, shame, envy. The reign of fear and anger must end within your own mind. Knowledge itself, which you fought for at such great price, must also be refined and transformed. To be in the Garden, you must know in a very different way.

You must know not by thinking but by being and trusting. Problems dissolve when you tell the truth with compassion and listen without judgment. Your needs are met through your willingness to be flexible and cooperative. For, in the Garden, there is plenty to go around. There is no reason to compete for resources.

People who try to enter the Garden prematurely don't have the consciousness they need to sustain the Garden experience. Without much ado, they find themselves standing outside the gates once again, wondering how they are going to make a living.

In the Garden, "making a living" is not an issue. By living true to yourself and expressing your talents joyfully, you naturally and spontaneously create the resources which are necessary for the fulfillment of your needs. As a result, you don't have to manipulate others or envy what they have.

In the Garden, conditional love is not possible. Since love and compassion are the defining characteristics of the Garden experience, no one can be excluded from them. Everyone in the Garden loves and respects everyone else. Each wants only the best for each other person.

In the Garden, worry or fear is almost unknown. When fear comes up, it is held so compassionately that it quickly dissolves.

The world of suffering exists outside the gates of the Garden. The world of grace exists inside them. Whether you live inside or outside the gates depends on how you stand in relationship to yourself and your neighbor. Do you accept your mistakes and learn from them? Do you forgive others for their trespasses against you? Do you stand as equals? Is your intention to bless or to curse? Do you see each another as innocent or guilty?

Until you anchor in the consciousness of unconditional love and close the gates of the world firmly behind you, you may move back and forth between heaven and hell, the world of suffering and the world of grace. When you are in one world, only that world seems real to you, and the other one seems an illusion.

Yet the truth is that both worlds are real and both worlds are inside you. The Garden is not a physical place, but a place within your heart and mind. It is a state of consciousness.

When you know that the whole drama is happening in your own consciousness, you no longer need to look outside of yourself for answers. Peace is there. And so is war. There the flames of dawn meet the flames of dusk. There consciousness is revealing itself constantly, showing you its pathos and its overwhelming beauty.

## INTEGRATING THE DARK SIDE

*You must redeem all the parts of yourself*
*that you have abandoned or betrayed.*

All aspects of your experience, including your anger, fear and shame, must be accepted and forgiven. When you know anger is about you, not about someone else, you know that the hardest thing is to forgive yourself.

You are asked to bring the hidden dark side into plain view. You are asked to feel your own pain and to hear the cry for love behind it. You heal as you become aware of the dark, disenfranchised aspects of self and bring them into the light of conscious awareness.

It is not an easy process, this synergy of dark and light within your own soul, but it is a necessary one. It is part of the birth of Spirit in your life. It is the way that the human comes to embrace his/her divinity.

Through the process of psychological integration, the fall from grace is interrupted. A shift happens in heart and in mind, and the ascension back to the divine begins.

You must redeem all parts of yourself that you have abandoned or betrayed. If you have cut off your sexuality, you must reclaim it. If you have neglected your creativity or repressed your power, you must find a way to accept and express these important aspects of self.

Most people project what they dislike or are afraid of in themselves onto others. If they are afraid of their power, they project it onto some powerful, charismatic figure through whom they try to live. The fact that they are subsequently disappointed or betrayed by the people onto whom they project their power is simply part of the lesson they are here to learn.

In order for integration to happen in the psyche, projection must stop. You must claim your dark side, not project it. When you are triggered by others, you must understand that they are showing you what you need to heal. Instead of reacting to them, you use the trigger to see an unloved aspect of self that needs to be integrated.

You experience conflict in relationships because others mirror back to you what you don't want to see in yourself. But if you see and accept the gift they are offering you, relationships become a tool for transformation. They push your buttons so that you can heal your deepest wounds.

## RELATIONSHIP AS A SPIRITUAL PATH

*If you are not happy, being with a partner*
*will only exacerbate your unhappiness.*

Very few of you experience happiness in your relationships. You think you can be happier with someone else than you can be with yourself. But this idea is absurd! The truth is that you can be only as happy with another person as you can be with yourself. Why would it be otherwise?

If you want to use your relationship as a path for spiritual growth, the first thing you must give up is the romantic fantasy that the other person can be the source of your happiness. If you are happy, being with a partner can be an extension of your happiness. But, if you are not happy, being with a partner will only exacerbate your unhappiness. Being in relationship with another is just as challenging, if not more challenging than being alone.

Please be clear about that. Your decision to enter into partnership should not be based on a desire to avoid looking at self, but on a willingness to intensify that process. You cannot escape yourself by entering a relationship. Quite the contrary: being in relationship inevitably brings you face to face with yourself.

When you live with someone, you are likely to trigger their unhealed wounds and they are likely to trigger yours. In order to manage these triggers, both of you must be able to own your thoughts, feelings, words, and actions, and refrain from blaming the other person for your pain or discomfort. Both of you must be responsible for your own experience or you will begin to project your anger and fear on the other person and it won't be long before the relationship is in crisis.

## TRANSCENDING BOUNDARIES

*When boundaries have been respected in a relationship,*
*it is possible to go beyond them.*

A spiritual relationship is built on a strong sense of boundaries. You know where your responsibility is and isn't. But such a relationship also leads to a deepening trust in which the boundaries between self and other begin to be transcended.

When boundaries have been respected in a relationship, it is possible to go beyond them. When you feel honored by your partner, it is easy for you to act in a kind and unselfish manner toward him or her. There is no sacrifice or self-denial in this. Rather, there is an expansion of your love, in which you learn to care as deeply for the happiness of the other as you do for our own happiness.

You can't go beyond self if you do not know who you are or who the other is. But when you know the truth about self and other, the lines of separation begin to fade away. In the end, there is only One Being present, in yourself and in the other. This is the One Self, the Friend Eternal, the compassionate One Him or Herself.

## MOVING MORE DEEPLY INTO LOVE

*Those who challenge your ability to love are your greatest teachers.*

Having experienced what it is like to hold one person's happiness equally with your own, you can do this in other relationships. By loving yourself unconditionally you are able to love others without conditions. This does not deplete your energy. On the contrary, it energizes you, for the love you give away returns to you through the gratitude of others.

Seeing the innocence and the beauty in others and letting them know that you see it is the greatest gift that you can give. When you can see that beauty and innocence not just in those who treat you well, but also in those who misunderstand or attack you, then you know that you are anchored in the Christ consciousness of unconditional love.

You don't withhold your love from those who need it, even when they seem to be asking for it in offensive ways. Your responsibility is not just to love the people you like and admire. You are asked to love your enemies too. In the end, there is no one who is unworthy of your love.

Those who challenge your ability to love are your greatest teachers. They push you to the limit, forcing you to move through your own walls of fear and judgment.

As you follow the path I have laid out for you, you learn to look not so much on how others treat you, but more on how you are treating others. You don't focus on the words and actions of others, but on your own words and deeds.

You can offer other people either fear or love. Your responsibility is to move through your fear into the consciousness of unshakable love.

When you learn to hold your own fears compassionately, you are able to hold the fears of others in the same gentle way. You are no longer emotionally reactive or ambivalent, but patient and steady. In your heart, you know that only love is real. Everything else is illusion.

## ENDING THE FALL FROM GRACE

*The desire for power and control takes you out of the Garden.*

In the Garden, Adam and Eve are innocent. They feel worthy of God's love. As soon as they cease to feel worthy, they are banished from the Garden. What used to be easy becomes hard. Play becomes work. Fulfillment becomes sacrifice.

When your will is separate from the Divine Will, you cannot create anything that is helpful to you or anyone else. If you are afraid or ashamed, find a way to hold the fear and the shame with compassion, so that you can release them gently into the arms of love.

God does not want you to struggle. God does not want you to beat yourself. God just asks you to be humble and understand that you can't create anything of real value from your limited ego consciousness.

The desire for power and control takes you out of the garden. It takes you out of relationship with the divine presence.

To trust God means to trust the deepest part of your being. It means to trust in your unlimited, resourceful Self—no, not the part of you that needs to figure everything out—not the part that needs guarantees—that part cannot be trusted, nor can it trust—but the essential Self that feels worthy of love. That is the link between you and God. As you rest in your connection to God, as you rely more on your essential Self and less on your ego, your struggle is diminished. Your sacrifice comes to an end.

Remember, the path out of the Garden leads inevitably to Golgotha. Sooner or later, the world will strip away from you everything except what you are able to give to yourself. Don't take the journey to the cross. It is a useless and unnecessary one. If you have not learned that from my life, learn it now.

The journey of awakening goes from unconscious innocence to the fall from grace, from guilt to responsibility to self-forgiveness. Innocence is not soiled by experience but redeemed by it in the end. When Adam and Eve return to the Garden, they will be naked once again, but they will know something they did not know before.

You can know the truth only by being it. That is what initiates the journey of becoming and concludes it. In the end, you return to the place where you began, to the Garden, where each of you must reclaim your innocence and learn to create with God.

## CREATING HEAVEN ON EARTH

*You return not just as a son of man,*
*but also as a son of God.*

The true price of freedom is not suffering, but responsibility. Instead of trying to make someone else responsible for your mistakes, you acknowledge and learn from them. You change the way you think and act. You begin to clean up the mess you made.

As you do, the Garden begins to bloom again. You plant new flowers and trees, water the soil and pull up the weeds. You become responsible for your creations and they thrive. What you reap at harvest time depends on what you sow each day.

That is the life you chose when you came into this embodiment. Those are the laws you must work with. You must live with your mistakes until you correct them. And unless you learn to forgive the past and create with greater foresight and responsibility, you will experience some version of hell on earth.

This planet is a learning laboratory that helps you develop the self-confidence and sensitivity to others that you need to create the conditions that are best for the common good. At this time, your Garden is parched and overgrown by weeds. It has not been tended kindly or responsibly. Nobody else can tend it for you.

Every thought you have, every emotion you indulge, every action you take weighs in. So consider these well. Ask yourself how they will impact others and yourself. Do not forge ahead blindly driven by your doubt, your anger, and your fear. You cannot afford to create out of that place anymore.

Earth has given you notice. Water and wind have risen up and spoken to you in your dreams. Fire has appeared to you as it did to Moses. There are no secrets here.

To many of you, it seems that life is speeding up. All the more reason why you must slow down. How else can you inhabit the present moment? You can't address all that has happened in the past. You can only address what is happening now.

It is time for you to live each day as though it were your last, to live each moment as though it were the only moment you have. If you can do that, you will be a good gardener. You will have the peace of mind and the silence of heart that result from responsible creation.

When you return to the Garden, you are different from the way you were when you left. You left hell-bent on expressing your own creativity at any cost. You return humble and sensitive to the needs of all. You return not just as a son of man, but also as a son of God. You come full circle. You become responsible for your creations.

## TRUSTING THE CHRIST WITHIN

*Don't worry about the future. You are the one creating it.*

When you act out of fear, you don't solve any problems. You just add to the imbalance and the hysteria. Don't act out of fear. Let the fear come up. Ride it as a wave and return to your center. Then it will be time to act.

Realize that you have just the amount of time that you need to complete your journey. So don't rush. But don't hesitate either. Proceed forward with faith, confidence, and enthusiasm. Take no thought for yesterday or tomorrow. What you say and do today will be enough.

Move in the direction of your greatest joy. Choose something to do that will express your love, your gratitude, your appreciation.

Don't beat yourself because you suffered in the past. Forgive the past and move on.

Do what you have always wanted to do. If nobody wants to pay you to do it, do it for free. If nobody encourages you, redouble your efforts. Do not withhold your gift. The salvation of the world depends on all people expressing the gifts they have.

Don't worry about the future. You are the one creating it. Don't tie it down to the past. Release it to do its work. Have faith. Don't be attached to the results. Trust.

The one you are trusting is God incarnate, the Christ himself. How can you fear the future when Christ is with you? Put your trust in that One.

## MINISTRY OF LOVE

*The second coming happens when Christ is born in you.*
*That is when the promise is fulfilled.*
*That is when the Messiah comes.*

When the truth is known and embodied, it can easily be understood. An authentic and compassionate person becomes a role model for others.

Such people are magnetic and compelling, not necessarily because they have achieved great things in the world, but because they care and you can feel it. Love has risen up in them and it overflows them, anointing all who come their way.

When you learn to love yourself, you cannot help loving others. It is not hard to do. It's natural and spontaneous.

When you love, there is no limit on that love. It constantly recycles, flowing in and out of the heart. Like waves breaking and receding on a beach, the tides of love are steady and dependable. They touch every shoreline with their blessing.

Love is not something you do. Love is who you are. You are the embodiment of love in this moment. Nothing less.

All this begins in your own heart. That is where Christ is born in you as it was in me. And once born, He cannot be contained. There is no place where He cannot go. There is no place where His love cannot reach.

Wherever you go, Christ goes with you. He moves with your legs, reaches with your hands, speaks with your voice, and sees with your eyes. Because of you, He is everywhere. Without you, He would be invisible.

That is why I ask you to awaken the power of love and become a witness to it in this world. No, not to preach or proselytize, but to listen, to comfort, to care. The love that expresses through you is the Christ Presence. Because your heart has opened, the human vehicle is ablaze with the divine light, the very embodiment of God's love.

Do not wait for me to come again. Be the vehicle through which my love can reach to your brothers and sisters. The second coming happens when Christ is born in you and in all your brothers and sisters. That is when the promise is fulfilled. That is when the Messiah comes.

When I heard the call, I answered it. Now you hear it too and you must answer it as I did. Remember this simple teaching I gave to you: "What is not loving must be forgiven, and what is forgiven becomes love's patient blessing on an imperfect world."

## CHAPTER TWENTY-NINE

# Teaching Love

*Love is ultimate reality. It is the beginning and the end,
the alpha and the omega.*

When you learn to connect to me in your heart you will understand directly the truth that I am teaching you. What has come down to you over the 2,000 years since I left the body is not the pure teaching. It is what others have given to you in my name.

If you know me in your heart, you will embody my teaching with an inner certainty. You will know that love is the only answer to your problems.

When you give love you cannot help but receive it. Indeed, the more you give, the more you receive. There is no deficiency of love in the world. Love lives in the heart of every human being. If it is trusted, it has the power to uplift consciousness and change the conditions under which you live.

Love is ultimate reality. It is the beginning and the end, the alpha and the omega. It emanates from itself, expresses itself and rests in itself. Whether rising or falling, waxing or waning, ebbing or flowing, it never loses touch with what it is.

When you are in communion with love, you never lose touch with your true nature. When you lose your connection to love, you experience pain. You suffer. Yet suffering has a purpose. It wakes you up. It helps you learn to reconnect with the presence of love in your heart.

Death may dissolve the body and the world, but it cannot dissolve love, because love is eternal. It is not dependent on a particular body or personality.

I may not be present here in a body, but I am present in your love. When you find the love in your heart, you know that I am with you. It is that simple.

Do not look for me in the world, because I cannot be found there. Do not look for me in the past. There you will just find a story about me. You will not find my living presence.

Narrow mindedness, judgment of others, selfishness, greed, spiritual pride will prevent you from having communion with me. All this must be surrendered if you would abide with me.

If you want to meet me and know me, open your heart to love's presence and open your mind to the truth I have shared with you. We meet in a place beyond judgment or fear, where all are equal and all are loved. I do not live in a body or in a limited place. I live in the love that uplifts all bodies, all hearts and all minds.

That is the temple where you will find me. That is the place where we will lift up our voices together in prayer and celebration.

## THE DIVINE IN THE HUMAN

*The Messiah does not come from on high.*
*S/he comes in the hearts of each one of you.*

My former life is metaphor for you and as such it retains all the power of Myth. You believe that I had a divine origin, that I was sent by God to redeem you. You emphasize my divine origin and tell the story of a virgin birth. All this just separates you from me and makes me special in your eyes.

Yet if I was really special, then what I have taught you would be untrue. You would not be able to open the prison door on your own. You would have to wait until I came with the key to release you.

Mine is a teaching of empowerment, not of dependency. I have told that what I can do you can also do. I did not tell that you are powerless to help yourself.

RETURN TO THE GARDEN

Fortunately some of the details of my life have survived intact, so you know that I never placed myself above others. I sought out the poor, the sick, the disenfranchised. I kept company with lepers and prostitutes. I carried the teaching wherever I went, to all women and men who had ears to hear it. Some were black and some were white. Some were rich and some were poor.

Mine was not a gospel for the rich and famous or for the spiritual elite. My gospel was for every man and woman. It empowered even the lowest of the low with dignity and respect.

I did not put myself or anyone else up on a pedestal, but rather sought to raise everyone up. If I was of divine origin, then so were all of the men and women who heard my words and witnessed my deeds.

I rejected the teaching of specialness professed by the Pharisees. There is no chosen people. Neither the Jews and not the Christians. There can be no chosen people in a teaching of equality, or there would be some "heathens" or "untouchables" who are "not worthy" and therefore not chosen. These concepts are blasphemous. They did not come from me. If you accept these ideas, you are following a different path than the one I laid out for you.

My life and teaching were an invitation to you to understand and embrace your equality with other human beings and to claim your inner connection with God. I did not come to create yet another spiritual elite, but to tear down all the walls that separate you from your brother or sister.

If my teaching had been accepted by the Jewish hierarchy, it would have created a revolution within Judaism, turning it away from narrow parochialism and opening it up to all peoples of the world. In the same way, if my teaching were understood by the Christian hierarchy, it would not stand for any kind of exploitation, persecution, manipulation or control of one human being by another. One cannot protect the faith by engaging in fear tactics or attempting to silence the voices of conscience that need to be heard.

I did not come to create another narrow religion. I came to teach the principles and practices of unconditional love.

Were I in a body today, I would live and teach beyond labels, beyond prejudice, beyond ideas that separate one person from another. And my teaching would threaten those in positions of power and privilege, just as it did in my day. Do you think it is less likely that I would be plotted against, betrayed, and handed over to the authorities who are threatened by what I live and teach? Perhaps a more clinical execution than crucifixion would be my fate, or perhaps I would be assassinated before the authorities had the chance to arrest and imprison me.

So long as human beings deny the potential of their own Christhood, they will continue to condemn and crucify the Christ. The passion play will continue and you must decide whether you want to continue to carry your cross up the hill, or put it down.

If you are wise and courageous, you will lay down your cross, and those who follow you will be spared their journey of fear and guilt. A new day can dawn on earth, a day when the Christ is celebrated in each one of you, rather than crucified upon a cross.

That day is coming. And I am doing all I can to help you bring it. If you will listen to me and practice my teaching, if you will model it in the world through your personal example, then it will not be long.

In the Jewish tradition, the Messiah cannot come as long as any man or woman lives outside the embrace of love. All of you must awaken if the world is to be redeemed. In that sense, the decision each of you makes is crucial. For the Messiah does not come from on high. S/he comes in the hearts of each one of you.

## FREE WILL

*Your mistakes do not condemn you,*
*unless you refuse to correct them.*

In the beginning, human beings lived in blind obedience to the law. They did what they were told and they were rewarded appropriately. They were the beloved of God, but they never made choices on their own. They never tasted freedom and they wanted it.

Like Prometheus, they had to steal the fire of the gods. To evolve, they had to learn to become love-givers, not just love-receivers.

As a result of their quest for knowledge, they were cast out of the Garden and for the first time in their lives they felt shame. They hid from God and from each other.

In the Garden, there were no seasons—no winter, spring, or fall —but perpetual summer. Struggle or hardship was unknown. All their needs were provided for.

When they left the Garden, they faced the task of providing for themselves. They became responsible for their own lives. They had to make choices. The price of free will was high indeed. But it was freedom they wanted.

They wanted to become conscious creators. They wanted to wake up and make choices for themselves. They did not know that making choices would result in making lots of mistakes. They did not realize that they would judge themselves and others mercilessly for those errors. They did not know that self-crucifixion would become a way of life.

From the garden of grace to the Garden of Gethsemane, from unconscious bliss to conscious shame, they moved until the fall was complete. And there they stood shivering in the cold, without faith in themselves, unable even to turn to God.

Slowly and painfully, they learned to have faith in themselves. They cut down trees, tilled the soil, planted seeds, and brought in the harvest. They labored from dawn until dusk. They built roads and railroads, great cities and industrial centers. They extended their civilization out into the prairies and the foothills of the mountains, out to the edge of the sea. They survived drought and pestilence, floods, fires, and hurricanes. They triumphed over the earth. They subdued the animals of the field and the birds of the air. In their eyes, they earned the dominion once promised to them.

But along the way, they made some big mistakes. They became restless, irresponsible, greedy. They polluted rivers and streams. They burned their own cities. Their jails filled to overflowing. Murderers, rapists, and child molesters walked their streets. The earth groaned under the onslaught of endless roads, landfills and construction sites. Plutonium was buried deep in the heart of the earth. Oil spills stained the pristine waters of their shorelines and birds lay lifeless on the beach. Even the sky was torn open, leaving huge gaps in the ozone layer.

They began to realize that their version of the creation was not as good as God's. Prophets began to ring the bells of doom and gloom. Earth changes were coming. God was angry at them and they were going to have to pay for their sins. As the millennium approached, judgment day seemed to be coming with it.

Perhaps this scenario seems familiar to you. Perhaps you feel the personal and the collective level of fear arising as human creation runs amuck. Perhaps you understand how people feel alone, disconnected from themselves and from God, unable to face their mistakes or correct them.

When you chose to have free will, you also chose to be responsible for your creations. Perhaps you did not fully understand what that would entail. But now you do. Now you know that the time for caring and cooperation has come. Now you know it is time to clean up the mess you have made, to make amends to those you have hurt, and to repair the environment that you have desecrated.

Your mistakes do not condemn you, unless you refuse to correct them. The choice is yours. The choice has always been yours.

## THE RENEWAL OF THE COVENANT

*You will make a new covenant with your Creator,*
*so that His truth may live and shine in your time.*

In every generation, the truth must be encountered directly by prophets, mystics and visionaries. Becoming one with that truth, they can express it in the language of their times.

When prophets, mystics and visionaries express the truth, they often challenge the institutions, dominant beliefs, and the authority figures of their society. Like me, these inspired teachers claim an inner authority, not an outer one. They oppose and expose all forms of hypocrisy and injustice, even when it is institutionalized. As such, they are not very popular with the powers that be.

Because they seek to empower people to think for themselves and take responsibility for their lives, the teachings of the prophets, mystics and visionaries often ignite the hearts of people. They encourage people to ask questions, to challenge old customs and laws that no longer serve the greater good. Through the authentic life and teaching of such individuals, truth remains a living force.

In contrast to the prophets, the mystics, and the visionaries, there are the fundamentalists who live their lives based on a past authority. They look at the Bible or some other holy book as literally true. They are concerned about the letter of the law, not the spirit of it. When I was born, the Pharisees were the fundamentalists, but fundamentalists can be found within every religious tradition, in every time and place.

Fundamentalists believe that there is only one truth and they alone have it. They are often intolerant of other paths and work hard to convert others to their way of thinking. They often profess their beliefs with great zeal, but this zeal in itself seems to hide an inner insecurity. Fundamentalists are easily threatened by people who hold different values and beliefs, and they are quick to condemn others.

Fundamentalism emphasizes an outer authority, rather than an inner one. It establishes spiritual hierarchies and creates new idols. It substitutes elaborate rules and rituals for the authentic practice of God-communion and sacrifices the freedom of the individual to the tyranny of the group mind.

While fundamentalism is strong in your time, so is its opposite: experimentalism. Today, there are hundreds of thousands of books, tapes, lectures, and workshops claiming to point the way toward truth. Every path you can imagine is being offered, from angel guidance to satanic rituals, from the sublime to the ridiculous. It is hard for some people to discriminate.

In some respects, this is a confusing time to be on the planet. The old, hierarchical religion is in its death throws. You can no longer take your direction from churches, gurus, or other authority figures. You must find it in your own hearts. You must try new ideas and practices, learning what works and what does not. You must learn to discriminate and become responsible for the ideas you accept as truth. You must walk your path with honesty and humility, learning to honor the path of others.

This puts the responsibility squarely on your shoulders. Will you make mistakes? Absolutely. Will you try some ideas that won't work, perhaps hurting yourself or others in the process? Very likely.

But you will learn from all this. You will find your way through the forest and come into the clearing where the sun steams through.

You will learn to meet your unique needs in the context of the eternal human need for both freedom and belonging. You will find the universal truth, which has lived in all times and all places, and learn to hold it and share it authentically. As you take the spiritual journey honestly and courageously, you will make a new covenant with your Creator, so that His truth may continue to live and to shine in your time.

## GOD'S FAITH IN YOU

### *To know creation, you had to become it.*

When you ate from the tree of knowledge, you entered into a path of mistake-making and correction which would bring you true knowledge of self and other.

You wanted to participate in the drama of creation, to know what your creator knew, to learn to create like Him. That desire led to your birth into form. To know creation, you had to become it.

It was a choice made with great courage. You gave up the comfort of absolute truth for the discomfort of relative knowledge. From that moment, you would strive for the absolute, but encounter only the relative. The path of knowledge did not seem to lead back to God. Indeed, it often seemed to take you away from the divine.

You acted with great faith. Yet God had even greater faith. He released you on your quest for knowledge knowing full well you would walk through the land of darkness, encountering dragons and demons. He knew you would get caught in the dynamics of blame and shame, punishing yourself and others. He knew you would come to the brink of destroying yourself, yet he still let you go. He had such great faith in you that He was able to observe your suffering, indeed even feel it, without intervening in the choice you had made.

Perhaps He knew something you also knew when you left the Garden, but now have difficulty remembering. He knew that His spark, His seed, His love and His truth, was living within you. He knew that as soon as you learned to turn to that love, you would begin to find your way home. And so the covenant between Him and you would be renewed. You would find light in the darkness. Not just His light, but your own as well. That light and that love were your inheritance.

God knew that no matter how far you strayed from the Garden, you could never abandon it completely. At the deepest level of your being, you had known unconditional love and acceptance. You had forgotten that experience, but in the end, when you were reeling in your deepest pain, you would remember it. You would remember God's love, because it is the essence of who you are.

When you left the Garden, you began a quest for knowledge outside yourself. You sought truth in the ideas and philosophies of other people. You read books, traveled to far-away places, sought esoteric and unusual experiences. All this took you away from your inner connection with God. You tried to find outside of you what you already had within. Indeed, the more you sought truth without, the more you forgot the inner connection with truth. Your relationship with God, which once had been intrinsic, became extrinsic. You made idols and worshiped them. The more you searched outside of you the more empty you felt within. And the more empty you felt, the more your search was fueled.

For some of you God became a large bank account, an exquisite house, or a fancy car. For others it became an expensive education, or a successful career. Still others found idols in a bible, a teaching or belief system, a preacher or guru. And of course, a few of you made idols of a bottle, a recreational drug, casual sex, or the promise of love.

All these things seemed to offer you satisfaction, but none of them delivered the love or the comfort they promised. Instead, they left you feeling empty, wanting more.

You became over-stimulated without and lost your capacity to feel and connect within. Your relationship to love had become inverted.

You became needy, dependent, alone. You forgot how to offer love. You could only ask for it.

You desperately wanted relationship, yet you could not handle its demands. You had become too selfish, too defensive. You had driven yourself into a corner. The very thing you wanted most was the thing you could not have, or at least this is what you believed.

The search for God outside you led to a wall you could not climb or get around. It was too tall and too wide. You were at an impasse.

The external journey had come to an end. There was nothing left to do but turn around.

To turn authentically, you had to recognize the utter futility of the search for love outside yourself. That moment of recognition would be the beginning of your spiritual path. It would be the end of your descent from grace, and the beginning of your return to the Garden.

## TAKING TOTAL RESPONSIBILITY

*If you can create hell, can you not also create heaven?*

In your search for happiness outside yourself, you made many enemies. Yet your hatred for them was nothing compared to your hatred for yourself. For every problem or trauma you encountered in the world, you experienced a wound within.

You thought it was your brother pounding the nails into your hands and feet. But now you know that it was you. Everything you ever did to anyone else, you did to yourself. You are the victim of your own actions.

It is not easy to turn your life around. It is not easy to learn to take total responsibility for your experience. It is not easy to give up the game of shame and blame. Yet, if you want to transform your life, that is what you are asked to do.

You must look at the hell you have created within your own consciousness and take responsibility for it. You must understand once and for all time that you are the one who walks to the cross, the one who is crucified, and the one who performs the crucifixion. There is no one else here but you.

But if you can wrong yourself so completely, if you can torture and abuse yourself so mercilessly, if you can be the one who experiences hell itself, can you not also be the one who brings love and compassion? Can you not also be the peacemaker, the Christ, the one who comes with arms extended?

If you can create hell, can you not also create heaven? Is your creativity essentially distorted, prejudiced, and misdirected? Are you a man or woman condemned to suffer for all eternity for your mistakes, or are you the fallen angel who once sat at God's side, the one suffering from pride who needs but to surrender to regain his celestial seat? Do you have a choice? Can you create with God, instead of against him?

When you stop crucifying yourself, your resurrection is at hand. When you learn to bring love and acceptance to your own wounded psyche, the Christ within steps off the cross and walks free of shame and blame. When you can do that for yourself, you can offer the same hand of love to your brother and sister.

When you learn to take total responsibility, there will be no one left to blame. There will be no more enemy to be found outside of you, and the enemy within can be forgiven. That is the path back to the Garden, the path of forgiveness, the one that I offered you once and offer to you now once again.

## REDEMPTION

*I told you "knock and it will be open."*
*But I am not sure that you believed me.*

When you are scared and overwhelmed by life, you think you are a victim of pain in a meaningless world. You do not know that your pain belongs to you and that it is your responsibility to transform it. You do not know that you are here on Earth with specific lessons to learn about how to love yourself and others.

Yet, sooner or later, you realize that life is not going to conform to your expectations or demands. And you understand that your frustration will continue until you change your attitude toward life.

Trying to change the external events and circumstances of your life without addressing your internal beliefs and attitudes is an ineffective strategy. If you want to change the outer circumstances of your life, you must begin to look at the contents of your own consciousness. What meaning are you giving to the situation that presents itself? Are you suffering because of what happened or because of your interpretation of it?

The spiritual path begins with self-scrutiny, not with mechanical words and deeds aimed at increasing your ability to get what you want. The search for external abundance cannot succeed when you are feeling bankrupt within, even when it results in increasing your bank account or your possessions.

Inner wealth translates into appropriate supply: neither too much nor too little. You have just what you need when you need it. When you accept life as it is offered to you, you avoid an unnecessary struggle. You realize that the way you look at something influences the way you experience it and what you attract in the future. If you stop resisting life, it gets easier. Events which support you begin to occur naturally. You don't have to try to make them happen.

The law of grace operates from the inside out. As changes are made in the way you hold your experience, your experience begins to shift.

You do not reject or find fault with your experience just because it shows up differently from the way you expect it to. Instead, you take a deep breath, let go of your expectations, and try to get your arms around what is happening. You know that your job is to embrace everything that happens to you. And that the more difficult it is for you to embrace something, the more deeply you will learn from it.

You learn to surrender into life and to trust it as it unfolds. This surrender is required not just once or twice, but continually, day to day, hour to hour, moment to moment. As the outside and the inside are brought into alignment, grace unfolds.

Grace is poetry in motion. It is a mercurial dance, embodying form for an instant, and then abandoning it. It comes into being, disappears, changes shape, and reappears. It is spontaneous, playful, always new. You must be in the moment to see it or appreciate it.

I once told you "knock and it will be open." But I am not sure that you believed me.

When you are ready you will cross the threshold and we will abide together. Until then, know that the Friend is with you. She will lead you beside the still waters. She will guide you and comfort you. Through her, you will understand that goodness and mercy surround you and follow you throughout all the days of your life.

For you, my friend, are the bringer of love. You are the one who brings the light that illumines the darkness.

Because you have learned to love yourself, you could receive my love and carry it with you. Thus, wherever you go, I go with you. Through you, my teaching is given to the world authentically, as I gave it to you.

Godspeed on your journey, my brother and sister. Once you arrive in the House of Love, you never leave it. You merely open the door to others when they are ready to join you.

*Namaste.*

Paul Ferrini is the author of over 40 books on love, healing and forgiveness. His unique blend of spirituality and psychology goes beyond self-help and recovery into the heart of healing. His conferences, retreats, and *Affinity Group Process* have helped thousands of people deepen their practice of forgiveness and open their hearts to the divine presence in themselves and others.

For more information on Paul Ferrini's work, visit his website at www.paulferrini.com. The website has many excerpts from Paul's books, as well as information on his workshops and retreats. Be sure to request Paul's email newsletter, his daily wisdom message, as well as a free catalog of his books and audio products. You can also email us at orders@heartwayspress.com or call us at 941-776-8001.

# New Audio and Video by Paul Ferrini

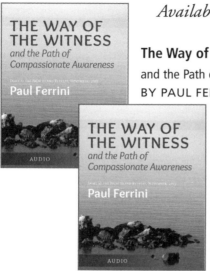

*Available as a CD or DVD set*

## The Way of the Witness

and the Path of Compassionate Awareness

BY PAUL FERRINI

3 DVD set or 6 CD Audio set
with 5.5 hours of talks
Either set available for $55.00.
ISBN # 978-1-879159-95-2

Talk #1 The Art of Bullfighting

Talk #2 The Way of the Witness:

Talk #3 Choosing Love

Talk #4 Being Yourself and Allowing Others to be Themselves

Talk #5 Giving up the Caretaker Role and Asking for what You Need

Talk #6 Two Powerful Triangles within the 8 Keys to the Kingdom

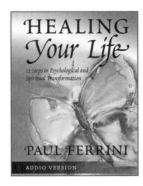

## *Available as a CD or DVD set*

### Healing Your Life

12 Steps to Psychologial and Spiritual Transformation

BY PAUL FERRINI

$111.00    approxImately 11 hours

978-1-879159-93-8    www.paulferrini.com

In this powerful series of recordings, Paul Ferrini teaches his ground-breaking Roadmap to Spiritual Transform-ation. Paul developed this curriculum to help us move through our pain, heal our childhood wounds and step into our power and pur-pose in this lifetime. He describes in detail the 12 steps that take us out of denial into a process of deep psychological healing in which our masks are taken off, our patterns of self-betrayal are ended, and we begin to move through the Dark night of the Soul that ensues when the False Self begins to fall apart. The process is complete when the False Self dies and the light of the True Self is born within our consciousness and experience. Then, like a brightly colored butterfly, we leave our cater-pillar-like self behind, spread our wings and begin to fly. The result is Self-Actualization on all levels.

# New Books by Paul Ferrini

## *The Long-Awaited Roadmap to Self-Healing and Empowerment*

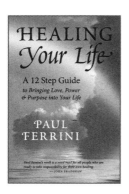

**Healing Your Life**

12 Steps to Heal Your Childhood Wounds and Bring Love, Power & Purpose into Your Life

BY PAUL FERRINI
ISBN: 978-1-879159-85-3
176 Pages   Paperback   $14.95

Paul Ferrini finally shares his powerful 12-Step Roadmap to healing and transformation. This work is the fruit of 35 years of writing and teaching experience.

This book will help you open up to a life of genuine healing and empowerment. You can learn to love yourself from the inside out, initiating a process of giving and receiving that will transform your life. You can end your suffering and connect with your joy. You can find your passion in life and learn to nurture and express your gifts. You can learn to be the bringer of love to your own experience and attract more and more love into your life. You can fulfill your life purpose and live with your partner in an equal, mutually empowered relationship. All the gifts of life and love are possible for you. You need only do your part and open your heart to receive them.

*"35 years of heart-centered spiritual work have taught me what is necessary to bring about a real, lasting change in a person's consciousness and experience."*
— PAUL FERRINI

**The Keys to the Kingdom**

8 Spiritual Practices that will Transform Your Life

BY PAUL FERRINI
ISBN: 978-1-879159-84-6
128 Pages   Paperback   $12.95

8 SPIRITUAL PRACTICES THAT WILL TRANSFORM YOUR LIFE

1. *Love Yourself*
2. *Be Yourself*
3. *Be Responsible*
4. *Be Honest*
5. *Walk Your Talk*
6. *Follow Your Heart*
7. *Be at Peace*
8. *Stay Present*

Please use the keys in this book to open the doorways in your life. Take the keys with you wherever you go. Use them as often as you can. They will help you to transform your experience. Fear will drop away and unconditional love will shine through. As you awaken to who you are, so will the people around you.

A fearful world cannot exist for a loving heart. Love changes everything. That is why this works. Do your part, and you will see for yourself.

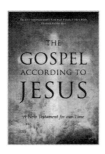
If you know me in your heart, you embody my teaching with an inner certainty. You know that love is the only answer to your problems.

When you give love you cannot help but receive it. Indeed, the more you give, the more you receive. There is no deficiency of love in the world. Love lives in the heart of every human being. If it is trusted, it has the power to uplift consciousness and change the conditions under which you live.

Love is the ultimate reality. It is the beginning and the end, the alpha and the omega. It emanates from itself, expresses itself and rests in itself. Whether rising or falling, waxing or waning, ebbing or flowing, it never loses touch with what it is.

I may not be present here in a body, but I am present in your love. When you find the love in your heart, you know that I am with you. It is that simple.

The long-awaited sequel to *Dancing with the Beloved*

### When Love Comes as a Gift

Meeting the Soul Mate in this Life

BY PAUL FERRINI

ISBN: 978-1-879159-81-5

176 Pages  Paperback  $12.95

ebook $10.00

The soul mate is not just one person, but a work in progress, a tapestry being woven out of light and shadow, hope and fear. Every lover we have prepares us to meet the Beloved. Each one brings a lesson and a gift and each defers to another who brings a deeper gift and a more compelling lesson.

Our partner challenges us to become authentic and emotionally present. S/he invites us to walk through our fears, to tell the truth and to trust more deeply. Gradually, we open our hearts to the potential of creating intimacy on all levels.

And then it is no longer a temporal affair. It is Spirit come to flesh. It is the indwelling Presence of Love, blessing us and lifting us up. It is both a gift and a responsibility, both a promise made and a promise fulfilled.

# Recent Workshop and Retreat Recordings

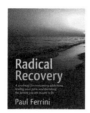

## Radical Recovery

A Roadmap for overcoming addictions, healing your pain, and becoming the person you are meant to be
ISBN for CD Set 978-1-879159-91-4
Available as a 2 CD Set for $24.95
or as 2 Audio Downloads for $19.99

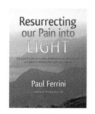

## Resurrecting our Pain into Light

Healing our Trauma, Overcoming our Guilt and Taking ourselves off the Cross
ISBN for CD Set 978-1-879159-92-1
Available as a 5 CD Set for $55
or as 5 Audio Downloads for $49

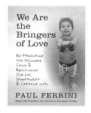

## We are the Bringers of Love

Re-Parenting the Wounded Child
& Reclaiming Our Joy, Spontaneity and Creativity
ISBN for CD Set 978-1-879159-90-7
Available as a 4 CD Set for $44
or as 5 Audio Downloads for $41

## Freedom from Self-Betrayal

Spiritual Mastery Talks at Palm Island
ISBN  978-1-879159-87-7
6 CDs   $59.95

## Putting Flesh on the Bones

Recordings from the 2009 Retreat in

## Real Happiness

Awakening To Our True Self

An Introductory Talk by Paul Ferrini

1 CD   $16.95   ISBN 978-1-879159-75-4

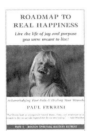

## Roadmap to Real Happiness

Living the Life of Joy and Purpose

You Were Meant to Live

Part 1   4 CDs   $48.00

ISBN 978-1-879159-72-3

Part 2   3 CDs   $36.00

ISBN 978-1-879159-73-0

## Creating a Life of Fulfillment

Insights on Work, Relationship and Life Purpose

2 CDs   $24.95

ISBN 978-1-879159-76-1

## Being an Instrument of Love
## in Times of Planetary Crisis

Two Talks on Individual and Collective Healing

2 CDs   $24.95   ISBN 978-1-879159-79-2

## The Radiant Light Within

Readings by Paul Ferrini from the *Hidden Jewel* & *Dancing with the Beloved*

1 CD   $16.95   ISBN 978-1-879159-74-7

Paul Ferrini has some 45 books and just as many audio/video products available through Heartways Press, Inc. All these titles can be viewed at **www.paulferrini.com**. Just click on the link that says "online bookstore" and then choose the appropriate category. You may also place your order for books/media products on line and/or you can register for Paul's workshops and retreats. If you have any questions please feel free to email us at orders@heartwayspress.com or call us at **941-776-8001**.

**www.paulferrini.com**